C++
REAL-TIME
3D GRAPHICS

Andrew Tyler

SIGMA PRESS
Wilmslow, England

Typeset and Designed by Sigma Press, Wilmslow, UK

Cover Design by Design House, Marple Bridge.

First published in 1994
Sigma Press, 1 South Oak Lane, Wilmslow, Cheshire SK9 6AR, UK

First printed 1994

ISBN: 1-85058-506-7

British Library Cataloguing in Publication Data
A CIP catalogue record for this book is available from the British Library

Printed by: Interprint Ltd, Malta

General disclaimers

Preface

Computer Graphics is one of the great revolutions in the way we live. Forget what the historians say. History is never made by winning battles. It comes from the relentless progress that humans make in changing the world to suit their needs. It's called Technology. Computer Graphics is just such a change. It is the beginning of an unparalleled synthesis between man and machine which has crept into our lives most innocuously but which heralds a profound change.

Superficially, what Computer Graphics appears to do is provide interactive pictures which simulate the world around us. In the case of games, the world can be entirely artificial. What it really does is something far more profound. An interactive image on a screen is the way in which a computer can communicate most powerfully. Humans don't relate at all to the binary digits within the machine. But when those digits are converted to a moving image with life-like forms and dazzling colours they have meaning. That is what is really happening. Through Computer Graphics, the machine is at last able to communicate with us in a way which we understand. A human can glance around and instantly assess the environment. When the computer can present on its screen a realistic environment changing in real-time, it is at last operating at a level humans are designed for - advanced pattern recognition. A human is hopeless at precise numerical computation, but takes little effort to catch a falling ball. It has taken a long time for machines to communicate in the way in which we are best suited, but it is here now. It is a small step of the imagination to realise that although communication is currently limited to pictures on a screen, it won't always be that way. When it is possible to communicate directly with the cerebral hemispheres, machines will finally be integrated.

This book has three things to offer: It is about computer graphics, the C and C++ programming languages, and Object-Oriented Programming.

Something has been said about graphics already so now let's talk about the programming languages. There are many programming languages, so why should you worry about C and C++ in particular? The answer to this question is simple. These languages, and C++ in particular, are set to dominate programming in the near future. Of course, no programming language lasts forever but for the time being C++ will play a very major role, particularly in the writing of large programs. There are several important reasons for this and they are connected both with old programming issues and new developments in the way we think about programs.

In the most primitive of programming languages, assembler, it is possible to get right at the data being manipulated by the program as it passes through the registers of the CPU. By a careful choice of assembler instructions, programs can be fine-tuned so as to minimise processing time and give very fast execution. That's fine for specialised programs which do particular things very well but how do you evolve a viable ''literature'' in such a programming style which allows last year's program to be used as a basis for next year's, especially if the programmer who wrote it has left and in the meantime the CPU has been upgraded? Programming in assembler concentrates programmer skills into tightly-packed odd-shaped boxes which have to be taken apart and essentially rebuilt to work with different hardware. It's like illuminating medieval manuscripts. There will always be a need for assembler programming in the most demanding of environments, just as a Works Team is required to service racing cars.

But there is a more profound task which software must perform which does not have to do with fine-tuned performance, but instead allows the development of a ''literature'' of the language. Literature is vital to convert programming from a grammatical syntax to a cultural activity so that it can evolve in meaning and value. It is not sufficient to relegate programming to archives of arcane and obscure one-off listings understood by a specialised minority and dependent on particular hardware. To have a value which accumulates and increases with time, it is necessary for programming to develop its own literature which is generally meaningful to all programmers and from which better programs can develop.

Different programming languages have addressed different perceived needs of the programmer. For example, a language such as BASIC has attacked the obvious problem of making it simple to use and FORTRAN has modelled itself in the way which scientists analyse data. Languages of this type fix their attention on the need to provide a service. But they cannot easily focus on the more general need to generate a lasting literature which can be built on to produce programs of increasing complexity without increasing confusion.

Let us also consider the impact that hardware has had on computing. A long time ago computers were no more than banks of thermionic tubes connected by wires. It just wasn't possible to make powerful calculating machines that way because of the sheer physical impossibility of connecting a sufficiently large number of them and replacing those that failed fast enough, aside from the power requirements. With the advent of semiconductor devices, all that changed and then with ever increasing miniaturisation and integration a new landmark was passed. It became possible to assemble complex electronics by connecting together with a small number of wires (a bus) discrete "chips", or ICs (integrated circuits) each one containing hundreds of thousands of separate electronic semiconductor switches. There was a subtle advantage in assembling electronics this way. If a chip failed it could be immediately replaced by another so that maintenance was easy. Also, and more important, it became possible to make more powerful electronic devices as assemblies of complex, but stand-alone, chips. Increasing complexity was not accompanied by increasing confusion. At each stage, more complex behaviour is expressed in terms of building blocks from the last stage. The question is, where is the parallel in software? Why isn't it possible to make software the same way as hardware? Where is the software "chip", the software IC? Why can't you open a manufacturer's catalogue of software "chips" that you can connect together to make a robust program? These are the questions that C++ seeks to address and comes close to answering, and explains why you should be very interested in what the language has to offer.

That said, it must be added that the parallel between hardware and software is not as close as one might imagine. It certainly has been possible to make major advances in hardware through ICs but still the analogue in software is less forthcoming. The reasons must have something to do with the fact that different people perceive the same program differently and also the plain truth that hardware must be purchased from a manufacturer and one has to adapt to what is on offer. Nonetheless, the great strength of object-oriented C++ is that it makes it possible to write programs in the form of software ICs. That is the great achievement of the language: it allows the programmer to see his program as a number of connected parts, each taking care of its own data, and having particular behaviour set by its functions. These "objects" in the program go about their business and attend their duties according to what messages they receive and who they should talk to. It makes it possible to contain within the program, in software, the same entities that one sees in real world problems. That is the essence of C++ and Object-Oriented Programming (OOP). It can make the program look like the real-life problem in the mind of the programmer.

C++ is derived from C but is very much more than just an extension of it. C++ does however keep all of the features of the C language. C is like a high level assembler language. It has the power, speed and flexibility of assembler to fine tune the instructions for speed, but is not tied to any particular processor. It is future-proof. So C++ wins all ways. It is capable of manipulating data almost as fast and efficiently as assembler but also includes the possibility of high level structures of great subtlety and beauty in its object-oriented features, which raise it to the level of a true vehicle for literature. There are other languages (e.g. Smalltalk) which are even more heavily object-oriented but C++ is here now, available at modest cost on excellent commercial compilers. For the time being, it's the way to go!

What this book is about is Object-Oriented programming (OOP) in C++, and C along the way, and showing you how to apply this technique to graphics. I gave a course of some of the material to Final Year graduates at Manchester University in 1993, and it worked out very well. Students, even those without any programming experience at all, were able to get to grips with the graphics programs and modify them to finally produce their own version of a ripple tank (Chapter 11). They found it hard work but, universally, very rewarding. Graphics is well-suited to learning programming. It gives a visible output if the program works and a mess if it doesn't. The incentive is there to complete the project. This book is structured to take you through the stages of a ''graphics pipeline''. It starts with drawing a polygon and works its way finally to a world containing a city through which you can fly under keyboard control. Along the way, you learn how graphics works and some technical ideas such as hidden surface removal and shading and many other interesting things, ending up with a Virtual Reality world you can model in your own way. All done in C++ OOP.

How fast do these programs run? Will you be able to rush off and write a commercial flight simulator program and get rich? No and Yes. No in the sense that the emphasis of the book has been on learning C++ in the software environment provided by Borland's Turbo C++ IDE, the powerful value-for-money compiler. Such an environment provides safe, ''bullet-proof'' functions. For the very fastest code, it would be necessary to include assembler sections and that has not been done. Yes in the sense that many of the ideas can be developed to bypass the limitations imposed by the need to produce easily-understood software. The software is at times complex, but only to do justice to the elegance of the language though I have never tried to make it terse, as C can easily be. The programs have been written on a 486 PC running at 33 MHz and on such a machine they run fine. On a 386 running at 25MHz the more complex programs, such as PC-CITY in Chapter 12 will run slowly, being much more complex. I don't apologise for this since the emphasis has been on learning the C++ language, without the benefit of assembler code. By the end of this book, the enthusiastic programmer will be able to spot many opportunities to clean up the code and speed things up; I regard that as a fair task. This book isn't supposed to teach high speed graphics above all else, it's supposed to be a balanced presentation illustrating the power of the C++ language.

I wish you well and hope you will have cause to stand back in amazement at the beauty and elegance of object-oriented C++.

Acknowledgement

I gratefully acknowledge the many valuable suggestions and comments made by my talented colleague James Youngman, and for his stamina in checking the manuscript.

Andrew Tyler

CONTENTS

8. Getting Things into Perspective 130

9. Simple Rotations 147

10. Hidden Surfaces and Illumination 160

11. A Ripple Tank 176

12. A Virtual Reality 191

READER CONVENIENCE DISK

A disk containing all of the program listings in this book is available from:

Mediastyle Ltd
c/o Live Graphics
PO Box 19
Alderley Edge
Cheshire   SK9 7XY

Please send a cheque for £15.00 payable to Mediastyle Ltd.
Non-UK purchasers: add 10% to cover airmail postage.

1

An Overview

This book is about programming real-time graphics in the C++ language.

C++ is an enormous extension of C, so you learn C programming as well. It is not an encyclopaedia of these languages, but it does include a detailed discussion of those aspects which will enable you to follow the programs of the book. You may find that some aspects seem to have a disproportionate amount of space allotted to them whilst other, major, features of the language have little. This reflects my biased view, having taught the material in a course to third-year undergraduates and observed what they found easy and what they found difficult. In particular, emphasis has been given to what pointers are and how they are related to memory locations, a topic which I feel is often glossed over. Having spent some time in assembler programming I found pointers easy to understand when viewed as manipulators of addresses. I have observed that learners who do not have this background find pointers very difficult. My students found pointers hard but nearly everything else (except the object-oriented aspects of C++) straightforward.

The graphics is real-time in the sense that it was developed on a 486 PC clone running at 33 MHz. On such a machine, it runs fine. On a 386 running at 25 MHz, the more complex programs, particularly in the last Chapter "Building a World", run slowly. It certainly would have been possible to write much faster programs, for example using machine code (I have already written a book for the Atari ST and another for the Amiga, both published by Sigma Press, on just this topic), but the point of this book is to program in an industry-standard language throughout. Here are three very good reasons for doing this:

❑ It leads to programs which do not depend on the architecture of a particular microprocessor but which can be run on any computer (providing a C++ compiler exists for the machine).

❑ The programs will be durable, robust and can be understood by other programmers.

❑ The programs can be extended and developed using the features offered by C++ without the need to alter the original code.

Of course, these statements need to be expanded and that will be done in later parts of the book.

This book is about mainstream programming but using the very elegant C++ language. There are advantages to using this approach which may not be immediately apparent to the "hacker" who wants to rush off and find all sorts of secret and tricky ways of achieving spectacular and fast graphics effects. In the first place, C++ programs are not much slower than assembler and, more important, it is unlikely that the lone programmer will be able to keep track of what is going on in a very large assembler program, although Borland's Turbo Assembler does allow the high level constructs of object-oriented programming. C++ really wins here since it allows a program to increase in complexity without increasing confusion. For the big programs of today, it makes more sense go for reliability and manageability than clever little bits of code that only one person really understands and which can't easily be extended.

C++ is an Object-Oriented Programming (OOP) language because it allows one to create software objects in the program which parallel the concepts from the problem one is trying to model. If, for example, you are writing a program about traffic flow it is most likely that cars will appear somewhere in your model. OOP allows you to include in your program "car" objects which behave and feel like cars. Thus the program has a structure which is similar to the problem in mind and therefore easy to relate to.

C++ is well suited to computer graphics for that reason. In computer graphics you have a good picture of what should appear on the screen – after all, you can "see" it. However not all the objects which appear in a program are as clear cut as a graphics image. A program has many parts and stages and the objects which naturally appear are often not so visual. They can be objects which perform a function or task, such as a sorted list, whose job is to keep track of a list of what is to appear on the screen. The real world is full of objects of various kinds; some are material solid objects, such as a car and others are just well defined concepts that only exist in our minds, such as "mathematics" or "science" or "conscience". Whatever the type of object it clearly has an important role in the way we think since we have a clear understanding of what it means and we know what its characteristics and behaviours are. Object-oriented programming allows the programmer to bring these things directly into the program.

The aim of this book is to develop 3-D solid graphics routines which run reasonably well in real time and include features such as vector drawing of filled polygons, hidden surface removal, illumination from a light source, keyboard control, full perspective and rotational transforms and ending up with a layout for a city which you can explore and build yourself.

In this introduction, we'll have a quick look at some of these things before getting to the "meat" in successive chapters.

1.1 Computer Graphics: a new medium

Computer graphics is not a minority interest of computer freaks. It is a multi-billion dollar industry. Even in 1982, when Hollywood spent 3 billion dollars on movie production, the world commercial computer graphics industry spent 2 billion dollars and was growing at the rate of 30% a year. In the same year in the U.S., 10 billion dollars were spent on video games. There has been no halt since that time. Computer graphics is very big business indeed.

The microcomputer owner meets some of the best graphics for his machine in games, many of which use advanced concepts straight out of the professional computer journals. For small machines there are always limitations on what can be achieved, determined by the speed of the processor and the size of RAM. But in recent years the popular microcomputer has been extremely good value for money, having considerable computational power at very low price and providing complex graphics at minimal cost. This explosion in the power/price ratio of computer hardware has put immense computing capability in the hands of the popular micro owner and made advanced graphics techniques, which were the domain of the professional, available to anyone.

1.1.1 Is it Art, or What?

Humans are very good at generating and recognising complex visual patterns but not very good at doing arithmetic. In contrast, digital computers were designed to be perfect at binary arithmetic. What else they can do depends on how well complex mathematical functions can be constructed from basic binary arithmetic. There is a limitation here, since numbers in a computer cannot be more accurate than the number of bits assigned to them but, apart from that, it is clear that complex mathematical calculations can be done quickly on even very modest microcomputers.

In computer graphics, the computer adds tremendous speed to any calculation associated with geometry, which is the mathematics of drawing. Because geometry is concerned with the exact mathematical relations between lines and surfaces, it is ideally matched to the way the computer works. This is the good and the bad news of drawing with computers: precise mathematical functions can be expressed graphically at lightning speed but making them look like natural objects requires considerably more work. In fact much of the effort in computer graphics is now concerned with 'messing up' the perfect but sterile images of geometry to make them fit for human consumption. Doing this has less to do with computers and more to do with the traditional skills of animation discovered many years ago by Walt Disney.

It is very easy to draw precise mathematical shapes with a computer, because such shapes can be generated from a formula. A circle is an example of a simple mathematical function. For a circle centred at the origin of an x-y coordinate system, the formula is

$$x^2 + y^2 = r^2$$

Such a function is a good starting point for a billiard ball but a poor starting point for an apple, although superficially the difference is not all that great (both have an overall spherical shape with a shiny exterior). Let's consider how we might use a computer to draw an apple.

First of all, there has to be a good starting point. There is no such thing as a mathematical formula for an apple. All apples are different. However, apples do have a typical shape and that is what the human artist knows from experience. But an artist would not draw all the apples in a still life with the same shape, it would be too boring. Programming a computer to avoid repetition and simplicity is difficult.

One way to draw apples would be to use equations of curves having the apple shape. By choosing functions with high powers of x, y and z, as much sharpness or flatness as desired can be included. This is the world of bicubic patches, Bezier functions and beta-splines. This would certainly allow variation, but with considerable computational effort. One way to do this would be to hold different apple outlines as (x,y) coordinate pairs in a data base and then use curve and surface fitting techniques to connect then as in a "join the dots" picture. This is how the famous teapot of Martin Newell, which was a prototype in the early development of modelling solid surfaces, was constructed. In technical language it can be constructed from an outline consisting of three Bezier curves. Since the teapot is symmetrical, its surface (with the exception of the spout) is then generated by rotating the outline about the central vertical axis.

Another way is to avoid curves altogether, and instead subdivide the surface of the apple into many flat facets like a gemstone. By making the facets sufficiently small and numerous, an apple of any shape can be modelled. The little facets, being flat and many sided, are polygons and the surface of the apple is a polygon mesh. This approach is less time consuming than using curved patches but there remains the problem of disguising the sharp boundary edges between polygons.

This leads to the next level of refinement in producing a convincing image. A mathematical function on its own knows nothing of the laws of physics. These are so familiar to us that we take them for granted: glass is transparent but wood is opaque, metals look bright and shiny but human skin is dull and diffuse. Somehow these subtle but essential clues must be included. The most important first step is to make the rear surfaces of opaque objects invisible. This is called *hidden surface removal* which, despite the apparent simplicity of the task, turns out to be quite difficult. Much time has been spent investigating efficient and thorough ways of doing this. Next there must be visual clues to the surface structure. One obvious step is to illuminate it with a light source so that one side is brighter than the other.

At the next level of refinement, the surface must be textured and patterned, or rendered, in a "natural" way to look real. In this the programmer is aided by the mathematics of fractals, developed and promoted by Benoit Mandelbrot. This is the geometry of self-similar structures and quite different from the geometry of Euclid where structures are built from perfect lines and surfaces. Natural objects appear to have a lot in common with self-similar structures and even if the similarity is not exact, they are convincingly modelled by them. A self-similar structure is one which has the same appearance at any level of magnification. Of course, natural objects may only satisfy this definition over a limited range of dimensions but it often produces very convincing results. For example, the side branch of a fern when magnified looks like the main branch and small pebbles under magnification look like boulders. Nature is full of such structures. An additional bonus is that algorithms have been discovered which allow self-similar structures and landscapes to be generated from a relatively small amount of information. This relieves the programmer of carrying a colossal database from which to generate each separate detail of a complex scene.

All of these steps are essential to give a convincing image. The fact that so much visual richness is required to make an image look real testifies to the very advanced pattern recognition capability of human beings.

When all this is done, what have we got? Just a very roundabout way of painting an apple? The difference is that once created in software the graphic entity has an independent existence. The picture on the screen is just the final stage. Even if not being currently displayed, it can evolve according to rules included in the program. There is not even the constraint to create objects which are modelled on real life. It is possible to invent new "life-forms" inside the computer. In Computer Aided Design (CAD) this is what happens all the time. Machines are designed, built and tested inside the computer long before they exist as material objects. In simulators and games this aspect is pushed as far as possible. Computer games specialise in generating artificial realities; the more exotic the better.

Virtual Reality is the coming thing. The idea that computer graphics can simulate an interactive reality in real-time is the essence of computer games. It only required the art to move from bit-mapped sprite images to realistic 3-D vistas for the awareness to dawn that here was a way of replacing real life with a computer generated copy. There is nothing profound here, just the impact of the incredible speed of very large scale integrated electronics. Now, with the aid of spectacles which give separate input to each eye and tactile stimulators on the hands, it is possible to enter totally into the world inside the computer. With the Cyberspace novels of William Gibson a new genre was born which went one stage further in depicting a synthesis of computer data networks with the neural structure of the brain so that one could interact directly with computing machinery without the need for the intermediate eye-screen interface. It's quite clear that this will happen in time. Why waste time displaying data on a screen, why not plug directly into the brain? Who knows what possibilities exist once the advanced pattern recognition skills of the human brain are combined with the digital processing of the computer. What will it be like when the computer couples directly into the human nervous system without the need for an intermediate interface? Aside from the minor consideration of feeding the body, it will be possible to live out an entirely artificial existence inside the computer.

Future developments in input-output devices will undoubtedly have a major impact on what is currently called computer graphics. At the moment the emphasis is on generating realistic images. Computer graphics is the thin end of a very long wedge which started when computers first produced a visual output in response to human input. Where it will end is unknown, but along the way it is sure to be lots of fun.

1.2 What Can You Do on a PC?

The answer to this question is best illustrated by looking at what has been achieved in the past on powerful commercial systems, of which a good example is the Reyes system developed at Lucasfilm Ltd and currently in use at Pixar. This has been used to make a number of well known short film sequences including "The Adventures of Andre and Wally B", "Luxo Jr.", "Red's Dream" and the animated knight sequence from "Young Sherlock Holmes". The Reyes system was set up to compute a full length feature film in about a year, incorporating graphics as visually rich as real life. Assuming a movie film lasts about 2 hours and the film runs at 24 frames per second, this means each frame must be computed (rendered) in approximately three minutes.

The basic strategy in this system was to represent each object (geometric primitive) in a scene by a mesh of micropolygons which are sub-pixel-sized quadrilaterals with an area of a quarter of a pixel (the smallest visible unit on the screen). All the shading and visibility calculations are done on these micropolygons. The overall picture is constructed like a movie set with only the visible parts actually being drawn. Micropolygons are deemed to be invisible if they lie outside a certain viewing angle or are too close or too far away. The final system includes subtleties such as motion blurring, the effect whereby objects in motion appear to be blurred at their trailing edges. This is one of the devices used to enhance the impression of motion and is another lesson learned from traditional cartoonists.

A very complex picture in this system typically uses slightly less than 7 million micropolygons to render a scene of resolution 1024 x 612 pixels. With 4 light sources and 15 channels of texture a picture takes about 8 hours of CPU time to compute on a CCI 6/32 computer which is four to six times faster than a VAX11/780. Frames from "Young Sherlock Holmes" were the same resolution and took an hour per frame to compute. In the final movie all the stored frames are played back as in a conventional film.

But it's not necessary to go as far as this to produce high quality pictures. There are now "personal" graphics stations available at prices almost within the reach of mortals. The Personal Iris machine manufactured by Silicon Graphics was a good examples. It offer 256 colours (8 planes) from a palette of 4096 and, using a hardware "geometry engine", were able to perform transforms such as scaling, rotation, hidden-line removal and lighting, amongst others, to produce 3-D motion in real-time. The CPU was a 20 MHz R3000 RISC processor with a R3010 FPU (floating point unit). Here, RISC technology has been used to maximise the speed, but it is interesting to note that, before 1986, Silicon Graphics used the 68000 processor as used on the Atari ST and the Amiga 500. It will not be long before machines such as these drop into the personal computer market.

Current machines you can buy include even further enhancements. Right now, in 1994, desktop users have the advantage of the local bus to speed up the transfer of data from the processor to the video card. The most popular of these is the VESA standard local bus (Video Electronics Standards Association) which is an adaptation of the 486's bus structure. This bus was originally a 32 bit bus which means that data was transferred along 32 parallel channels simultaneously, but now it's being pushed to 64 bits to handle the output of the next generation of 64 bit processors such as the Intel Pentium or the Mips R4000 RISC processor. To give you an idea of the immense amounts of data which must be transferred to the screen to make a convincing picture, consider that a screen with resolution of 640 x 480 pixels with 24-bit colour goes through 7 million bits each time it is drawn and to avoid flicker this must be done at least 20 times each second. Amazingly the 64-bit VESA bus can in principle handle up to 250 million bits per second, although video data doesn't go across the bus for every frame. Eventually we're going to see such buses as standard for personal computers.

Right now, the emphasis is in creating images on the screen which look lifelike and convincing. This takes a lot of work. The objects to be drawn start off as a description in a database of some kind. Then they must be set down to their positions in the artificial world inside the computer and seen from the observer's (your) point of view.

Even before the more subtle artistic touches are applied the objects have to be ordered for drawing so that the ones furthest away are drawn first. Then as each is finally drawn on the screen back faces which can't be seen in the real world have to be removed from the drawing list and any shading from light sources and surface textures have to be put in. To do a really convincing detailed picture on a desktop micro takes hours so high quality graphics is still the domain of specialist machines.

What about a micro like an 80486 with 2 MBytes of RAM and a CPU working at 33 MHz? The potential for detailed graphics is somewhat less, especially if frames are to run in real time, sufficiently fast to avoid intolerable flicker. But it is surprising how much can be achieved. For speed, building up solid objects using polygon meshes is most attractive since it only requires that the vertices be stored, and a large object can be described by a very small amount of information. Moreover, since polygons are sets of vertices joined by straight lines, the most complex algebra involved will be that of simple geometry. This is the strategy we will use.

1.3 C and C++ for Elegance and Speed

C and C++ commend themselves particularly well to the demands of computer graphics. C is a fast and streamlined language and C++ is very much more than an extension of it. In C the operator ++ means "increment" so one might imagine that C++ just means "incremented C". This is not the case. C is like a high-level assembler language. But it is more than an assembler language in that it does not depend on any particular processor instruction set while retaining many of the features of assembler. Assembler is just about the closest one can get to what is going on inside the microprocessor controlling the microcomputer. Ultimately all the operations which determine the function of the microprocessor have their origin in digital electronics. Since no one can think at this level, large groups of instructions are grouped together and given simple letter codes which have some meaning to the programmer.

For example, one of the most common operations is to copy data from one place in memory to another. Although such an operation requires very many settings of the electronic switches which really govern the operation of the processor, it is represented to the programmer as a single instruction as a unique combination of binary digits. A binary digit is just either one of the two possible settings of a switch, 0 or 1. A light switch is a binary switch; one might say it has the value 0 when the light is off and 1 when the light is on. A microprocessor which lies at the heart of a microcomputer operates in exactly the same way except that there may be nowadays millions of such switches involved. Therefore of all the many possible combinations of binary operations which could possibly exist there are those which amount to useful manipulations of data in the system. It is rare even for the programmer to even worry about these unique combinations of binary digits. Instead they are summarised into mnemonics which are easier to understand and called the Instruction Set. Being a good assembly code programmer largely consists of understanding what can be done with the Instruction Set.

1.3.1 Indirect Addressing

Of the many instructions in the instruction set, there are some very basic and powerful ones which dominate the manipulation of data. For the 68000 processor, which is a particularly straightforward processor these are the **move** instructions. They are used to copy data from one place in memory to another although the name inaccurately suggests that data disappears from the source location are reappears at the destination location. Of these **move** instructions there is a large and powerful group which use indirect addressing. What this means is that data is copied to or from a memory address which is itself held in a specified memory location, most likely one of the registers of the processor. The reason why such an instruction is powerful is that when the program is written, the programmer does not know what memory address will be held at that location at any particular time. The address itself becomes changed as the program runs. Such an entity is called a pointer. The pointer "points" to places in memory from where data is copied to or from and, like a searchlight, focuses attention on continually changing memory locations. In the context of assembler programming this is called indirect addressing because the actual address is only indirectly available by looking at a memory location. In C it is just called a pointer. If that's all there was to pointers the device wouldn't be of much use. However you can manipulate pointers with simple arithmetic so they point where you want. The most basic type of arithmetic is to increment (the operator ++ means increment) or decrement them before or after they are used so that you can move forwards or backwards along a data array. The use of indirect addressing through pointers gives C almost the same low level access to data as is available in assembler and accounts for its speed and power. Of course, there are many other features to the language, but the use of indirection in this way adds substantially to the power of C.

1.3.2 OOP

If you were familiar with C and were contemplating moving on to C++, you might think that the use of the ++ operator implies that C++ is just an incremented C. You would be in for a big surprise. C++ is very much more than a small increment of C. In fact it is so much more that it might easily have been called a separate language. However, its inventor Bjarne Strousrup called it C++. It retains all the features of C and adds a whole new aspect called Object-Oriented Programming (OOP). This is not a small step but an entirely new way of thinking about programming. It allows the programmer to build into his program objects having the same behaviours as the real life entities he is trying to model. If the problem he is modelling is about traffic flow then he can certainly include car objects into his program. These car objects can carry with them the characteristics of cars so that should one car "collide" with another in the program, the result might be damaged car objects. This is a very powerful view of programming. It brings the program closer to the way we view the world.

This book aims to show you how to program powerful graphics in C++ using these ideas.

1.4 The Example Programs

The programs in this book have been written using Borland's Turbo C++ 3.0 and are ready to run. They are written for the PC but, with changes only to the basic screen drawing routines, will run on any machine that has a C++ compiler. Turbo C++ is a very powerful and inexpensive compiler. It is one of several good compilers on the market. With its integrated Development Environment (IDE) it is easy to write and debug programs. It is a delight to use. Of course, it is also possible to use the more extensive Borland C++ package also though this, with the Applications Framework, contains material for Windows programming which is a whole new world yet again. I have used Borland library functions exclusively throughout for the basic screen operations, though it would have been possible to speed things up by using custom assembler code. The reason for this is to make the programs as simple, transparent and as well documented as possible to the programmer. Of course, if you're an experienced programmer you will quickly find ways of making little "hacks" and speeding things up considerably.

The programs have all been run extensively to ensure they are as bug-free as possible, and the listings have been obtained from within the IDE to ensure that there are no further stages of transcription during which errors might creep in. However as with all human endeavours, there can be no guarantee that the programs are completely bug free, or more likely that they will always run without problems under all ranges of input parameters. That is a disclaimer.

The programs are certainly neither the fastest nor most elegant examples of their kind in existence but, in a tutorial of this kind where the emphasis is on teaching, the main point is to understand how things are done. The astute reader will quickly discover clever ways of improving them.

Apart from this all the programs are tailored closely to the graphics applications. They attempt to use OOP in a creative and suggestive way in the spirit of the language.

2

An Introduction to
C and C++ Programming

C and now C++ programming are increasingly popular programming languages. Why is that? The answer lies in two quite different aspects of these programming languages: the ability to manipulate data at primitive levels and the very high level abstractions allowed in C++ classes. C++ is based on C but is much more than just an extension, as we will see. In fact even putting aside the enormous enhanced features that object-oriented programming (OOP) adds to C++, C++ has a number of smaller features that C doesn't which make life much easier for the programmer. For that reason we will simply pick up immediately with C++ as offered in Turbo C++ but deal in the first instance with those elementary aspects which do not involve OOP and are therefore clearly C. It's easy to use expressions like "elementary" when introducing a language knowing full well that it's definitely not elementary if you've never seen it before. That apology made, what we mean by elementary are those aspects of the language which are basic and without which no program of more than a few lines could be written.

A learner of C is at first surprised to find how small the language is. There are very few mathematical operations indeed and hardly any hardly any functions intrinsic to the language. It's really a bare-bones language, sometimes called a portable assembler language. That is a good description because assembler is the language of manipulating data at memory and microprocessor level and as close as a programmer can get to the hardware. C and C++ allow almost the same access to data but with unlimited potential for abstraction in C++ through the Object-Oriented features as well. Anything beyond the primitive intrinsic features of the language must be added as libraries of functions. In C++ it is also necessary to build libraries of classes. However the programmer would not expect to have to shoulder this burden and indeed does not have to. A package such as Turbo C++ has them all available, ready for use. Much of learning the language consists of knowing what library functions are available.

If you have ever programmed in assembler then many features of C and C++ will be familiar. One in particular, indirect addressing, plays a very important role in both assembler and C. If you understand how data is stored in memory and how indirect addressing works at the hardware level then you will not be surprised by pointers in C.

The following is certainly not meant to be a detailed description of the C and C++ languages by any means. Many aspects of the languages have been omitted entirely. The emphasis here is only on those aspects which have a direct bearing on the graphics programming in later chapters. For the ultimate reference the reader is directed to the most excellent and highly detailed "Bible" of the C++ language "The C++ Programming Language" by its creator Bjarne Stroustrup, though it may be too much for the beginner.

2.1 Code Fragments

In the following sections we will often have cause to illustrate various features of the language with small fragments of program code. These fragments will not run on their own. To do so requires a fuller description of the Turbo C++ integrated development environment (IDE) which we discuss in Appendix 1. For the moment it is only important to learn a few simple facts about the appearance of C++ code.

❑ the code can be written in free form, like a spoken language, starting anywhere on a page and without line numbers,

❑ each new statement must end with a semi-colon,

❑ comments can be inserted in either of 2 ways:

1. Preceded by /* and ended with */ for a block of comment, or

2. Preceded by // for a single line of comment.

Further clarification is given where the code fragments appear in the text.

2.2 Memory

To start with, we must look at a fundamental issue: how numbers are handled in a computer.

There are several places in a computer where data is stored or accessed. These constitute the memory of the system. Very approximately they amount to the following:

Microprocessor registers – a small number of memory locations within the main processor where data is currently being worked on.

RAM   – random access memory. Contained in semiconductor chips. Data may be written and read very quickly. Used for immediate program execution. When the power supply is shut off this data is lost.

ROM   – read only memory. Also based in chips but permanent so it's always there. Can only be read, not written. Usually holds permanent parts of the computer operating system.

Floppy disk   – read or write memory. A magnetic storage medium. Slower to access but can hold modest amounts of data or programs.

Hard disk   – also read or write memory. Like a floppy disk but mechanically rigid and capable of holding very large amounts of data. Also used to hold running program data in a transient manner.

From now on we won't be concerned with any further hardware details. For us, memory is just a place where data can be stored. But each item of data must be stored at a different location and each location is distinguished by a different address.

2.3 Numbers in the Binary Scheme

Data in a microcomputer system appears in several forms. This might seem confusing at first but results from distinctly different ways of manipulating data. The simplest unit of data is the BInary Digit or BIT and can have one of two values, either off (0) or on (1), also called logical FALSE and TRUE respectively. This is the most elementary unit in the computer system since the electronics is based on switches which are either on or off and therefore have a binary setting. No one has ever bothered to make any other kind of logic. The number system which can be constructed out of such units is called binary (base 2), meaning out of 2. The system which goes in powers of 10 and with which we are most familiar is called denary (base 10). We probably invented denary because we have ten fingers. In the binary system numbers are constructed from powers of 2. For example the number 13 measured in units of 10, or denary is really 1 x 10 plus 3 x 1. The number 213 is 2 x 100 plus 1 x 10 plus 3 x 1. If we list this as powers of 10 it looks like

$$13(\text{base } 10) = 2*10^2 + 1*10^1 + 3*10^0$$

$$= 200 + 10 + 3$$

The surprise here is that 1 is 10^0 which makes the powers of ten symmetrical. Any number to the power of 0 is 1.

In base 2, or binary, the number 13 looks like

$$13(\text{base } 2) = 1*2^3 + 1*2^2 + 0*2^1 + 1*2^0$$

$$= 8 + 4 + 0 + 1$$

Instead of writing numbers out in this long form, just as in denary it is usual to collect only the coefficients of the powers of 2 in columns. The column number, labelled from the right, gives the power of 2. Hence the number 13 is written as

$$13_{10} = 1101_2$$

The basic data types in C result from groups of bits although it isn't really the number of bits that distinguishes a basic data type since on different machines and with different operating systems (platforms), and especially as time goes by, the exact number of bits in a particular type may change although the data type will still have the same name.

Especially important in counting memory is the humble byte which is a group of 8 bits. That is independent of the C language altogether. The byte is the basic element of memory.

When you say "my machine has 1 megabyte of RAM", you mean it has 1048576 bytes of memory which is the value of 2^{20}. That doesn't look like a million does it? It is close to a million, but not exactly so, because we are in the binary system and have to count in powers of 2; one million bytes or 1 Mbyte is the closest number in denary.

Another useful entity is half a byte or *the nybble*. It is a group of 4 bits and is especially loved by assembly language programmers who have frequent use of it. The reason is clear. In the above example we referred to 1 Mbyte of RAM when it was really something slightly different. When dealing with smaller numbers we cannot be so sloppy. It is very useful to have a continuous set of numbers covering the full range between all the bits in a nibble set to 0 and all the bits set to 1. This is the hexadecimal system, or hex for short.

Humans count in powers of 10, and find it unnatural to count in powers of 2. But some link with the binary system is necessary, especially when memory locations are being inspected. To this end the hexadecimal number system is commonly used. In it nibbles are abbreviated into single symbols. For the values from 0 to 9 ordinary denary numbers are used but for the values 10 to 15 (the maximum value of a nybble) new symbols are needed. Here a great opportunity has been lost. Instead of inventing new computer age symbols, the letters of the alphabet A, B, C, D, E, F have been hijacked. Hexadecimal means base 16.

In the three systems – binary, denary and hexadecimal respectively – the equivalence is:

Binary	Denary	Hexadecimal
0000	0	0
0001	1	1
0010	2	2
0011	3	3
0100	4	4
0101	5	5
0110	6	6
0111	7	7
1000	8	8
1001	9	9
1010	10	A
1011	11	B
1100	12	C
1101	13	D
1110	14	E
1111	15	F

Negative Numbers

Negative numbers in binary are hard to get the hang of. This is because there is no special symbol reserved for the minus sign and it must be encoded within the number itself. It is done in the following way.

For simplicity, suppose we are working only in nybble size numbers (in fact since there usually aren't any instructions to handle only numbers of this size directly, a nibble must be part of a larger number). To deal in negative numbers the total possible range, 0-15, is split equally. The interval 0-7 inclusive (8 numbers) is reserved for positives and the range 15-8 inclusive (also 8 numbers) is reserved for negatives (the range –1 to –8). This is actually a good idea. A negative number is obtained by counting backwards from 0. If there is nothing below 0 the next best thing to do is to go to the top and count down. In a practical sense this is a good method because all the negative numbers then have their top bit set. The top bit is like a minus sign turned vertically. There is a special name for this convention: 2's complement

There is a simple recipe for getting the negative of a number: write it in binary, switch all the 1's to 0's and 0's to 1's (1's complement) and then add 1 (2's complement). Let's try it. We know that −2 is in fact 14 so here's the check:

Step 1

+2 is 0010

Step 2 (1's complement)

change bits to get 1101

Step 3 (2's complement)

add 1 to give 1110

which is 14 in decimal and, therefore, correct.

The 2's complement method of labelling negative numbers works for any number of bits and therefore the larger data types. But be warned, if you increment a number outside its positive range you might get nonsensical results. To help you keep track of what is going on numbers can be explicitly signed or unsigned. Signed numbers treat the top bit as a sign bit. Unsigned numbers are always positive.

2.4 Fundamental Data Types

We use the word fundamental here because you will see that there are more complex data types in C called derived data types and in C++ abstract data types, or classes, which the programmer can design. Even for abstract data types the grammar of the language does not change and they are used in exactly the same context as fundamental data types. The fundamental data types however are simply numbers which are a greater or lesser number of bytes long, with the exact size determined by the platform (hardware and compiler) and even possibly subject to change with time. The figures we quote are what is used in Turbo C++ and likely to be stable for a long time. The smallest one is the character called **char** type for the ASCII set shown in Appendix 2. This is of byte, 8 bits, length. **char** is typically used to represent characters that appear in sentences (strings). It is effectively a byte-length integer. The more general integer type is **int** which is 16 bit but can be used together with **short** and **long** as **short int** or **long int** to mean explicitly a 16 bit or 32 bit integer. When used alone **short** and **long** mean **short int** and **long int** respectively. All of these can be preceded by the specifiers **signed** and **unsigned**. If there is no specifier, **signed** is assumed.

To handle fractions and astronomically large numbers of the kind that would appear in a scientific calculation there are the following **float, double,** and **long double** which are represented in 32, 64 and 80 bits respectively.

It is worth mentioning three other types at this stage which are not really fundamental: **enum,** pointer and **void. enum** is used for ordered sets of values, such as the numbers of the alternatives in a list (like 0, 1, 2 etc.). Pointer is the data type for indirect addressing. It holds the address of something else and can occur as 16 bits for a **near** pointer or 32 bits for a **far** pointer. The next section discusses pointers more fully as a derived data type. Unlike the names of the other data types, the word pointer is not a keyword of the language and so has not been written in bold. **void** is used to specify that a function does not return a type or for pointers to data of unknown type. It represents a nonexistent or unknown type.

C++ is said to be a strongly *typed* language. What this means is every variable in a program has a type and this fixes very rigidly what can and cannot be done with the variable. It is also possible to convert from one type to another, in what is called a cast, under certain circumstances. By giving each variable a type the compiler can spot when you require more from a variable than it is capable of and flag an error which helps to nip bugs in the bud. C++ is very hot on bug control.

2.5 Variables

2.5.1 Variable Types

Every variable in C or C++ has a type. Suppose there is a variable in the program which measures the number of people in a census and has the name *num_persons*. What sort of variable should that be? Clearly it cannot be a fraction, and there cannot be a negative number of persons. It could be an unsigned integer. Therefore a possible choice of type for this variable would be **int**. The variable would make its first appearance in the program as a declaration in the form

```
int num_persons;
```

Note that it is followed by a semi-colon. The semi-colon signifies that a statement has been made. It is a declaration because we have simply declared the existence of the variable *num_persons* without saying what its actual value is. That will presumably happen at a later stage in the program. We could have initialised the variable at the same time as it was declared in the following way

```
int num_persons=200;
```

Now *num_persons* both exists and has a value.

If there is no explicit statement to the contrary then an integer variable is taken by default to be signed. If on the other hand we do not wish it to be signed, so that it is only a positive number over the whole range then we can force it to be **unsigned**:

```
unsigned int num_persons=200;
```

In fact this is a more sensible type since there will never be a negative number of persons and the full range of **int** can be used.

One might ask the question "where does *num_persons* exist?" The answer to that question depends very much on where in the program it is declared and we will consider the question later when we look at the scope of variables. For the time being it is sufficient to note that it has a location in RAM.

We should be careful however about how big this person count is going to be. If the platform we intend using, for example Turbo C++, represents **int** by a word of 16 bits, then the largest unsigned int we can have is 2^{16}-1=65535. Should the count exceed 65535, the 16 bit number will become 0 again. It would then have been better to have chosen a **long int** as the type, then if such a type is represented internally as a 32 bit number, a long word, the maximum value which could be held is 2^{32}-1=4294967295 or 4 Gigabytes. There aren't that many people on earth yet so that would work fine.

The alternative is to use floating point numbers. These are still held in memory as long words or greater but the number of significant digits is limited so as to reserve space for powers of ten. For example the smallest non-zero number an **int** type can hold is 1. The next number down is 0 so it cannot be used for fractions. This is an interesting point since in the graphics we will use **int** a lot for speed. But we will have to watch out that fractions less than 1 are not inadvertently lost. The advantage of a **float** type is that it is possible to describe very small and very large numbers with a limited number of significant figures. Hence a **float** can be used for a number such as 0.325 or 2.67 x 10^8 or 3.2 x 10^{-6} so there is never any risk of a variable going out of range. A **float** can have any sign. There is however a penalty to pay as far as our graphics project is concerned which will cause us to use **int** wherever possible. It is that **float** is much slower than **int** and since we are after as real-time graphics on a 486 **float** is too slow.

Variables can be of more complex type than the fundamental types discussed above. The simplest of these are the derived data types pointer and array which will be discussed shortly. Abstract data types, represented in C++ by classes, open the door to object-oriented programming and will not be discussed until a later chapter.

Later, when more has been said about the appearance of a C++ program, more will be said about other aspects of variables, such as their storage classes, scope and duration. For the moment we will look at derived data types.

2.6 Derived Data Types

There are several derived data types which build on the Fundamental types listed above. We will discuss them in turn, taking first the pointer and array together because they play a very important role on C and C++ programming and are intimately connected.

2.6.1 Pointers and Arrays

One of the first things which is surprising about the C language is that it is really quite small; there isn't much in it. It has hardly any mathematical functions actually in the language; everything comes from libraries of external functions. In the case of pointers and arrays they are really part of the same idea in different clothing.

2.6.1.1 Pointers

A pointer is a program variable which holds the address of something else. This is quite different to a fundamental data type which just holds a value. What do we mean by "holds" in this context, it seems a curious turn of phrase? The answer results from the fact that a computer gets data from memory locations, may change it and return it to other memory locations. This is quite different from the way we become accustomed to think of variables when studying mathematics.

When we say x has the value 6 or y is 3.25 there is no mention of "holding". But really that's not true. x is the name or label we are using to distinguish a set of numbers which have a special meaning. x can be any number which fits this meaning. It exists in our mind as a concept which can hold a value. Similarly for the computer. There is a special place in memory, consisting of a number of bytes depending on the data type, which is reserved when the variable is declared in the program. That's like thinking of x without yet having given it a value. So when we write a declaration like:

```
int num_persons;//the person count
```

a space of 2 bytes is reserved in memory with an address which is referenced from the label *num_persons*. For the moment the two bytes are empty because we haven't put anything there (or filled with garbage from whatever was there before). What must be done next is to initialise the variable:

```
num_persons=259;//259 persons
```

Now *num_persons* has 259 in it, or strictly speaking for the PC, the low byte has the value 1 and the high byte the value 3, in the order 3,1 with the least significant byte first. So there are two numbers associated with *num_persons*; its value 259, which is an **int,** and its address. Much of the power of C and C++ comes from the ability to work directly with the address of a variable without knowing what the value of the variable is.

A pointer is a variable which does not hold a value but instead holds the address of something else. This something else could be just a simple variable or another pointer or almost anything, as we shall see. Holding the address of something else is called **indirection.** Its importance in a program is that instructions can be written which manipulate the data held at the address in the pointer without knowing what is there at the time. This means a program can dynamically respond to data "on the fly". Without this possibility a program would be unable to efficiently respond to change.

So a pointer really has at least 3 pieces of data associated with it: its address in RAM, the address it holds and what lies at that address. We say "at least" here because what lies at that address may be another pointer or a number or elements in an array or something more complicated. This minimum amount of information to allow the compiler to build the pointer must be given when the pointer is declared. Because C++ is a strongly typed languages the compiler needs to be able to watch that the pointer is not asked to do something of which it is not capable. To declare a pointer to an **int** called *ptr* we declare:

```
int* ptr;  // pointer to an integer
```

The asterisk following **int** states that *ptr* is of type pointer-to-int and is a derived type. We could move the asterisk closer to the identifier and instead declare:

```
int *ptr;  // also a pointer to an integer
```

which means the same thing. I prefer to use the former because it emphasises that *ptr* is the identifier, or name, of the variable which is of pointer-to-int type. Sometimes in a list of variables being declared simultaneously it's more convenient to use the latter, to make sure that ptr is a pointer though others may only be **ints**.

Now we have to say which particular integer variable it points to by initialising it:

```
int* ptr=&num_persons;// pointer to person count
```

where the ampersand, &, means "address of". So what we have said is that *ptr* is assigned the address of *num_persons*. Figure 2.1 shows how memory might be allocated with fictional addresses written in for realism. Note here that the addresses shown are 16 bit numbers. This is because it is assumed that **near** pointers are used in which the address only changes within the range 64K. Near pointers are always used in the small memory model which is what is used to compile all the programs in this book. The possibility of different types of pointers stems from the segmented addressing of the Intel x86 series processors and is a complicated topic; it is beyond the scope of this book. Note also that the bytes are reversed in order in memory from the way you might expect. That is also a property of x86 processors.

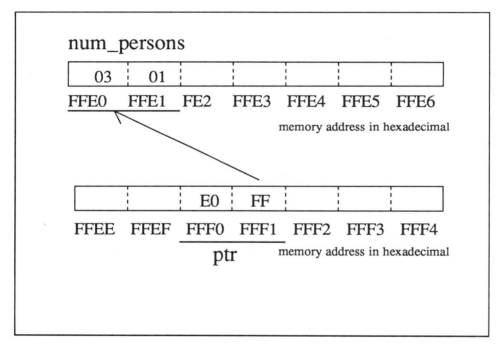

Figure 2.1 Indirect addressing with a pointer

Now that all is set, we can get the value of *num_persons* from the pointer indirectly rather than *num_persons* directly

```
int result=*ptr;// result equals person count
```

There's a lot going on here. A new **int** has been declared and simultaneously initialised with the value of *num_persons*. We could have broken it into 2 steps as

```
int result;
result=*ptr;
```

but the advantage of this language is the ability to cram a lot of meaning into a single line (sometimes with loss of clarity, but with brevity). The asterisk before the pointer name on the right hand side of the assignment means "what-the-pointer-points-to" and is called dereferencing. What the pointer points to is, of course, *num_persons*, so 209 will now be also held in *result*.

This use of the asterisk on both sides of the assignment operator is confusing at first, but there isn't a problem if you remember that on the LHS it defines the type and on the RHS means dereference; in both cases the asterisk says what is being pointed to. There is also confusing use of the ampersand in the same way. We have already seen it on the RHS as an address but it can also be used on the LHS to declare another type called a reference, but we will look at that later in Chapter 3.

2.6.1.2 Arrays

An array is a set of data types all of the same kind. It is possible to have a set of different types called a structure but we will meet that later in its context as a special kind of class. There is also the **union** which is a set of different types occupying the same memory; the **union** has not been used in the programs in this book.

The array is an important derived data type since there is frequent need to store an array of data. An array identifier also acts like a pointer but of a constant type.

Let us suppose that we wish to store a set of values of the variable *x*. *x* may represent the heights of people, temperatures read from a thermometer at different times, or perhaps a list of the number of homes rented by an agency for different years. If it is either of the former we will wish to save *x* as **float**. If it is the latter, **int** will probably do. Let us assume it is **int**. The array of values has the identifier *x* and can be declared with the size of the array, that is the number of elements

```
int x[8]; // 8 elements
```

for an array with 8 elements. If we wish the array can be initialised at the same time it is created

```
int x[]={1,2,3,0,4,9,3,21};
```

Note that the array size doesn't have to be specified if the elements are given.

Alternatively the elements of the array can be filled one by one

```
x[0]=1; x[1]=2;// initialise the first 2
```

Please make note of a very important fact here; the first element of the array is called number 0 and an array element is specified by the element number, or index, inside the square brackets. Whilst it may sound strange that the first element is called number 0 it is very useful and indeed natural. Consider how you count in tens. All the numbers between 0 and 9 constitute the first ten numbers. 1 isn't the first number, it is 0. 10 is the first number of the next decade, not 11. There is also a good practical reason for having the first element as 0 which is to do with the way an array is laid out and accessed in memory and connected with how it is related to pointers. An array has several pieces of data associated with it. First there are the data elements of the array and then the addresses of the memory locations of each of the elements. Since the elements follow each other in memory in sequence, it is pointless to keep more than the address of the first element $x[0]$. This address is associated with identifier of the array itself, x, as if x were a pointer to the array and like any pointer, held the address of the start of the array.

As was done in the element-wise initialisation, to access one of the elements of the array we use indexing by square brackets

```
int result;      // create result

result=x[1];     // assign result to x[1]
```

x is like a pointer constant since it must always hold the address of the start of the array. But that doesn't stop us from getting array elements by dereferencing x. We could have written

```
result=*x;       // get what x points to
```

x points to the start of the array which is $x[0]$, the first element. Indexing and dereferencing to get array elements achieve the same end. This apparent duplication is very confusing to the novice and seems to be unnecessary. The language allows you to think of an array as either an entity with a name whose elements can be accessed by indexing, or a just a contiguous sequence of data in memory. The first is closer to the mathematical picture, the second is what really exists in the computer. Which one is the best to use depends on the problem in hand. In fact we can go even further and get any element by dereferencing

```
result=*(x+3);   // get the fourth element
```

It is the fourth element because $x[0]$ (= $*x$) is the first, $*(x+1)$ is the second, $*(x+2)$ is the third and so on.

There is a subtlety here which you might have spotted. The second element was accessed at the address $x+1$, but was that address x plus one byte, or x plus what? It was in fact

```
address x + 1*(number of bytes in the type)
```

The type is **int** so if **int** is implemented in 16 bits, $x+1$ is an address which is 2 bytes higher than x. Because the type of the array was declared as **int*** (pointer-to-int) the compiler knows that it must do a calculation to get an address which is based on **int**.

The number of bytes associated with a type is called the scalar of the type. That this calculation is automatically done relieves you from ever having to worry about how memory is allocated for data in this instance.

2.6.1.3 Pointer Algebra

x is like a pointer to the first element of the array but it isn't a real pointer because it must always represent the address of the first element. That can never change. However we can now invent another pointer which can hold any address but initially it will hold the address of the start of the array

```
int* array_ptr=&x[0];//init. pointer to array
```

The array pointer is of type pointer-to-integer and is set to point to the address of the start of the array which is &*x*[0]. Figure 2.2 shows a memory layout. Alternatively since we know that *x* itself is like a fixed pointer it can simply be copied as

```
int* array_prt=x;    //assign one pointer to another
```

In this case the address that x represents is simply copied into *array_ptr*.

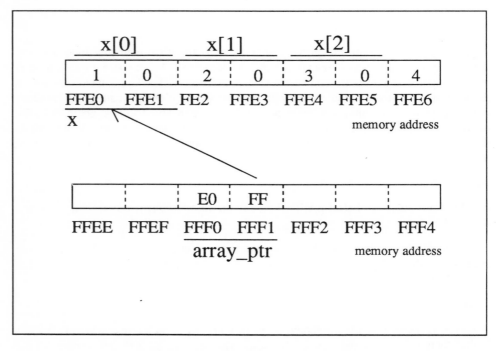

Figure 2.2 : pointer addressing an array.

Yet again it could be done in stages:

```
float* array_ptr;      // declare the pointer
array_ptr=x;           // copy x
```

Why have we gone to all the trouble to set up *array_ptr* when *x* seemed to do the same thing? Remember *x* cannot be changed but *array_ptr* can, that is we can manipulate the address it holds so as to point it anywhere along the array. This is pointer arithmetic or pointer algebra. We can do something new with *array_ptr*; we can make it point to the second element of the array

```
++array_ptr;
```

This is the pre-increment operation (a prefix operator) and it moves the pointer along one position in the array. What that means is that *array_ptr* now holds the address of the second element of the array. The ++ operator means increment the address the pointer holds. Of course, it is incremented by the number of bytes corresponding to the **int** type and you don't have to worry about it. If the pointer had been declared as **float*** then it would have been incremented by 4 bytes, if that is how **float** is implemented. The advantage of being able to change the pointer is that it is now permanently changed and if it is accessed in a loop this simple instruction will ensure that it marches along the array without us having to keep count of the position. You will see the increment operator and its inverse, the decrement operator – –, used very frequently. Together with pointers it is one of the most powerful device in the C language. You can now see where C++ came from – it is incremented C.

There is one final twist to consider which emphasises the similarity between pointers and array names. Just as it is equivalent to use either subscripting or dereferencing of an array name to access one of its elements, so it is possible to do the same with a pointer. In the above example once *array_ptr* is initialised to *x* we can write

```
array_ptr=x;              // init. pointer
result=array_ptr[4];      // 5th element by subscripting
result=*(array_ptr+4);    // same thing by dereferencing
```

A pointer can get what it points to either by dereferencing or by subscripting. It's the same thing, only the appearance is different.

2.7 The Structure of a C++ Program

Here is a toy program to illustrate the appearance of C++ code. It uses a standard C output function **printf()**.

```
/* a program to calculate the square root of 350 in three
iterations without using a mathematical function */
// SQU_ROOT.CPP
// calculate a square root
#include <stdio.h>

int main(void){

    float num=350.0;float squ_rt;
    float guess=20.0;
    squ_rt=(guess+num/guess)/2;      // 1st iteration
    squ_rt=(squ_rt+num/squ_rt)/2;    // 2nd iteration
    squ_rt=(squ_rt+num/squ_rt)/2;    // 3rd iteration

    // show the result
    printf("\n square root of %4.1f is %6.4f",num,squ_rt);

    return 0;
}
```

Even though this is only a tiny program, there is a lot in it. Without going into great detail, let's look at what it contains.

First note that there are two ways of including comments. A comment is for explanation and is not meant to be turned into executable code by the compiler. You can include a long comment over several lines within /* at the start and */ at the end. This is standard C. For a single line comment you can start the line with //. This is an enhancement of C++.

Next there is the precompiler directive **#include <stdio.h>**. It tells the compiler to add in the full contents of a file with the name *stdio.h* which is to be found in the include directory of your disk. Files with the extension .h are called header files since they contain declarations and other information which make variables and functions visible to the current program. In this case we want to get an output on the monitor so we have to include information which will allow the function which does that, **printf()**, to be used.

Next comes the program itself; it is called **main()**. **main()** is just another function like all others and it has to be defined in the way all functions are. It is preceded by the data type it returns when it finishes, in this case an **int** and it must state what type of data it takes as an argument. In this case it doesn't require anything, but rather than say nothing we specify type **void** which means nonexistent data type and is useful information for type checking.

The opening brace { signals the beginning of the function and everything up to the last closing brace } is the body of the function and will be executed. There must always be as many { as } in a function. In the function body each statement terminates with a semi-colon.

At the start of the function is the declaration and initialisation of the *num* to be square rooted. It, and successive code is indented to show that it belongs to **main**(). It is usual to indent each separate sub-block of code. *num* is taken to be type **float** so that decimals can be handled. Likewise the answer *squ_rt* is declared and an initial guess defined. Then the calculation begins. The trick is to start with a guess, divide that guess into the number and take the average with the guess. If it's a reasonable guess, the average quickly moves to a good approximation to the square root. This is done three times, each time taking the result form the last to generate the trial value for the next. Note that it is not necessary to declare a new *squ_rt* variable for each iteration. The appearance of *squ_rt* on either side of the assignment operator, =, is not a violation of algebra but just a reflection of the fact that *squ_rt* is a memory address which holds data. Data can be copied from it to start a line and at the end data can be copied back into it. Finally the result is output on the monitor using **printf**().

printf() is a standard function for outputting data. The data can be included in a string of characters which are enclosed in quotations. The places where the output is to be positioned are marked by the format specifiers starting with the % sign. For floating point output the specifier is in the form **%fw.p** where w gives the minimum width of the output and p gives the precision or the number of places of decimals. Since the value of *num* is 350.0 it needs a width of 4 and a precision of 1. We require the result to have 4 places of decimals and since it has the value 18.7083 to that precision, it will have a width of 6. The escape sequence \n means start a new line.

What appears on the monitor is

```
square root of 350.0 is 18.7083
```

On the penultimate line 0 is returned by the function in accordance with its return type which was stated to be **int**. A return value of 0 means the end of the program was reached without error. Finally the closing brace } is reached and the program ends returning control to whatever called it, most likely the operating system or the IDE in Turbo C++.

2.8 Functions (Passing by Value and Reference)

The function is also a derived data type. **printf**() is a function. Unfortunately it is a complex library function and would not be helpful as an illustration. Instead we will look at another small program which shows how functions work. This is very much like some of the examples given at the end of the chapter. You may regard them as variations of this one.

```
// VOLUME.CPP
// calculate the volume of a box

#include <stdio.h>          // declarations for input/output

// forward declaration of function
int volumef(int,int,int);  // takes three integer arguments

int main(void){// the main program

     int l=2;          // Note: letter 'l' not digit '1'
     int b=3;
     int h=4;          // initialise length, breadth and height
     int volume;       // declare the result
     volume=volumef(l,b,h);
     printf("\n the volume is %3d\n",volume);
     return 0;
}                     // end of main

int volumef(int length,int breadth,int height){//function body

return length*breadth*height;// the answer

}                     // end of function
```

This program calculates the volume of a box with side lengths equal to 2, 3 and 4. What it does is not as important as how it does it. Look at the second program line (ignoring comments). There the volume function is forward declared. It is announced long before it is used so that the body of the main program will at least know that **int volumef(int,int,int)** is a function which must be supplied with three integers to do its job, which are the arguments of the function, and returns an integer. The declaration only announces the function. The definition of the function is left until after **main** but that won't be a problem because the compiler will be looking out for it wherever it is.

Lets go straight to the definition of **volumef()** at the end. There a full description for how the function works is given in terms of three new variables *length, breadth and height* which are not mentioned elsewhere in the program. These are dummy variables whose only job is to show the implementation of the function. They are said to have block scope within the block of code which is the body of the function and are auto variables with local duration; they only exist within the function. These terms will be explained fully later.

When the main program is run the three variables *l, b* and *h* are declared and initialised. Then a new variable volume is declared and **volumef(l,b,h)** assigned to it. **volumef(l,b,h)** is an expression which is evaluated at this point and to do so the function itself must be called. What happens is that the numbers 2, 3 and 4 are copied into *length, breadth* and *height* and the function runs to produce an answer of **int** type which is returned. The fact that copies of the variables are passed means that while the function is running there are now two identical sets of data in memory: one is *l, b* and *h* and the other is *length, breadth and height.* Doing it this way means that the original data cannot be corrupted by the function but can be a waste of time if the data is long, as for an array. This way of passing arguments to a function is called **passing by value**. There is another very important way called **passing by reference** in which the actual address in memory of the data is passed. This is faster than passing by value for large variables but dangerous since the original data itself is accessible to the function. Passing by reference can be done with a pointer or with the reference data type which we will see very much more of later.

Where the function actually appears in an expression, as in the assignment to *volume,* it evaluates to the return value. The answer is then displayed using **printf().**

Having seen how this function works it is easier to discuss some other variables properties: scope, duration and storage class.

2.9.Storage Class, Duration and Scope

2.9.1 Storage Class

This is not class in the OOP C++ sense. It means where in memory the data associated with a variable is stored. It can be in an area of RAM called the data segment belonging to the program, in a CPU register, another area of memory reserved for temporary variables called the stack or even another dynamic area of free memory called the heap. Where the data is held depends on how a variable is declared and where it occurs in the program. If a variable exists only inside a function as in the above section where it was copied by value, then it is only needed as long as the function lasts and is only a transient thing. It will most likely be held in the stack or in the CPU registers while it is being used. Storage class relates to the physical location of data.

2.9.2 Scope

The scope of a variable means where in the program it can be used, i.e. where its name has meaning. Put more precisely it means where the identifier (name) of the variable can be used to access memory for the object it describes (object here only means memory usage and not as in OOP). This sounds complicated but it isn't. In C, variables come and go with great frequency. When a function is defined it uses variables to spell out how it works as shown in the section above. These variables come to life when the function is called and either copies of data (pass by value) or references (pass by reference) are assigned to them. At the end of the function they die. Variables of this kind have scope limited to the block of the function, and need only to be temporarily stored on the stack. In general, the shortest scope is block scope, and may apply, for example, to a short loop.

A much longer scope is file scope and applies to variables declared outside all functions, including **main**(). These are global variables. Their scope starts when they are declared and continues until the end of the file.

Class scope applies to classes in C++ and is complicated until you understand classes. We will delay this until OOP.

Scope is very similar to **visibility,** i.e. where a variable can be "seen". They only differ where two variables have the same name which may occur when one is declared inside a block contained within another block with the first declaration. The inner variable will "hide" the outer one until it goes out of scope.

2.9.3 Duration

Duration has a very similar meaning to storage class in that the way in which data is stored is closely related to how long it lasts. Of course, it is also a consequence of the scope as well. There are three types of duration: local, static and dynamic.

The variables we have seen with block scope in a function are good examples of local duration. They endure only as long as the function call. They are local to the block. They are kept on the stack or in a CPU register and are also called automatic. In fact if you wish to ensure that a variable is automatic you can precede the declaration with the **auto** specifier. The stack is like a data pile in RAM where data which is transient is temporarily stored. It works on a first-in-first-out basis with data being removed in exactly the reverse order it is put in. There is nothing mysterious about the stack, it is just an area of memory but with one on the registers of the CPU, called the stack pointer, keeping a record of the address of the last memory location filled. As data gets put on the stack the address held by the stack pointer changes, decreasing since the stack usually moves downwards from high to low memory.

Static variables are given space in memory in a more permanent location than the stack, in a part of RAM reserved for program data called the data segment. You can force static duration by using the specifier **static** in the variable declaration. This memory is permanent while the program lasts and a variable of this type effectively lasts forever. Variables with file scope are static.

Dynamic duration applies to variables which are also transient, like auto variables but which are so under the control of the programmer. They are held in another stack-like are of memory called the heap, or free memory, and are put there with calls to specific memory allocation functions. For us the most important of these is **new**, a C++ function. They are removed with another C++ function, **delete**. Free memory is a good place to temporarily hold large data objects. We will use **new** a lot in the programming of classes.

2.10 Operators

Operators are the "built-in" functions of the language. They are symbols which perform operations on variables. Mostly in C functions are provided from the libraries or user-defined by the programmer. In C++, the operators listed below can be "overloaded" to represent new operations between user-defined data types so as to extend their meaning. The very approximate categorisation below gives a brief description of built-in operators.

Arithmetic

For simple arithmetic manipulations of fundamental data types.

Add	+	Multiply	*
Subtract	–	Divide	/
Remainder	%		

Relational

For comparison, especially decisions inside loops. Watch out for ==, it is not assignment but asks the question "is it equal to..."?

Less than	<	Greater than	>
Less or equal	<=	Greater or equal	>=
Equal to	==	Not equal to	!=

Logical

These return a 1 if the operation is TRUE and 0 if it is FALSE. In C any variable which is non zero is TRUE whereas a variable which is zero (or null for a pointer) is FALSE. It's easier to tell the truth than a lie!

AND	&&	OR	|

Bitwise

These are operations on variables represented as their binary equivalents.

Shift left	<	Shift right	>
AND	&&	OR	|
Exclusive OR	^		

Assignment

Copying the contents of one variable into another. There are various shorthand combinations here involving simultaneous assignment and arithmetic, for example

x = x + 2;

can be shortened to the assign add combination

x += 2;

Assignment	=	Assign add	+=
Assign subtract	−=	Assign product	*=
Assign divide	/=		

plus the equivalent combinations with the bitwise and shift operators.

There are several other operators associated with pointers and classes which we will leave until these topics are covered.

2.11 Turbo C++ IDE

Here is a very brief description of the Turbo C++ Integrated Development Environment (IDE); more information is given in Appendix 1. A full description is given in the Turbo C++ User's Guide which comes with the package. It is a fully integrated platform for generating, debugging and running programs. This section only contains a few hints which will help you find your way initially. First a comment on the memory model.

2.11.1 Memory Model

The way in which memory is allocated for the program is called the memory model.

There are six memory models which can be used: tiny, small, medium, compact, large and huge. They have their origin in the segmented addressing of the Intel 8000 series CPUs and the differences between them depend on how much memory is allocated to the assembled program code and how much is allocated to data. In general both of these grow, but not uniformly, with increasing model size. For the modest sized example programs in this book the default model, small, is used. This gives 64K for code and 64K for data and stack and near pointers are always used. These are 16 bit pointers which cannot address beyond the 64K limit but are fast, which is what is required for the graphics.

2.11.2 Anatomy of a Program

Here is the way an executable program can be put together. First a program is written in a window in the Editor. Then it is saved to memory using the menu option **File|Save as..** when it is given a name. If there are other source code files which must be linked then a project must be opened and these files added to it. The simple example files at the end of this chapter do not require projects. Projects are described where they occur in the later chapters.

The program can be compiled and run from within the IDE with the menu option **Run|Run**. If the program is error free there will be a brief switch to the user screen where the output will be displayed and a return back to the IDE. If there are errors you will be told what and where they are in a message window. If the program compiles OK it will run immediately. To see the output of the program from within the IDE, switch to the user screen with the menu option **Window|User screen**. You can get back to the IDE from the user screen by pressing any key or clicking the mouse. Compiling the program will also produce a file in the same directory as the source file and with the same name except that its extension will be .exe. This is an executable file which can be run directly from the DOS prompt outside the IDE.

In the simplest approximation that is all there is to it. Of course, there are very many more details to worry about to fine tune the system but the IDE is supposed to make running programs as easy as possible. Where more information is required it is given in the text and Appendix 1 has a much fuller description.

2.12 Example Programs

The example programs for this chapter are not graphics programs but are short and illustrate the basic C and C++ programming ideas met in this chapter. Enter these programs in the IDE and run them as described above. Try changing them and introducing your own variations to see what happens. The best way to learn is to experiment. The programs are described below.

PC_WORLD.CPP

This is a version of the usual "hello world" program that starts many C books. It starts with comment lines giving the program's name and purpose. Comments are essential for other people to understand what's going on and for yourself at some later date when you've forgotten.

It uses the standard C output function **printf()** to display on the screen the words "hello PC WORLD". To be able to recognise **printf()** as a function the **include** directive must be added above the beginning of the program body. **printf()** is a big and powerful function but here it is only being used to output the string within quotes. The **\n** is the newline character so it starts a new line before the text and goes to a new line after the text.

The main program starts with **int main()** which is the main function and returns an **int** at the last brace }. This **int** is 0 to state that the program terminated without error.

PCPPWRLD.CPP

This is the C++ version of the previous program. The C function **printf()** has been replaced with the more powerful C++ <<operator, cout. This is in fact a much more complicated thing but it looks simple. That is the style of C++. It is actually an overloaded operator of a class, but that will become clearer when C++ classes are explained later. For the moment think of it as a channel for an output stream of data, which once again is enclosed in quotes.

C_NAME.CPP

Here is a program showing input of data using the C input function **scanf()**. This function waits for data from the keyboard and returns when **Enter** is pressed. The data is put into an array of characters, which is declared on the line above, as a string. A string is a character array with the null terminator, 0, after the last character. The **%s** in **scanf()** is a format specifier which says "get ready for a string". The string is placed character by character in the array *name*. **printf()** is told to output a string by the same format specifier and is passed the array identifier to do so.

CPPNAME.CPP

The C++ version of the previous program. Here the C++ operator cin>> is used to place the string in the array *name*. **cin>>** is for input and **cout<<** is for output. Notice how the operators can be placed in series (concatenated) to output or input combinations of messages and data.

VOLUME.CPP

Here is the function given earlier in the text. In this program it is spelled out. In the following versions the code is more compact and terse, as C can be.

At the start there is a declaration or prototype of the function, which specifies the data types it takes as arguments and what type it returns. A prototype is needed to make the function visible to the rest of the program. With it the program can be compiled as long as the full function definition, giving the details of its implementation, is somewhere else in source files. In this case it is at the very end. **volumef()** takes three **int** arguments as **pass by value,** which means they are copies of the original *l, b* and *h*, and returns an **int**. It calculates the volume of a box from the three side lengths.

In the program, first four integer variables, *l, b, h* and *result* are declared and then *result* is assigned the value of the function. The function is an expression which is evaluated by calling the function and the result assigned to *result* which is then displayed on the monitor.

VOLUME1.CPP

This is the same program as above except that it has been compacted to make the code shorter and more terse. As you become more experienced you will prefer terse code, though to start with it is harder to understand.

The declarations of the variables has been done in one line with commas separating the individual terms, and there is no longer a *result* variable. Instead the function itself has been placed in **cout<<** for evaluation. We can see that *result* was really an unnecessary intermediary.

VOLUME2.CPP

Here is a different approach using a pointer. **volumef()** no longer returns anything but does take an additional pointer argument. The pointer-to-integer variable *pointer* is declared and initialised with the address of *volume*. *pointer* is now passed to the function so it is only the address of *volume* which is being passed. This is **passing by reference.** The function assigns the product to what the pointer points to, which, of course, is *volume*. This is called dereferencing the pointer. In this way *volume* is changed though it has not been explicitly mentioned. Passing data by reference requires care because the function then has direct access to the variable and may corrupt it, if the function has a bug.

VOLUME3.CPP

A more terse version where now the pointer, *vpointer*, has been dispensed with and the address of *volume* passed directly to *volumef()*. This looks like trickery until you realise that *ptr* is being initialised with *&volume* during the function call with the missing line

```
ptr=&volume;
```

vpointer is thus seen to be an unnecessary intermediary.

INT_ARRY.CPP

Here is a longer program which illustrates the relationship between an array and a pointer used to access it. It is an array of integers which is filled and accessed with the streams operators. First an integer array is declared together with an index. The array is filled an element at a time. Notice that there are 5 elements but that they go from number 0 to number 4. It is very easy to make mistakes with arrays if you don't watch for this. In reporting the elements you are asked for the element number which is, of course, 0 for the first.

The object of the reporting is to show you that an element can be accessed using either subscripting of indexing from its name, or a pointer to which the name is assigned. Remember that an array name is like a pointer constant to the array.

CH_ARRY.CPP

This example illustrates an array of characters to hold a string. More on this in the next chapter. A string is an array of characters with the array element after the last character filled with 0, the null terminator. That's how the string knows how long it is. The numerical value of a **char** is called its ASCII (American Standard Code for Information Interchange) code. These are listed in Appendix 2.

In this example the string is typed in and on **Enter** is put directly into the array. Elements of the array are accessed as before but this time showing them as both characters and their ASCII values. This is done by making a cast to **int.** Each element of the array is a **char** but by preceding it by **int** it can be cast to **int** thus revealing its ASCII code. Either **int** can be in parenthesis or the character can be in parenthesis. These two alternatives are shown in the program.

STR_PTR.CPP

The program illustrates the manipulation of a string by means of a pointer. It includes pointer incrementing and decrementing and shows how a pointer can actually alter data. For a change the C function **printf**() is used for output.

Initially the string "mary" is placed in an array called *name*. The size of the array adjusts itself to fit the string exactly. It has 5 elements, 4 for the characters and the last one for the null terminator. Then the string and the second character by subscripting are output. On the next line a character pointer called *sptr* is initialised to point to 'a'. Now the fun starts. The pointer is incremented to point to the next character 'r'. Then what-the-pointer-points-to is incremented, by dereferencing, so the 'r' becomes 's' and the data is permanently changed.

CONSNANT.CPP

This final example program jumps ahead a little since it includes looping and decisions through **while** and **if**. However, it illustrates logical, relational and assignment operators. It counts the number of consonants in a word. The work is done in the function **count_it**() which uses the C function **getchar**() to read in a string of characters from the keyboard buffer, which is where input is stored when you press **Enter**. The characters are read in one by one while they remain in the alphabet and if it is not a vowel, the consonant count is incremented. At the end of the string the total count is reported. Look at the multiple arguments for the **if** test combining the "not equal to" test with logical AND's. See if you can rewrite this program to count the number of vowels in a string.

```
// PC_WORLD.CPP
// say "hello" in C

# include<stdio.h>                  // header file for printf()

int main(){                         // body of main

    printf("\n hello PC WORLD\n");  // output a string

    return 0;                       // terminate without error

}                                   // end of main
```

```
// C_NAME.CPP
// input a string in C

# include<stdio.h>

int main(){

    char name[20];                     // declare character array
    printf("\n What is your name? \n"); // output a string
    scanf("%s",name);                  // fill the array
    printf("\n hello %s\n",name);      // output a string

    return 0;

}
```

```
// PCPPWRLD.CPP
// say "hello" in C++

# include<iostream.h>                // header file for cout

int main(){

    cout<<"\n hello PC++ WORLD \n"; // output a string

    return 0;

}
```

```
// CPPNAME.CPP
// input/output a string in C++

# include<iostream.h>

int main(){

    char name[20];
    cout<<"\n What is your name? \n";
    cin>>name;
    cout<<" hello "<<name<<"\n";

    return 0;

}
```

```
// VOLUME0.CPP
// calculate the volume of a box

#include <iostream.h>

int volumef(int,int,int);    // prototype declaration: returns int

int main(){

    int l=2;                 // init. vars.
    int b=3;
    int h=4;
    int result;

    result=volumef(l,b,h); // evaluate the function expression
    cout<<"\n the volume is "<<result;       // print the volume

    return 0;
}

// function definition
int volumef(int length,int breadth,int height){

    return length*breadth*height;

}
```

```
// VOLUME1.CPP
// calculate the volume of a box; terse code

#include <iostream.h>

int volumef(int,int,int); // prototype declaration

int main(){

    int l=2,b=3,h=4;
    cout<<"\n the volume is "<<volumef(l,b,h); // print the volume

    return 0;
}

// function definition
int volumef(int length,int breadth,int height){

    return length*breadth*height;

}
```

```
// VOLUME2.CPP
// calculate the volume of a box using a pointer

#include <iostream.h>

void volumef(int,int,int,int*); // prototype declaration

int main(){

    int l=2,b=3,h=4;
    int volume;
    int* pointer=&volume;          // pointer initialization
    volumef(l,b,h,pointer);
    cout<<"\n the volume is "<<volume; // print the volume

    return 0;
}

// function definition
void volumef(int length,int breadth,int height, int* ptr){

    *ptr=length*breadth*height;   // pointer dereferencing

}
```

```
// VOLUME3.CPP
// calculate the volume of a box using a terse pointer assignment

#include <iostream.h>

void volumef(int,int,int,int*); // prototype declaration: must return int

int main(){

    int l=2,b=3,h=4;
    int volume;
    volumef(l,b,h,&volume);
    cout<<"\n the volume is "<<volume; // print the volume

    return 0;
}

// function definition
void volumef(int length,int breadth,int height, int* ptr){

    *ptr=length*breadth*height;

}
```

```
//INT_ARRY.CPP
// an array of integers.

#include <iostream.h>


int main(){

    int arry[5];        // an array of 5 integers
    int index;          // the array index

    cout<<"\n enter the first integer:";
    cin>>arry[0];
    cout<<"\n enter the second integer:";
    cin>>arry[1];
    cout<<"\n enter the third integer:";
    cin>>arry[2];
    cout<<"\n enter the fourth integer:";
    cin>>arry[3];
    cout<<"\n enter the fifth integer:";
    cin>>arry[4];

    cout<<"\n\n which element number would you like first? ";
    cin>>index;
    cout<<" element number "<<index<<" is "<<arry[index];

    cout<<"\n\n which element number would you like second? ";
    cin>>index;
    cout<<" element number "<<index<<" is "<<*(arry+index);

    int* ptr=arry;  // the array pointer

    cout<<"\n\n which element number would you like third? ";
    cin>>index;
    cout<<" element number "<<index<<" is "<<*(ptr+index);

    cout<<"\n\n which element number would you like fourth? ";
    cin>>index;
    cout<<" element number "<<index<<" is "<<ptr[index];

    cout<<"\n\n Return any number";
    cin>>index;

    return 0;

}
```

```
//CH_ARRY.CPP
// an array of characters.

#include <iostream.h>


int main(){

    char name[20];        // an array of 20 characters
    int index;

    cout<<"\n enter your name: ";
    cin>>name;

    cout<<"\n\n which character number would you like first? ";
    cin>>index;
    cout<<" character number "<<index<<" is "<<name[index];
    cout<<"\n with the ascii code "<<int(name[index]);

    cout<<"\n\n which character number would you like second? ";
    cin>>index;
    cout<<" character number "<<index<<" is "<<*(name+index);
    cout<<"\n with the ascii code "<<(int)*(name+index);

    char* ptr=&name[0]; // the array pointer

    cout<<"\n\n which character number would you like third? ";
    cin>>index;
    cout<<" character number "<<index<<" is "<<*(ptr+index);
    cout<<"\n with the ascii code "<<int(*(ptr+index));

    cout<<"\n\n which character number would you like fourth? ";
    cin>>index;
    cout<<" character number "<<index<<" is "<<ptr[index];
    cout<<"\n with the ascii code "<<(int)ptr[index];

    cout<<"\n\n the one beyond the last character is ";
    cout<<"\n null with the ascii code "<<int('\0');


    cout<<"\n\n Return any number";
    cin>>index;

    return 0;
}
```

```
// STR_PTR.CPP
// pointer manipulation with a string

#include <stdio.h>

int main(){

    char name[]="mary";              //init. an array

    printf("\n %s",name);            // output string "mary"
    printf("\n %c",name[1]);         // output character 'a'

    char* sptr=&name[0];             // init. string pointer
    printf("\n %s",sptr);            // output string "mary"

    sptr=&name[1];                   // init. pointer to 'a'
    printf("\n character %c, ascii %3d",*sptr,*sptr);
    // the character and its ascii code

    ++sptr;                          // increment pointer
    printf("\n next char is %c, ascii %3d",*sptr,*sptr);
    // move along the string

    ++(*sptr);       //increment what the pointer points to
    printf("\n next char in ascii list is %3d",*sptr);
    // changed the ascii code of 'r' to 's'

    printf("\n now the string reads %s", ----sptr);
    // the string is permanently changed to "masy"

    return 0;

}
```

```
// CONSNANT.CPP
// count the number of consonants in a word

#include <stdio.h>

void count_it();        // counting function prototype
int num=0;              // global record of count

int main(){

    printf("\n write the word to be tested\n");
    count_it(); //catch the word and count the consonants
    printf("\n this word has %d consonants\n",num);

    return 0;

}

void count_it(){        // function definition

    char c;             // hold a character
    c=getchar();        // read in first char from the buffer

    while((c>='a')&&(c<='z')){// providing it's in the alphabet

        if((c!='a')&&(c!='e')&&(c!='i')&&(c!='o')&&(c!='u')){
                        // and if it's not a vowel
            num+=1;     // it must be one more consonant
        }
        c=getchar();    // get the next character
    }                   // until there are no more

}
```

3

Advanced C and C++

This chapter is about the more advanced features of C++ which are essential in a large program but does not include Object-Oriented Programming. That follows in the next chapter. Here we look at pointer arrays, decisions, branching and looping, dynamic memory allocation, the reference data type, file structure for a large program and several other aspects of the syntax of the language.

3.1 Pointer Arrays

In the last chapter we learned that a pointer is a variable which holds the address of something else. It is said to point to the data of which it holds the address. To get that data the pointer must be dereferenced. However since a pointer holds an address, there is no reason why that address cannot be that of another pointer. Once you realise this you can see that pointers offer a device to access data at remote levels of indirection. Actually it is not usually necessary to go beyond one more level of indirection; the possibility of deeper levels of indirection is useful in multidimensional arrays but becomes hard to visualise. However two levels of indirection in the form of pointer arrays is a powerful feature and a useful way of accessing two dimensional arrays. Arrays of strings of characters can be accessed using pointer arrays.

First an important comment on arrays in general. Arrays of the kind we have been discussing cannot be used to hold data unless they have been declared with their size specified. It is correct to do the following

```
int x[100];          // declare an array of 100 elements
x[0]=10;x[99]=50;    // init. two of them
```

but the following cannot be done where the array size is itself a program variable and therefore unknown when the program is written

```
int x[m];        // this won't compile
x[0]=10;x[99]=50;
```

The reason why the latter will fail is because the compiler must allocate space for the array in its data segment when the program is being compiled and so the array size must be known. Arrays which have their size determined dynamically during the running program cannot be constructed this way. Such arrays are an essential part of programming however and can be implemented using memory management functions. In C++ there is a special operator specifically for just this purpose. It is the **new** operator. It will play an important part in our graphics programming and we will discuss it later in this chapter.

The way in which multidimensional arrays are implemented seems very strange until you realise that we are really looking at pointers with lower levels of indirection. Consider the 2-D array of integers

```
int x[2][4];    // a 2-D array of integers
```

which means two rows and four columns.

This looks innocuous but you might ask why it hasn't been written in the simpler and more obvious form

```
int x[2,4];     // does not mean a 2-D array!
```

The reason is that the form $x[2][4]$ really does represent how the array is accessed in an expression. Understanding this will help to see how pointer arrays work.

Multidimensional arrays are rather more complicated than 1-D arrays. Although our original idea was to have an element of the array specified by a row index and a column index, it is quite correct to use expressions like $x[1]$ even though x is the name of a multidimensional array and you would expect to see not one but two indices specified. When x appears in an expression it is interpreted as a pointer to the first element of the first of two 1-D arrays. When the expression $x[1]$ occurs it is also interpreted as a pointer but to the first **int** of the second row. We are clearly allowed to think of x rather like a pointer to an array of two pointers each of which points to a 1-D array of 4 integers. Suppose we decided to test this out and wanted to access an array element using dereferencing, how could it be done? Here it is:

```
int result;         // hold the answer
result=x[1][3];        // get last element by subscripting
// remember the first row or column is [0]
result=*(*(x+1)+3)     // same thing by dereferencing
```

Isn't the subscripting form easier to read and closer to our understanding of a 2-D array of integers? Clearly there's a lot going on behind the scenes, but to understand it gives greater power over data manipulation. Notice one important thing; in getting to the second row in *(x+1) it has been possible to use x+1 as a row address offset by 1 from the start of the array. But there are 4 integers between the start of the array and the start of the second row so it must mean that x+1 is of type pointer-to-4xint in order that it can jump four integers in a single increment. Notice one more important thing. In the above code fragment there are two pairs of square brackets in the first line and two indirection operators in the second line. There is a one-to-one correspondence here so it's possible to spot the implied level of indirection in arrays by counting the number of pairs of square brackets.

Let us look at another way of constructing a 2-D array explicitly from 1-D arrays using pointers. Let us first define three 1-D arrays of integers

```
int x[]={0,3,6,9,12};        // arrays of integers
int y[]={1,4,7,10,13};
int z[]={2,5,8,11,14};
```

x, *y* and *z* are the names (identifiers) of arrays of integers. Each one consists of a location in memory which holds the address of the first element of the respective array. So *x*, *y* and *z* are constant pointers to integers. Now let us define an array of pointers from *x*, *y* and *z* with the identifier *r*

```
int* r[]={x,y,z};            // an array of pointers
```

Clearly *r* is a 2-D array in our mind with 3 rows and 5 columns but we have constructed it as a pointer array. It is really a different thing altogether from the 2-D array above. Now to access the elements dynamically we can declare a pointer-pointer and initialise it to *r*

```
int** ptr_ptr=r;             // copy r
int** ptr_ptr=&r[0];         // same thing
```

Figure 3.1 shows a possible memory layout of these variables where *ptrptr* is actually held in a CPU register. To get the third y element (=7) which is in the second row and third column we can write

```
result=*(*(ptr_ptr+1)+2);  // element by dereference
result=ptr_ptr[1][2];        // same thing by indexing
```

What happens if we use the increment operator to increment the address held by *ptr_ptr*?

```
++ptr_ptr;                   // now points to y array
result=*(*ptr_ptr+2);      // third y again
result=ptr_ptr[0][2];        // third y by subscripting
```

Yet again we can go backwards to restore *ptr_ptr* to its original value

```
--ptr_ptr;                  // now points to x array again
result=ptr_ptr[1][2];       // get third y again
```

These manipulations of pointers are very difficult to follow to start with and, even when you are an experienced programmer, they give pause for thought. But the pointer together with its indirect addressing is a central feature of the language and allows rapid and succinct manipulation of data. Without it the language becomes far less interesting and useful; we will use arrays of the kind described above quite extensively in the graphics programming. However such 1-D and 2-D arrays require manipulation of the data which is very "array-like" and not natural to the more complicated objects such as vectors and matrices which we will need for the graphics. Although vectors and matrices are 1-D and 2-D arrays of data they have behaviours which go beyond the data itself. This need is satisfied by the OOP aspect of C++ through its classes.

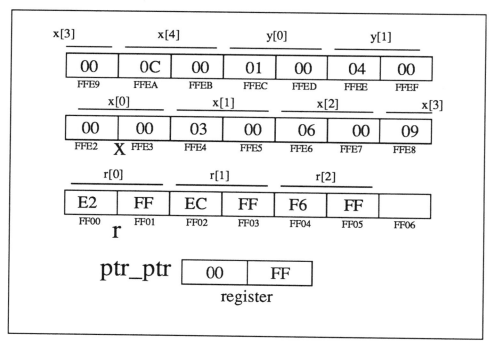

Figure 3.1: A pointer array.

3.2 String Arrays

Strings are collections of characters which usually look like lines of text. The string is treated in the language as an array of characters terminated with a special character called the null terminator which is a byte of value zero and is there to mark the end of the string. What we have been talking about in the previous section is very relevant here since the string identifier is a pointer constant to the first character. In other words a string is just a 1-D array of characters terminated with the null. Here is a string

```
char my_string[]="Hello World";// a string array
```

A string is an array of type **char**. The type **char** is implemented in 8 bits and is therefore a byte sized object. The different characters which you can use in strings aren't just limited to letters of the alphabet, there are many other symbols as well; they constitute the ASCII set and are listed in Appendix 2. In the above example the string has been initialised with the text inside the quotation marks which is a particularly intuitive way of writing a string. Alternatively we could have initialised the array character by character

```
char my_string[6];// declare a string
my_string[0]='H'; my_string[1]='e'; my_string[2]='l';
my_string[3]='l'; my_string[4]='o'; my_string[5]='\0';
```

Note that characters are enclosed by single quotes and space must be left for the NULL terminator.

Many strings together constitute an array of strings and are really a 2-D character array very similar to the 2-D integer array we looked at above. Here is an array of names set up as a 2-D character array

```
char names[4][7]={    "Tracy",
                      "Sharon",
                      "Kevin",
                      "Wayne"};
```

Here is the same array set up as an array of pointers

```
char* names[4]= {    "Tracy",
                     "Sharon",
                     "Kevin",
                     "Wayne"};
```

What is the difference between these two? In the first 28 bytes of space have been reserved for the entire array by the compiler and each row has been allocated 7 bytes. This leads to wasted space because "Tracy" needs only 6 bytes including the null terminator but we had to allocate 7 to cope with "Sharon". In the second case *names* is the identifier of a 1-D array of pointers to 1-D character arrays and evaluates to the address of the first one. Each pointer holds the address of one of the strings, for example *names*[0] holds the address of "Tracy". The difference now is that when *names*[0] is initialised, space in memory for just 6 bytes is allocated and filled with 'T','r','a','c','y','0' and a pointer to the 'T' returned to *names*[0]. Hence no space is wasted. Once the array has been defined it is possible to access it using a pointer-pointer which can be initialized to the string array. Here is the code from an example program, NAMES.CPP, at the end of the chapter. It illustrates manipulations of the string array.

```
// initialize a pointer to an array of strings
char** ptr_ptr=names;      // points to "Tracy"
++ptr_ptr;                 // points to "Sharon"
++(*ptr_ptr);              // pre inc. pointer :"haron"
(*ptr_ptr)++;              // post inc again: "aron"
(**ptr_ptr)++;             // change string to "bron"
```

Several complicated pointer manipulations are going on here. In the first line a pointer-pointer is initialized to point to the start of the array. In the second line it is pre-incremented to point to the second string identifier, i.e. the pointer to the string "Sharon". In the third line *ptr_ptr* is dereferenced and the result incremented; this means "increment what I'm pointing at". Since it is pointing at the address of "Sharon", incrementing the address will make it point one character further, that is to the 'h' not the 'S'. This increment is permanent. On the next line the same procedure is followed but with post-incrementing; in this example there is no difference between these two alternatives; in other cases there might be.

The next line does two levels of indirection which means "what I'm pointing at is pointing at". Well what I'm pointing to is the address of the 'a' in "Sharon" and what it is pointing to is the 'a' itself. So if I then increment that I get the next character in the ASCII set after 'a' which is 'b'. Now the string itself is permanently changed.

You can see how easily it is to get confused below a few levels of indirection. In the graphics programming we will be using integer arrays most of the time, for speed. There our manipulations of arrays will generally easier than this educational string example.

3.3 Reference Data Type

Having just looked at pointers this is a good place to introduce the reference data type. The appearance of this type is confusing in exactly the same way as is the pointer declaration and dereferencing. In the pointer case the ***** is used on the LHS to specify the pointer type and on the RHS to denote dereferencing. In the case of **a reference**, the **&** is used on the LHS to specify the type which leads to some confusion with its other use on the RHS to initialise a pointer.

To declare a reference, you write

```
int& my_ref;
```

and to initialise it to an **int** variable *x* you write

```
my_ref=x;
```

You could do this all at once:

```
int& my_ref=x;
```

This makes *my_ref* a reference to *x* and an **alias** for it. Now whenever *my_ref* is used it will be exactly the same as using *x* itself. Unlike passing by value, *my_ref* is actually another name for *x* and not a copy. Any change made to *my_ref* will also be made to *x*. *my_ref* is like a pointer which does not have to be dereferenced.

One of the major uses of references is as arguments within function definitions. For example a function which takes two **int**s

```
void my_func(int a,int b);
```

would be called with specific arguments

```
...
my_func(x,y);
```

where copies of *x* and *y* are passed to *a* and *b*. If *a* and *b* are changed in the function *x* and *y* will remain the same. If *x* and *y* are meant to be changed then a pointer would have to be used and dereferenced. If on the other hand references are passed

```
void my_func(int& a,int& b);
```

then when the function runs, if *a* and *b* are changed so will be *x* and *y*. In fact addresses are copied so the reference is really a pointer in disguise. When the arguments are large memory objects it is much more efficient to use a reference, which only requires an address, than to make a complete copy.

3.4 Control: Branching and Looping

Almost all programs need to be able to control their direction in response to the changing flow of data. There are a small number of statements in the C++ language which support this. These statements are sufficiently flexible to handle any combination of circumstances. The last example program, CONSNANT.CPP, at the end of the previous chapter illustrates some of these.

3.4.1 while Iteration

The **while** statement will continue to do something in a loop while a condition is **TRUE**. The condition is tested the first time at the start and nothing will be done if the condition is **FALSE**; the **while** will be by-passed altogether. If the statement is **TRUE** the statement immediately after the **while** (or the block of code enclosed by the braces) will be repeatedly executed until the condition is found to be **FALSE**. Figure 3.2 illustrates the flow of the **while** statement.

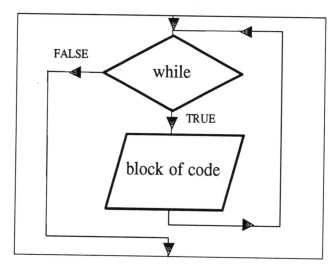

Figure 3.2: While loop.

```
while(*xptr++=*yptr++){

     // block of code

}
```

This surprising example includes an assignment in its test condition. **while** loops are often used in situations like this. What is happening is that two pointers are being dereferenced inside the test; "what *yptr* points to" is being copied into "what *xptr* points to" and both then incremented to point to the next. Thus an array is being copied while the test is being done and the block of code is also being executed. The loop will terminate when the array element being assigned is zero since that is logical **FALSE**, so it is in fact "what is being assigned" that is being logically tested.

Note also the position of the closing brace under the 'w' in the **while**. Though this arrangement is not mandatory, it helps to show where statement ends.

3.4.2 do-while Iteration

The **do-while** iteration works just like **while** except that the condition will tested for the first time after the block of code is executed. The block of code will then be repeatedly executed as long as the condition, tested at the end of each iteration, is **TRUE**. When the condition is found to be **FALSE**, control moves to the next statement after the **while.**

This can lead to disaster if the code being executed is not properly initialized until the condition is tested at the end of the first iteration. Figure 3.3 shows **do-while**.

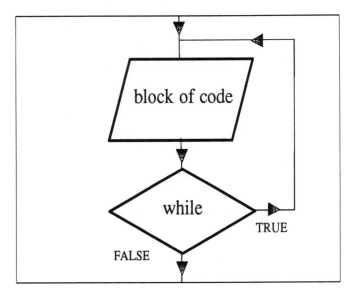

Figure 3.3: Do-while.

3.4.3 for Iteration

This is useful to repeat a loop a specified number of times. The **for** loop is essentially a **while** loop with a condition to test, which is usually a counter, and its initialization and increment/decrement. Figure 3.4 shows the flow of a **for** loop. The statements are placed inside the parentheses following the **for** and separated by semi-colons

```
for(int i=2;i<100;i++){
      // body of code
}
```

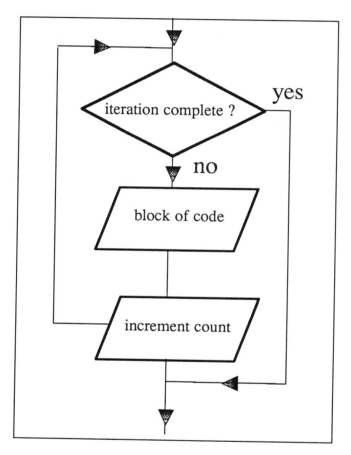

Figure 3.4: For.

A useful limiting case is when all statements are null as in

```
for(;;){   // forever
           // body of code
}
```

This will continue forever, or until a termination occurs inside the body of code.

3.4.4 if-else Structure

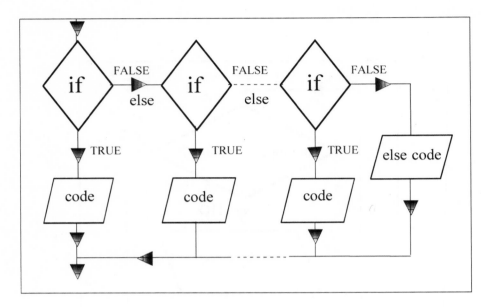

Figure 3.5: If-else.

if-else is a choice between alternatives. The diagram of Figure 3.5 explains it best. In a program, it might look like:

```
if(i<10 && x>3.20){
     // do something
}
else if(i<20 && x>9.70){
     // do something
}
else if(.......){
     ....
}
else ...... ;
```

where alternatives are chosen on the basis of the values of an integer and a floating point variable.

Sometimes this structure is more obviously replaced by the following, less elegant construction: **switch-case**.

3.4.5 switch-case

When the alternatives in a choice can be listed by an index it is more straightforward to use the **switch-case** statement. Figure 3.6 illustrates this.

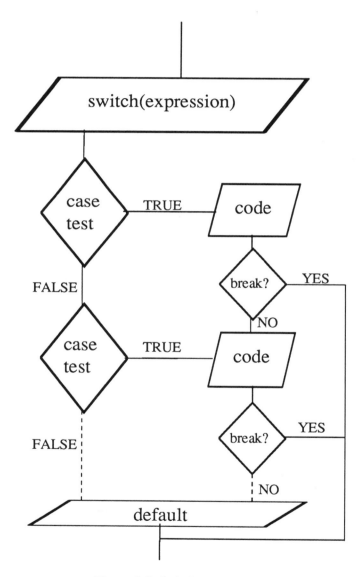

Figure 3.6: Switch-case.

Here is how it might look

```
switch(index){// index on integer values

    case 0:
            // do something for index=0
            break;
    case 1:
            // do something for index=1
            break;
    case 2:
            // do something for index=2
            break;
    default:
            // if no others chosen
            break;
}
```

Notice how each alternative ends in a **break** which breaks out altogether from the switch statement and prevents any further cases being considered. **break** is typically used to get out of a loop. The complement of the **break** is **continue** which will cause a loop to restart and ignore code following the **continue**.

3.4.6 goto

The dreaded goto returns! The use of this is to be discouraged except under very unusual circumstances where it solves simply what would be difficult to implement any other way. It causes an unconditional jump to a labelled statement somewhere else within a function but not past an initialisation.

```
    goto who_knows_where;
    ....
who_knows_where:
    // how did I get here...?
```

It is very unhelpful in debugging since it is difficult to identify unique conditions for the arrival at the point of the label. The **goto** is really a kludge and encourages bad programming technique and muddled thinking.

3.5 Dynamic Memory Allocation

There is very frequently a necessity to create space of unknown size for variables whilst a program is running. Typically this might be in the form of arrays of length unknown to the writer of the program. For example if a program asks for a string to be input from the keyboard, how much space should be reserved for the string? One solution is to limit the space and declare an array at the maximum in the program. This however is inefficient use on memory since the string may be very short in practice. Worse, the space may be insufficient and cripple the program. There is a much better solution.

Space for variables may be allocated dynamically "on the fly" with the C++ operator **new** and released when it is not needed any longer with the operator **delete**. There are also C functions **malloc** and **free** but we will not use them.

new opens space **on the free store** which is a managed area of RAM called the **heap**. This is less restricted than the **stack** which holds other short-lived and return addresses from function calls is essential to the program generally. The heap provides an alternative area of dynamic memory for user allocated storage. It does require that blocks of memory (objects) allocated to variables are deallocated as soon as possible. Except in the constructor and destructor of class instances, as we will see later, the programmer is responsible for this.

new opens space and returns a pointer to it. For example, for an integer pointed to by *xptr*

```
int* xptr=new int; // point to space on the heap
```

There is never such a desperate need for integers, but for an array

```
int* arry_ptr=new int[size];// an array of size integers
```

In this case *size* is a program variable whose value is unknown at the time the program is written. It provides a way of opening arrays of variable size. When the array is finished with it must be deallocated

```
delete []arry_ptr;
```

The [ ] shows it is an array.

3.6 Files for a Large Program

So far the example programs have been small. In general as programs get larger it is better to divide them into small units, or files, which are reasonably self-contained. In general there will be three kinds of files: header files, source files and a program file. The program file will contain the **main**() function.

Header files appear with the file extension .H and typically contain declarations of functions, **#defines**, **typedefs**, constants and other data which are needed to compile a source code file and appear at the head of it in the **#include** statements. They may **#include** other nested header files.

Source files usually have the file extension .CPP and contain the definitions of the functions which are declared in the header files. They must **#include** the appropriate header files. They can be separately compiled and are finally linked with the program file to produce the executable .EXE file which can be run from the DOS prompt by **Entering** its name. In the Turbo C++ IDE program file and source files are added into a project file to run, so that the linking is transparent to the user.

3.7 Other

There are some other features of C which are widely used in the language but have not been extensively used in the programs in this book. The reason for this is mainly the desire to produce an educational text where simplicity is emphasised, though the professional might aim the criticism that their omission leads to a restricted view of the language. I stick to my guns on this. There is enough to learn without assuming the full body armour of bullet-proof code. Here are some features which have been omitted.

const

const is a important keyword which is added to the declaration of a type to make a constant of the type. The point of making a type a constant is to prevent it being modified. There are even more subtle uses, particularly with pointers. For example, a function may return a pointer to a variable and we may require a safeguard that the dereferenced pointer not be used to corrupt the variable. One way to do this is to make the pointer a **const** type in the function definition

```
const int* my_func();//can't modify what it points to
```

The returned pointer cannot be used to modify what it points to; the compiler will signal an error. On the other hand it may be that a pointer itself should never be changed

```
char* const string_ptr="never change";
```

string_ptr cannot be used to point to anything else.

const is clearly an important safety feature of the language and should be used for "industrial strength" software, but it makes for much longer source code. It has not been used in this book.

#define

This is a precompiler directive, like **#include**, and is used to replace a user-defined identifier with a longer expression. It is a convenience to the programmer and is a macro since it is expanded before the compiler sees it. Although widely used, it is not encouraged since it makes what the compiler sees different from what the programmer sees and makes life difficult for debuggers. It is used later in chapter 10.

typedef

Another widely used shorthand device. You can define a more obvious word for an otherwise confusing combination in a type declaration. For example

```
typedef char** PString;
```

This will enable you to write
```
PString str_ptr;
```

whenever you wish to declare a string pointer since **char**** is the type of a string array. This is a very sensible thing to do since it makes the code more readable. Once again this has not been done in this book because it disguises the fundamental data types; it is perhaps best left for more experienced programmers.

3.8 Example Program

There is only one example program listed for this chapter: it is the string array program given in the text, NAMES.CPP.

```
//NAMES.CPP
// illustaration of pointer arrays

#include <iostream.h>

int main(){

    char* names[4]={"Tracy",        // array of string pointers
                    "Sharon",
                    "Kevin",
                    "Wayne"};

    char** ptr_ptr=names;   // init. string array pointer

    ++ptr_ptr;              // point to "Sharon"
    cout<<"\n"<<*ptr_ptr;           // output "Sharon"
    ++(*ptr_ptr);           // increment string address by 1 byte
    cout<<"\n"<<*ptr_ptr;           // output "haron"
    (*ptr_ptr)++;           // increment string addres again
    cout<<"\n"<<*ptr_ptr;           // output "aron"
    (**ptr_ptr)++;          // increment the ascii code
    cout<<"\n"<<*ptr_ptr;           // output "bron"

    return 0;

}
```

4

Classes

Object-Oriented Programming (OOP) is the jewel in the crown of C++. It is not just an additional feature of the language beyond C, it is a whole new way of thinking about programming. The class is the mechanism by which OOP is implemented in C++. In this chapter we explore what OOP is about and use a class to apply it to a simple example.

4.1 The World of Objects

Humans describe the World as a set of objects. Objects seem to be essential to language itself. Every sentence needs a subject and object (explicit or implicit) which has behaviour through a verb. The aim of OOP is to extend this paradigm to programming itself. There are additional devices such as inheritance, overloaded operators and virtual functions which further support the model.

To begin with, consider the problem of modelling the operation of a Bank (where rich programmers keep their money). There are many levels of functionality and many identifiable "data types". At the bottom there is the currency which flows through the bank and the accounts of the customers. This is more than a fundamental data type such as float since it is more than just a set of data. It can be internally represented as reserves, loans to debtors, loans from creditors the daily working fund and so on. To the customer it is visible as figures of credit and debit and hard currency but even that appears as notes and coins of different value. Money is not just a set of figures.

The Bank has its customers and the accounts associated with them. It has its employees of different status and the different tasks they perform. It has its own

BANK MODEL

branch

staff

deposit

  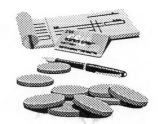

accounts

Figure 4.1: Bank objects.

internal structure: a Head Office and the different Branch offices filtering down to the High Street. It has different sections: a foreign currency department, a loans department, a mortgage department etc. The Bank does not exist in isolation, it communicates with the various institutions in the society in which it exists. Figure 4.1 illustrates a few of the "objects" in a Bank.

What is clear from this cursory view is that while the Bank is certainly a complex organism it has quite well defined objects associated with it. These are the things that have behaviour and actions. They are what we have been able to list as nouns and have a clear perception of when we think of a Bank. Sometimes the objects in a problem are not just the nouns and there are often objects which do not exist as visible material entities. It is clear that an employee is an object associated with the bank, but is an overdraft an object? It is if it fits with the programmer's perception and contributes meaningfully and naturally to the model. Obviously what constitutes an object in the OOP sense depends on the programmer. Different programmers will see the same problem as constituted form different objects. But that is how humans are; each has their own view of the World.

There is more to OOP than just talking about what constitutes the essential components of a program. After all no one would attempt to write a program in any language without making sure it closely modelled the task being solved. Traditionally in procedural languages this has been done by using functions or procedures that process data which floats around in the global space. Data and the functions which process it are somewhat independent and unconnected. The corruption of data on rare occasions is hard to spot and debug. Moreover further development of a program requires detailed knowledge of the way in which the functions interact with the data. That is how C works. A large program becomes hard to debug, extend and just understand and maintain by new programmers. Object-oriented programming has been invented to address these problems.

4.2 Classes

In C++ there is a device to make objects. It is called the class. The class pulls together data and the functions that operate on the data, into an encapsulated entity which is an abstract data type. The program then consists of interacting instances of the classes which behave and treat their data in much the same way as the objects in the real task that the program is being written to solve.

That all sounds very formal so we'll describe what's meant with an example from the banking problem. In the interests of simplicity and clarity, this example omits many of the features that one would employ in a real class, many examples of which we will use in the graphics programming. But as an introduction to classes it does capture the spirit of the idea. The graphics classes are more mathematical; this example is easier to follow.

4.2.1 An Account Class

Banks have accounts and we are quite certain that our program model of a Bank will be a good representation if it contains account objects. We expect there will be many account objects and we can see that in some respect they are the fundamental units of the Bank. One might have said instead that the customers are the fundamental units and the accounts follow from them. We prefer to think of a customer belonging to an account rather than the other way round. In fact several customers can belong to a single account, especially if it is a shared account, although it is also true that a customer can have several different types of account. There is clearly ample scope for debate here and this emphasises the non-uniqueness of the choice of classes. If we find that the idea of the account does not work as well as that of the customer in building up our bank model then we should abandon it and switch.

What do we expect of an account? In our very simple model we suppose it must have the following data some of which is confidential (it is limited to one name per account): a balance, customer name, internal code, an overdraft limit. These are the **member data** of the account class.

But the idea of an account does not end with the data. It must be possible to: deposit into or withdraw from the account, inspect the balance. For the moment we will suppose that these are sufficient behaviours; they will become the **member functions** of the class.

Member Data

Now it is necessary to be more precise about how these **class members** will be implemented. The balance can be a **float** since it is measured as a decimal and may go positive or negative (in overdraft). Likewise the overdraft limit can also be a **float.** The customer names are clearly strings and the internal code we expect to be an unsigned integer. Without the functions our class has become a prototype declaration

```
class account{
    float balance;
    float overdraft;
public:
    char name[50];
    unsigned int code;
};
```

The standard form of a class declaration or prototype is the reserved name **class** followed by the identifier, **account** in this case, an opening brace enclosing the class members and finally the closing brace followed by a semi-colon.

Private, Protected and Public Access

One very important feature of the class which is important to the account is to keep certain data members free from tampering by other functions in the program. The balance and overdraft are **private** to the class by default and can only be directly assessed by member functions of the class and friend functions (we'll discuss there later). There is no explicit statement of privacy because that is the default, but it could be written with the keyword **private:** if desired. The other data members do not have to be guarded this way and are explicitly declared **public**. They can be accessed by any function in the program. There is another access category: **protected** which allows access by members of descendant classes. Inheritance is a topic which will be discussed again later.

Member Functions

Now for the member functions. First of all we wish to be able to inspect the balance in the account. We prototype a function to do this without yet showing how it can be done

```
float get_bal();
```

This function takes no argument and returns the account balance. Also we wish to be able to deposit and withdraw money

```
void deposit(float);
void withdraw(float);
```

These two functions will take a **float** argument, the amount being deposited or withdrawn presumably, and return void, i.e. they simply adjust the balance. It is only necessary to state the type of the variables, not their identifiers in the declaration. The identifiers will have to be specified in the definitions later. These functions, being members of the class are allowed access to class data members whether they are private or otherwise. The class prototype has become

```
class account{
    float balance;
    float overdraft;
public:
    char name[50];
    unsigned int code;
    float get_bal();
    void deposit(float);
    void withdraw(float);
};
```

The class is starting to look real. It is not a working class yet because there is no way to enter the either name of the user of the account or its number. Whilst we could have added another function to do this we will use a special function, which has no return, called the **constructor** and has the special responsibility for ensuring that each new instance of the class, the object in fact, is brought to life properly. In this case we want every account to have a user associated with it and the right time to do that is when the account is created. The constructor is a special function and has the same name as the class itself

```
account(char*);
```

It takes the name of the account holder as an argument and copies the string into the account name. In fact, for reasons that will be explained shortly, we need two constructor functions. They both have the same name but take different arguments and so are distinguishable to the compiler. Functions with the same name but different arguments or return types are a powerful feature of C++ and are called **overloaded** functions. The second constructor takes no arguments and is needed to instantiate arrays. It looks like

```
account();
```

Finally, the class prototype is:

```
class account{
     float balance;
     float overdraft;
public:
     char name[50];
     unsigned int code;

     account();
     account(char*,unsigned int);
     float get_bal();
     void deposit(float);
     void withdraw(float);
};
```

Now that the class has been prototyped we must define the functions and show in detail how they work. Each function now has its definition and an access specifier (::) to show that it belongs to the account class. Now the identifiers must appear. These are the names of the variables that appear in the function definitions. They aren't members of the class but are dummy variables, and don't really exist in the program. They are just there so that the full workings of the function can be specified. First the constructors.

The Constructors

First, the default constructor for building empty arrays:

```
account::account(){
    code=0;                      // initialize
    balance=overdraft=0.0;       // all data
}
```

Then the constructor to set up an account:

```
account::account(char* new_name,unsigned int new_code){
    strcpy(name,new_name);       // enter the new name
    code=new_code;
    balance=overdraft=0.00;      // initialize to zero
}
```

The constructor takes the new name and copies it into the member *name* using a standard string copy function. It also copies in the new account code and sets both the account balance and overdraft limit to zero. At the moment there is no function to adjust the overdraft so that's something for someone to worry about later.

Other functions

Next we wish to get the balance on demand but must do so as outsiders only through a legal channel namely the access function **getbal()**. This function has been invented to give access to private data in a controlled way. It works simply:

```
float account::float get_bal(){return balance;}
```

Notice the complete identification of this function as a member of the **account** class by means of the scope resolution operator ::.

Then we wish to deposit and withdraw money:

```
void account::deposit(float incoming){
            deposit+=incoming;
}

void account::withdraw(float outgoing){
            deposit-=outgoing;
}
```

Our elementary class is now finished. The class is a factory for producing instances of itself. An instance carries its own version of the data members and access to the member functions. It must have its own data since every account will be different. The class prototype will be saved in a header file, in this case ACCOUNT.H and the function definitions will be saved in a source code file, in this case ACCOUNT.CPP. From the IDE a project file is opened and the files ACCOUNT.CPP and ACCOUNT0.CPP, which is the main file and written below, are added to it. The project is then run from the IDE. To see the output it is necessary to switch to the User screen from the Window menu.

Here is the main program file; it creates two instances of the account class, deposits and withdraws money and prints out the deposits in each. It is also included as an example program listed at the end of the chapter.

```
#include <stdio.h>
#include "c:\tc\3D\ACCOUNT.H"
int main(){

account Sigma("Sigma Press",1000);     // Sigma Press
account Wiley("Wiley",1001);           // Wiley Press
Sigma.deposit(563.55);                 // deposit to Sigma Press
Wiley.deposit(205.55);                 // deposit to Wiley Press
Sigma.withdraw(279.45);                // withdraw from Sigma
printf("\n Balance of %s is %5.2f"
        ,Sigma.name,Sigma.get_bal()); // 284.55
printf("\n Balance of %s is %5.2f"
        ,Wiley.name,Wiley.get_bal());// 205.55
return 0;
}
```

Sigma and *Wiley* are each said to be **instances** of the class **account.** They are the accounts in the program. Let's quickly go through the program to see what happens.

First are the header files which make visible all the functions, definitions and class prototypes, in particular the **account** class, necessary for compilation. Then begins the main program. On the next two lines are instantiated (instances are created) objects of the account class. Both the names and account numbers are passed to the constructor which copies them to the internal data members. Each instance has a data member called balance and name etc., but each is different between instances. Then deposits are made to the accounts using the "dot" member access operator to specify ownership. Sigma.deposit(563.55) means use the deposit function belonging to the Sigma account object and therefore add money to the balance belonging to Sigma. Money is added to the Wiley account and then 279.45 is withdrawn from the Sigma account. Finally a statement is output to the monitor giving the balances in each account.

Even in this tiny program there are many aspects of class programming on show. Let us go through them in more detail.

4.3 Anatomy of a Class

4.3.1 An Abstract Data Type

A class is an encapsulation of data and functions which represent an identifiable self-contained entity in the program. The class represents an abstract data type. That succinct definition really captures the essence of what a class is. It doesn't sound very informative but the idea of abstract data types gets right to the heart of classes.

Consider for a moment two data types that already exist in the language. The **int** type represents numbers which are always integer whereas **float** is quite different, being able to handle fractional numbers in the gaps between the integers. Within the precision offered by the computer **float** numbers are continuous whereas **int** numbers only exist at integer intervals. These are quite different concepts of numbers although usually we don't ponder the difference too much. The data types **int** and **float** also have particular functions associated with them though we don't notice it. Different functions are required to add **int** numbers than **float** numbers. This is also true of all the other built-in functions we expect to be able to perform. So **int** numbers really are a different concept from float numbers. The numbers exist in a different way in memory and they have different functions associated with them. Notice that we can *add* **int** numbers just as we can *add* **float** numbers. The + operator is used in both cases; we mean the same thing in both cases though it is actually a different operation. We use the same operators for all the mathematical functions. This is an example of operator overloading and plays a very important role in making the algebra of the data types seem natural.

So the built-in data types with which we are familiar really are a little more complicated than first thought. That is perhaps the surprising thing because classes simply extend this idea. The account class we have built, above, exemplifies this. The banking program will contain many different accounts just as a mathematical program may contain many different **float** numbers. Whilst it is unlikely that we will wish to multiply or divide accounts it is most likely that we will want to do other operations such as sorting and searching. The **account** objects, each an instance of the account class with a different name and different data, are completely analogous to the many different numbers of the **float** type in a mathematical program. The **account** really is just another data type. It is called an abstract data type because it has abstracted the concept of an account.

4.3.2 Instances of the Class

The class prototype or declaration is like a factory for stamping out instances or objects of the class. In the language there are already factories for generating the fundamental and derived data types. The class give us a way of generating our own user-defined data types.

When an object is born, the constructor function acts like a midwife. It makes sure the instance comes to life equipped with the right data to exist and function properly. If no data has to be passed to the new object at instantiation then it can be created simply. For example to create a new **int** data variable we say

```
int number;
```

so in the same way an object of class **thing** might be created by:

```
thing new_thing;
```

thing appears as just another data type in the language.

What makes it look more complicated is when the new instance requires data as in the **account** class, above. There when an object is created it needs a string and account number for its internal data members so this information must be passed:

```
account my_account("my_name",3210);
```

or

```
account my_account=account("my_name",3210);
```

but not

```
account my_account;// error - initialiser missing.
```

The role of the constructor function is crucial here. It must take care of the details to bring an object to life with all its faculties. There is another important class function which acts like an undertaker, clearing up the mess when an object dies as for example when it goes out of scope at the end of a function. This is called the destructor. If you don't define a constructor or destructor for your class, the compiler will define minimal functions as best it can. There has to be a default constructor. If you leave it to the compiler instances can certainly be constructed but they might not work right. In the account example, we did not define a destructor because there was nothing special for it to do. In the graphics programming there will often be need of special destructors. We will discuss the constructor and destructor in more detail later.

Each instance of the class has internal data members of the same name but there is no confusion since the object name always precedes the data member name with the **member selection operator** (.) operator when it is used. As in the account example Sigma.balance means the balance belonging to the instance *Sigma*. Whatever the sum of money in *Sigma's* balance, it is quite separate from Wiley.balance. Both have a balance but they are each different. There is an exception to this in static data members which are shared by all objects of a class.

4.3.3 Derived Types

Now that we have the **account** type it can be used in exactly the same way as any other data type. From the fundamental types we were able to derive such things as pointers and arrays. Without any extra programming work, we can immediately have the derived types pointer-to-account, **account***, and an account array, **account**[]. Isn't that a surprise! Suddenly there is a whole new world opening up in which the language is not just being extended by new functions but by new data types which represent units in the programming model. With overloaded operators which we will meet in the next chapter it will be possible to use the algebra to symbolise the interactions of the new data types, and the stage will be set for OOP. For the moment let us look at some lines of code which illustrate what can be done with derived data types from **account**.

Here is the declaration of a pointer to an **account**

```
account* ptrAcc;// declare a pointer-to-account
```

Here is an array of 4 **account**s

```
account acc_arry[4];
```

Now initialize the pointer to the array

```
ptrAcc=acc_arry;
```

or alternatively initialization all in one go

```
account* ptrAcc = &acc_arry[0]; // equivalent
```

Here's the array created on the free store, on the heap, with **new**

```
ptrAcc=new account[4];
```

where the pointer to the memory location is assigned to *ptrAcc*. These "empty" accounts in the array were brought to life by the default constructor which did very little except initialize the data members to zero. They will have to be given their names and codes one by one later. This is illustrated in the second example program ACCOUNT1.CPP at the end of the chapter.

You can see that this looks exactly the same as what we have already seen for **int** and **char**. The example program ACCOUNT1.CPP in the next section illustrates derived types of **account**, together with the use of **new** and **delete** to store an **account** array on the free store. Study this example closely; although it is simple it marks the beginning of real object-oriented programming style.

4.4 Example Programs

The example programs in this chapter illustrate simple classes through the **account** class. The first example is that discussed in the text. The files ACCOUNT.H and ACCOUNT.CPP contain the class prototype, or interface, and the implementation of the class member functions. They are needed for the example programs. These files should be placed in a directory named 3D off the Turbo C++ root directory, C:\TC\3D*.*, since that is the path given in the main file. All files for this book expect to be in this directory.

4.4.1 ACCOUNT0.CPP

This is the program discussed in the text. It needs a project file with itself and the following file added: ACCOUNT.CPP. The project file therefore contains ACCOUNT0.CPP and ACCOUNT.CPP. Once this project file is made, it can be run directly from the IDE which will also produce an .EXE file.

4.4.2 ACCOUNT1.CPP

This program illustrates the natural extension of the abstract data type **account**. It can be made into the derived data types which already exist for the fundamental types **int** etc.. In this program an array of **accounts** in free memory is made using the **new** operator.

This is the main program. It first declares a pointer to the new type **account. account** is now like any other data type. Although it is an abstract data type it can be used as a basis for derived data types such as pointer and array.

Then 4 **account** instances in an array are instantiated in free memory using **new** and the location assigned to an **account** pointer named *ptrAcc*. For every member of the array the user is invited to enter a name, a code and a deposit, inside a loop. To make the notation easy an **account** called *Account* is defined to handle each element of the array as it appears in the iteration. This makes the program easier to read and appear more natural. Notice how on each iteration the data members name and code of the instance are initialized automatically without referring to them explicitly. The member selection operators are used throughout. Finally the balance is given for each **account**. At the end **delete** is used to release the memory allocated to the array. This elementary "garbage collection" is the responsibility of the programmer and must not be neglected otherwise the memory resource of the system will inexorably diminish to zero.

Study what is going on here carefully. If there is such a thing as a natural division in this book between C and C++ programming, here it is. This is the point at which some serious OOP and the use of abstract data types is being shown, although it is still quite simple.

```
// ACCOUNT0.CPP
// introduction to the account class

#include <stdio.h>
#include "C:\TC\3D\ACCOUNT.H"

int main(){

    account Sigma("Sigma Press",1000);//instantiate Sigma Press
    account Wiley("Wiley",1001);        //instantiate Wiley

    Sigma.deposit(563.55);   //deposit money to Sigma
    Wiley.deposit(205.55);               //deposit money to Wiley

    Sigma.withdraw(279.45); //withdraw from Sigma

    // print out the balances
    printf("\n Balance of %s is %5.2f",Sigma.name,Sigma.get_bal());
    printf("\n Balance of %s is %5.2f",Wiley.name,Wiley.get_bal());

    return 0;

}




// ACCOUNT1.CPP
// derived data types of account

#include <iostream.h>
#include "C:\TC\3D\ACCOUNT.H"

int main(){

    account* ptrAcc;        // declare a pointer-to-account type

    ptrAcc=new account[4];// four new accounts in free memory

  for(int i=0;i<4;i++){ // for all the accounts

        float sum;
        account Account=ptrAcc[i];

        cout<<"\n enter the name of account "<<i<<" ";
        cin>>Account.name;
        cout<<"\n enter the code of account "<<i<<" ";
        cin>>Account.code;
        cout<<"\n make a deposit in accouht "<<i<<" ";
        cin>>sum;
        Account.deposit(sum);

        cout<<"\n Balance of" <<Account.name<<" is "
           <<Account.get_bal();
        cout<<"\n";
    }

    delete []ptrAcc;

    return 0;

}
```

```
// ACCOUNT.H
// header file for account class

class account{

    float balance;
    float overdraft;

public:

    char name[50];
    unsigned int code;
    account();
    account(char*,unsigned int);
    float get_bal();
    void deposit(float);
    void withdraw(float);

};


// ACCOUNT.CPP
// definition file for the account class
#include "C:\TC\3D\ACCOUNT.H"
#include <string.h>

//class constructor ...............................................
account::account(char* new_name,unsigned int new_code){

    strcpy(name,new_name);
    code=new_code;
    balance=overdraft=0.0;
}

// default constructor ...........................................
account::account(){

    code=0;
    balance=overdraft=0.0;

}

// get the balance ...............................................
float account::get_bal(){return balance;}


// make a deposit ................................................
void account::deposit(float incoming){

    balance+=incoming;
}


// make a withdrawl...............................................
void account::withdraw(float outgoing){

    balance-=outgoing;
}
```

5

Object-Oriented Programming

In the last chapter we met the class, the mechanism for implementing abstract data types. If you understood what was happening in the example ACCOUNT1.CPP, you have passed the point of no-return in grasping the essence of OOP. The instances of the class are the objects in our program. These objects carry their own data and functions in an encapsulated way and express our perception of what constitute the meaningful variables in a program. Object-oriented programming is the method which uses these objects to generate a literary style. Writing good OOP is as hard as writing a good essay. Both have the same requirements: good use of the language, clarity of presentation and efficient delivery of the theme. A good program is exciting to read and certainly has entertainment value. Getting from an understanding of the grammatical syntax of classes to OOP is like trying to write good literature having just learned the basics of English. It requires a study of what has been written by others so as to take advantage of their discoveries of what constitutes a good literary style.

One of the very important literary features that OOP encourages is the development of an algebra of the classes through overloaded operators. Consider how mathematics has evolved. It uses symbols to represent variables, as in programming, and operators to represent the manipulations of the variables. It is easy to see what the + operator in 1+2 means, but what does it mean for A + B where A and B are matrices? It means add each element of matrix A to each element of matrix B. That is a lot more complicated than adding 1 and 2 but we know from the context it is different. The + operator has different interpretations in the two contexts; it is an **overloaded operator**, just as the two constructors for the account class illustrated overloaded functions. By overloading the operator it has been possible to represent a complex idea in a shorthand symbol. Mathematics is filled with operators which represent complex manipulations of data in a shorthand notation. They constitute the algebra of mathematics and allow the development of complexity without increasing confusion. As concepts become more advanced the complexity is hidden in the operators. OOP also provides a similar mechanism so that manipulations of classes can be hidden behind overloaded operators.

We will try to bridge the gap between the bare grammatical syntax of OOP and the generation of a literary style. We will take as working examples vectors and matrices. These are advanced data types and will be essential in the graphics programming. This is an excellent opportunity to work on OOP and the graphics project at the same time. First of all let us consider the features offered by OOP which extend the power of the language in a practical sense.

5.1 Encapsulation and Source Code

In OOP the abstract data type is an encapsulation of data and functions of a class. It represents an abstraction of an entity in the program model which has data and behaviour. Hopefully, though not always, there will be many objects, or instances of the type in the program. Multiple instances indicates that we have struck pay dirt and that the abstract data type can play an important role in the program, just like the fundamental types **int** or **float**. Sometimes there is only need for a single instance of a type, as in the screen class to be described, because there is only one "screen". The important thing is that a class is an amalgamation of data and functions and appears in the program as instances, or objects, each of which carries its own data and access to the class functions. Data and functions together is something new to those who have experience of procedural programming.

5.2 Inheritance

Inheritance is not something which we use initially, though it will appear later. It will allow us to define a class which is a descendant of a simpler class; the descendant class is called the derived class and the class from which it is derived is called the base class. The point of inheritance is that the derived class has all the data members and functions of the base class and can add new ones of its own. It "reuses" the programming effort which went into the base class: it allows **code reuse.** A substantial saving of programming effort results and it is possible to avoid "re-inventing the wheel" each time there is a need for similar classes; they can be derived from a common base class or from each other. A class hierarchy can result, which is how humans categorise things anyway, and therefore certainly in the spirit of OOP.

5.3 Overloading

5.3.1 Function Overloading

We have already seen function overloading in the two constructors of the **account** class in the previous chapter. Function overloading lets you use the same function name for different functions as long as there is a difference in the arguments or the return type so that the compiler can distinguish them. This is very convenient since it relieves the programmer from having to invent artificially different names for functions which differ only in these details. There will typically be several versions of a constructor to handle the different ways a class can be instantiated with different data types.

5.3.2 Operator Overloading

Operator overloading is a very important aspect of OOP and very much more than a convenience. We will meet it frequently. It provides a mechanism whereby mathematical and other symbols can be used as shorthand notation to express the interactions of instances of a class. For example, in this chapter we will introduce the **vector** and **matrix** classes. We will wish to retain the idea, common to arrays, of subscripting, where the i'th element can be accessed as [i]. This is a standard way of referring to an element and we wish to carry into the new classes. Since there is no such operator available for these classes by default, it will have to be overloaded with a special set of instructions detailing how it will get member data to perform its function. It is really a function in disguise. This and many other operators will be overloaded in the course of the graphics programming. A list of over-loadable operators, is given in Appendix 3.

5.4 A Vector Class

A vector is a concise way of describing space. In 3-D computer graphics we want to do this all the time so it is natural to consider inventing a **vector** class to encapsulate our idea of a vector. Since a vector in 3-D is really only a set of three coordinates in space we might throw in the towel and head back to procedural programming. But to do so would lose many future advantages. Inventing classes requires hard work at the outset since a class cannot become real until its data and function members have been thought through thoroughly. It's easier to rush off and sketch out a program in the top-down procedural approach and leave the implementation details to the bottom layer of routines. Designing a class requires at the outset a careful consideration of what idea it represents and what it is expected to do. Having done that it is then easy to use the class with confidence to build the program.

In graphics programming, speed is all important. The routines in this book do not resort to machine code instructions for speed since that would produce code which is harder to understand and not portable. It would be aimed at a particular processor. To make things as fast as possible we will work with the integer data type wherever possible. This will gain a factor of about 3 as opposed to working with floating point, which would make the maths simpler. Therefore the data for the **Vector** class is held as integers.

5.4.1 What is a Vector?

The simplest type of vector is a concise way of specifying a position in space. The position is measured from a fixed position called the origin. Since space is 3-dimensional, the position is determined by moving specified distances forward, sideways-right and up from the origin (negative distances account for backward, left and down respectively). In mathematical language this usually means measuring all displacements in a Cartesian coordinate system, though other schemes can be used. A position in space is then specified by the distances along the three axes at right angles one has to travel to reach it. The vector notation arises from the way this information is presented.

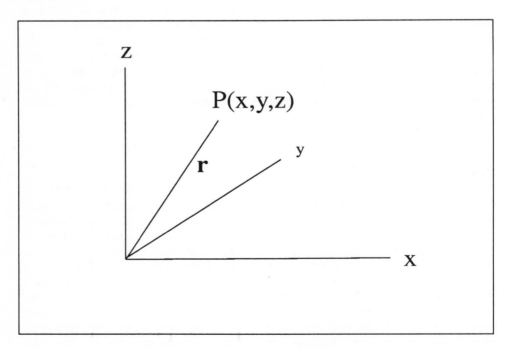

Figure 5.1: A vector in Cartesian co-ordinates.

If the displacements along the three axes to the point, P, are x,y and z respectively, then the vector **r** which stretches from the origin to P, as shown in Figure 5.1, can be expressed in vector notation as

$$\mathbf{r} = x\mathbf{i} + y\mathbf{j} + z\mathbf{k}$$

It is common to write vectors (which have both size (magnitude) and direction) in boldface to distinguish them from ordinary numbers which have only size. Here **i**, **j** and **k**, called the unit or base vectors, are signposts pointing along the x, y and z axes and the term **xi** means "go a distance x in the direction of the x axis" and so on. They are vectors in their own right with size (magnitude) equal to unity.

Since **i**, **j** and **k** really serve only to distinguish the three components of the displacement, we could omit them from the scheme providing the order is retained. The three components can be included in order inside brackets ready for multiplication with matrices in the column vector notation:

$$\mathbf{r} \quad = \quad \begin{pmatrix} x \\ y \\ z \end{pmatrix}$$

This is not the only way to represent vectors. In computer graphics, it is common to represent them in the row notation

$$\mathbf{r} \quad = \quad (x \quad y \quad z)$$

The convention used determines the way matrices, which we will also wish to use, are written. In this book column vectors are used because this is more common in science and engineering and therefore likely to be more familiar to the general reader. Switching between the conventions is tiresome but fairly painless.

However a vector need not be limited to three components. This is a problem if you stick to the picture of a vector as a displacement in 3-D space. But if a vector is written in column notation, as shown above, there is no reason why it cannot be a tall column and have many elements. This is how we will think of a vector. Sometimes we will have vectors with only three components and they will be positions in space. Other times the vector will have many more components and then we will think of it as a list of elements.

So far our idea of a vector is a set of numbers. This is not very difficult and barely enough to justify creating a vector class; a 1-D array would do. However a vector is very much more than that. A vector has behaviour which is quite different from other data types. There are several mathematical operations that vectors must be able to do.

5.4.2 Vector Addition and Subtraction

Let's take two 3-D vectors each with just 3 components and add them. This mathematical operation is more complicated than adding single numbers (scalars) and is uniquely a vector property. The addition goes like this:

$$\begin{pmatrix} x1 \\ y1 \\ z1 \end{pmatrix} + \begin{pmatrix} x2 \\ y2 \\ z2 \end{pmatrix} = \begin{pmatrix} x1+x2 \\ y1+y2 \\ z1+z2 \end{pmatrix}$$

The components of the final vector are obtained from adding the corresponding components of the two original vectors.

Likewise subtraction goes as:

$$\begin{pmatrix} x1 \\ y1 \\ z1 \end{pmatrix} - \begin{pmatrix} x2 \\ y2 \\ z2 \end{pmatrix} = \begin{pmatrix} x1-x2 \\ y1-y2 \\ z1-z2 \end{pmatrix}$$

5.4.3 Products of Vectors

The Scalar (Dot) Product

Vectors can be a shorthand and highly suggestive way of doing geometry. A point P(x,y,z) in a Cartesian system looks much more important when represented by a vector **r** which stretches from the origin to the point P. Another point P'(x',y',z') is similarly represented by the vector P'.

Very often we wish to know the angle, α, between these two vectors . It turns out that what is simplest to find is the cosine of α which is

$$\cos\alpha = (x.x' + y.y' + z.z')/\sqrt{((x^2 + y^2 + z^2).(x'^2 + y'^2 + z^2))}$$

The factors in the denominator look complicated but are just the magnitudes of the two vectors calculated using a 3-D version of Pythagoras' theorem. The numerator is the sum of the products of the components of the two vectors taken together. Because such a product occurs frequently in geometry it is given a special symbol and name. It is called the scalar or dot product and is written as

$$\mathbf{r.r'} = x.x' + y.y' + z.z'$$

It is called the scalar product because it produces a scalar answer from two vectors. Instead of writing the magnitude of a vector as a square root of a sum of squares all the time, which is tiresome, it is usual to represent it by the same symbol as the vector but without boldface. Hence the cosine is given by

$$\cos\alpha = (r.r')/r.r'$$

where $r = |r| = \sqrt{(x^2+y^2+z^2)}$ and likewise for r'.

The operation $|r|$ means 'the magnitude of r.'

Notice that the scalar product $r.r'$ is proportional to $\cos\theta$ and, most important, has the same sign as $\cos\theta$. The sign of the cosine turns out to be a very useful test of whether the angle between two vectors is less than or greater than 90°. If it less than 90° the scalar product is positive and if the angle is more than 90° (up to 180°) it is negative. This property makes the scalar product useful in testing whether a surface of a polygon is visible (facing towards) or invisible (facing away) from a viewers position, and is used in testing for the visibility of surfaces.

The Vector (Cross) Product

This is a product of two vectors which produces a new vector. Once again it is based on a useful application. In this case it generates the vector which is normal (at right angles) to both the original vectors. Another way of stating this is to say that the new vector is normal to the plane containing the two product vectors. This is shown in Figure 5.2.

The new vector r'' and the vector product are defined by:

$$r'' = r \times r'$$

Where the x here means the cross product.
The vector r'' is normal to the plane containing r and r' and its magnitude is equal to $r.r' \sin(\alpha)$. The components of r'' are

$$x'' = y.z' - z.y'$$

$$y'' = z.x' - x.z'$$

$$z'' = x.y' - y.x'$$

There is one important aspect of vector products, the order of multiplication matters; the product $r \times r'$ is not the same as $r' \times r$. In fact

$$r' \times r = -r \times r'$$

The direction of r'' is obtained by twisting r into r' through the smallest angle. The direction in which this is seen as a clockwise rotation is the direction of r''.

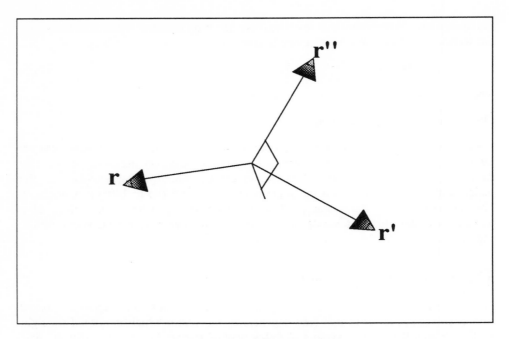

Figure 5.2. Vector cross product

The vector product is complicated but very useful in computer graphics. It is used to construct vectors which are normal to surfaces. We will use this in calculating the visibility and illumination of surfaces of polygons in the graphics programming.

5.4.4 Subscripting

A vector is entirely determined by its components and often we will wish to look at one of them in particular. For this we need to be able to use subscripting as in a 1-D array. If a Vector object has the identifier A then we would like to refer to the i'th element as $A[i]$. Of course, if A were nothing more than a 1-D array we could do this anyway. But remember A is an instance of the **Vector** class and has both data and functions as its members. It is considerably more complicated than an array.

5.5 The Vector Class Interface

We now have a clearer picture of what a **Vector** is. It is a set of data together with a number of mathematical functions. Some of these have been discussed, above. We will not include all the **Vector** functions within the class. For reasons explained later much of the **Vector** mathematics will be left outside the class as nonmember functions. There are still several other functions which are class members.

The class declaration is given fully in the file DECL_00.H at the end of the chapter and the source code for the full definitions of the functions is given in the file DEFN_00.CPP. DECL_00.H is a header file and contains the declarations necessary for the compiler to build the Vector and Matrix classes. DEFN_00.CPP is to be added together with other source files in the project for each executable program. The Matrix class is discussed later in this chapter.

Right now we will examine in detail what the **Vector** class contains. There are many features of C++ which we will meet in this example which have not yet been discussed. In accord with the spirit of this book as a practical "hands on" development of graphics programming, these topics will be discussed as they occur. The class members are listed below:

5.5.1 Vector Data Members

int* Vector::V

This is the way all class members will be specified: first the type, followed by the member identifier fully expanded together with its class identifier, the two being joined by the scope resolution operator ::. This one says that *V* is the name of the variable, it belongs to the **Vector** class and is of type **int***.

Clearly V gets us to the actual data since it can point to an array of integers. We have used integers for speed, which will pose a problem for fractions less than unity but that can be overcome by a trick of scaling all numbers by a factor, 32 in our case, and dividing out the factor at the end. To use float would avoid the problem but because float is a more complicated data type and takes more time to process, there is an intolerable time penalty. Since we wish the graphics to be a fast as possible **int** is used where possible. Where exactly that array of integers is we will see in a minute.

int Vector::dim

This is the number of elements in the vector. Before we discuss the constructors, look to the end of the class for the public access functions **int* getV()** and **int getdim()**. These have to be provided since there is no other way for a nonmember function to get to the data or size of the array. What is interesting about these two functions is that they are defined inside the class declaration. They are said to be **inline** functions. Only the very shortest functions should be inline because they are expanded in the code section of the program and can use up space if they exist in several places. They are fast to access however and save the time to call a function elsewhere in memory.

5.5.2 Vector Function Members

void Vector::build(int)

> We look at this function next because it is a special function that performs a very
> important service. It is a slightly longer function and is not expanded inline. You
> will have to look in the source file DEFN_00.CPP to see its implementation. In
> **build()** we meet a feature of the language which plays a central role in allocating
> space for arrays, and indeed any variable, whose size will only be known when the
> program is run. You have seen the solution to this problem in example
> ACCOUNT1.CPP where an array was declared. The answer is to use dynamic
> memory allocation through the **new** operator. That is what **build()** does. It takes
> the size of the array and opens up space in free memory using **new** and assigns the
> pointer to it to *V*. If no memory is available then a null is returned. A check is
> made for a failure to get memory since it would otherwise result in a program
> crash if things were to proceed. Here the condition is reported to the user.

There is an important point here, our **Vector** instances do not actually hold the data
array but instead just hold a pointer to it. That way each instance of Vector is quite
small even though the array of data it points to might be very large. Also the size of
the array is chosen to exactly match the data. Having used **new** to allocate memory,
this resource will have to be returned when the object goes out of scope. That will be
done by the destructor **Vector::~Vector()** which contains the instruction **delete []V**
and releases the space occupied by the array.

Next we will look at the many overloaded constructor functions. They all have the
identifier **Vector** but are distinguished from each other by taking different arguments.
If this were not true the compiler would flag an error. When a **Vector** is created the
compiler chooses the appropriate constructor. These overloaded functions are to cope
with the several ways data can be used to instantiate a **Vector**. The constructors are
not short functions and so are not expanded inline.

Vector::Vector()

> This is the default constructor which takes no arguments. Its main function is to
> create arrays of Vectors for which it is never possible to initialise the data
> members. That initialisation presumably comes later. All it does is make sure that
> both V and dim are legally set to zero.

Vector::Vector(int)

> Here an empty **Vector** of known size is constructed. The size is passed as an
> integer. Space for the **Vector is** allocated via **build()** and the elements will have to
> be entered by another part of the program.

Vector::Vector(int,int,int)

The next overloaded constructor which takes three integers to construct a simple 3-D **Vector** clearly meant for describing positions in space. Note how indirection is used to copy the data into the array pointed to by *V*.

Vector::Vector(int*,int)

Here is a constructor which will make an instance form an array of data. This is a most obvious conversion from a primitive vector which is just a 1-D array, to a **Vector** object. In this case the constructor is given a pointer to the array, and its size, and uses the library function **memcpy()** to copy the data to the array pointed to by *V*. Note the appearance of the **sizeof()** function for determining how many bytes a type occupies on the fly. You might think that this size is known by the compiler automatically. It is, but to make the code "bullet proof" and portable to another platform (machine or compiler) no chances are taken.

Vector::Vector(Vector&)

The final special constructor called the **copy constructor**. Its job is to make a new instance by copying an existing one. If you don't define a copy constructor the compiler will try to make one. It will do a byte-by-byte copy as best it can. This might not work the way you want. In our copy constructor a reference to the instance to be copied is passed and its data is copied using **memcpy()**. The copy constructor is frequently called in a program.

That completes the constructors for the **Vector** class. You can see that many possibilities for instantiating objects of the class have been anticipated. The constructor really has to be versatile, but only to the point where an unexpected compiler cast causes a call to the wrong constructor!

Vector::~Vector()

The destructor. It has the same identifier as the class name except that it is preceded by the ~ operator which means the complement or in this case inverse. The destructor does the inverse of the constructor. If the constructor opens space in free memory then the destructor must close it when the instance dies. The destructor is like an undertaker or executor for the class, just as the constructor is a midwife. In our case the constructor open an array in free memory and this must be released to the system by the destructor. It does this using the **delete** operator provided by C++.

Vector& Vector::operator=(Vector&)

This next function in the class is one that we have not hitherto mentioned. It is the overloaded assignment operator. This is included because we want to be able write statements like A=B;, where both A and B are **Vector** instances which already exist. Assignment is a very basic property of all data types and we want it to apply to the **Vector** type. By assigning B to A we mean to overwrite A's data with B's. There is a pitfall here and it isn't checked for; you the programmer will have to watch out for it. This is a feature of these programs which, being educational and reasonably transparent, do not come with a guarantee of "industrial strength" like a commercial library. In this case a copy of data can only successfully be done if the array sizes are the same in both instances. Only the programmer knows whether this is true! There is one other very important new thing. It has not been mentioned before. It is the appearance of **this**. **this** is a pointer to the instance calling the member function. It allows **self-reference**. ***this** means what **this** points to which is the instance itself. Returning ***this,** returns the object itself which could then be used as the argument of another operator. The assignment operator looks very much like the copy constructor but remember the copy constructor is used to make a new instance from an old one. The assignment operator is used to copy one instance into another which already exists. Generally the assignment operator is more complicated since it should worry about what happened to the object it overwrote.

int& Vector::operator[](int)

This penultimate member function is the overloaded subscript operator. It takes the index of the element in the array pointed to by *V* and returns the element. This is an important operator since it will enable us to write expressions like A[i], and mean the element i of the Vector instance A. This is more than it seems since the instance A only contains a pointer V to an array of integers. A isn't a 1-D array but we can overload subscripting to make it look conveniently like one. The overloaded indexing returns *(V+index) which means the integer at the address equal to V plus the offset index.

int* Vector::getV()

An access function for the data member *V*. This makes *V* available to nonmember functions in a controllable way.

int Vector::getdim()

An access function for the data member **dim**. It makes dim available to nonmember functions in a controllable way.

void Vector::show()

Last of all is the function to display the elements of a **Vector** on the monitor. It is a very crude function and just gives a straight listing.

That's the end of the **Vector** class. Many of the mathematical functions which **Vectors** perform are not included as member functions of the class. This means they can have no privacy, and can be called at any point in a program. The advantage of this is the equal bias they give for overloaded operators so as to make the algebra of **Vectors** look natural. More of that later.

5.6 A Matrix Class

A mathematical matrix is a 2-D array. It is a way of holding data in rows and columns. However a matrix has unique functions associated with it which distinguish it from other mathematical entities. It has a behaviour all of its own and is a prime candidate to be elevated to a class. We want a **Matrix** abstract data type. In the graphics programming it is convenient to hold descriptions of the graphics structures as 2-D arrays and for this the instances of the **Matrix** class will be very useful. In addition a **Matrix** can describe rotational and other transforms which are essential to show a changing view on the screen.

It's probably best to come clean at the start. Since a matrix is a 2-D array it can be pictured as a number of rows each of which is a 1-D array. But we have already invented the **Vector** class to abstract that data type. You won't be surprised therefore to discover that the **Matrix** class will contain a pointer to an array of **Vectors**. Already we are able to lose the complexity of handling arrays inside the **Vector** type; building a **Matrix** class is not as difficult as it might have been because we have **Vectors** already.

5.6.1 What is a Matrix?

A matrix is more than a 2-D array of data. It has its own behaviour. A **Matrix** class as an abstract data type can satisfy this requirement. Of particular interest to us is that instances of **Matrix** and **Vector** should behave just like the matrices and vectors from mathematics. One of the important uses of a matrix is to transform a vector. In the graphics we often want to multiply a vector by a matrix so as to rotate it into another orientation. If you look in a maths book you will find algebraic expressions like **M.r** which symbolises the multiplication of a vector **r** by a matrix transform **M**. Of course, this is not the same as multiplying two numbers; there is a special formula for multiplying the rows of the matrix by the column of the vector. However we wish to be able to write similar expressions to represent the multiplication of instances of the **Matrix** and **Vector** classes. This is an important feature since as the program grows we wish to be able to express the program statements in an algebraic shorthand notation so that increasing complexity is not accompanied by increasing confusion.

This is a good place to describe the rotational transform since it appears at several places in the graphics and must be implemented with an overloaded operator. It's also an opportunity to study the structure of a mathematical matrix.

5.6.2 Matrix transform of a Vector

As a result of rotational transforms which occur frequently in computer graphics, the coordinates of objects change in a particular way. A point P(x,y,z) will move to a new position P'(x',y',z') as a result of a rotation about some axis as shown in Figure 5.3.

Each one of the new components is related to all the old components in a set of linear equations:

$$x' = M00.x + M01.y + M02.z$$

$$y' = M10.x + M11.y + M12.z$$

$$z' = M20.x + M21.y + M22.z$$

where the M's are numbers giving the proportions of the original components and are the elements of a matrix **M**. The important thing is that the matrix elements are related uniquely to the rotation, so that any other point rotated in an identical way about the same axis would have its new components determined by the same matrix **M**. Using the rules of multiplication of matrices and vectors, we can emphasise this by disentangling the elements of **M** from the components x, y and z of the vector. The product is written as:

$$\begin{pmatrix} x' \\ y' \\ z' \end{pmatrix} = \begin{pmatrix} M00 & M01 & M02 \\ M10 & M11 & M12 \\ M20 & M21 & M22 \end{pmatrix} \begin{pmatrix} x \\ y \\ z \end{pmatrix}$$

The matrix product written this way is just shorthand notation for the set of linear equations which really matter when we actually come to work out the new coordinates. But writing it this way makes it clear that, once calculated, the matrix M can be used to rotate any point in the same way. In an even more concise shorthand we can summarise the transformation by:

r' = M.r

where the product here is the matrix product and not an ordinary product of numbers.

To convert this shorthand product back into the set of equations observe that the vector has three rows and one column and the matrix has three rows and three columns. To form the top row (x') of the transformed vector **r'**, multiply in turn each of the elements in the top row of **M** by each of the rows of the vector **r** and add them. The second row of **r'** is calculated from the product of each elements in the second row of **M** with the rows of **r** and so on (if we were working in the row representation of vectors everything would be the other way round). This meaning of matrix multiplication is something that just has to be learned.

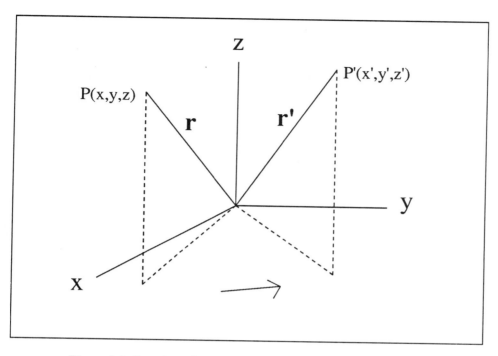

Figure 5.3: Rotation of a vector. Point P transformed to point P′

5.6.3 Matrix Subscripting

In the discussion of 2-D arrays it was possible to get an element using subscripting or dereferencing. Generally subscripting was simpler in appearance and more obvious. If we have an instance T of the **Matrix** class we would like to be able to get the element in the i'th row and j'th column of its data as T[i][j]. Remember a Matrix is not a 2-D array, actually it won't even contain a 2-D array, so being able to use subscripting as an overloaded operator is quite an achievement. Along the way we will also wish to get a row or a column from the **Matrix** and this will also require subscripting.

At this point it is easier to discuss the member data and functions of the **Matrix** class with reference to the files directly. We'll do that.

5.7 The Matrix Class Interface

Like the Vector class, the Matrix class interface is shown in the declaration in DECL_00.H and its implementation is shown in DEFN_00.CPP. First you will see that our perception of a **Matrix** is that it is made of an array of **Vectors**. That's good, it means we are capitalising on previous work. Code reuse eliminates wasteful code duplication. But note that a **Matrix** doesn't actually contain any data; it only contains a pointer *M* to an array of **Vectors**, and even these contain no data. The **Vectors** have pointers to the data which is floating somewhere in free memory. Instances of the **Matrix** class will be very small because the only data they hold are the pointer to an array of **Vectors** and the integer dimensions of the array: the *rows* and *cols*.

5.7.1 Matrix Data Members

Vector* Matrix::M

The pointer to an array of **Vectors**. That's where the data is.

int Matrix::rows

The number of rows.

int Matrix::cols

The number of columns.

5.7.2 Matrix Function members

void Matrix::build(int,int)

We discuss this important function first because as in the **Vector** class it allocates memory on the free store for the actual data arrays and is used by the constructors. **build()** is called by the overloaded constructors and takes the number of rows and the number of columns as arguments and opens space on the heap but it is a good deal more complicated than **Vector::build()**. Memory allocation all happens on one line and is deceptively simple-looking:

```
M=new Vector[rows];
```

rows is the number of **Vectors** to open space for since we perceive a **Matrix** as an array of **Vectors**. If space has been successfully found, a pointer to it is assigned to *M*, the **Matrix** class member. The square brackets specify an array of vectors with *rows* as the size of the array. But a **Vector** cannot be pulled out of thin air, it must be constructed, so without any further information the **Vector** default constructor will be called for each **Vector** in the array. We now have an array of **Vector** instances whose identifiers are their array index. Each instance has a null *V* pointer member and a zeroed *dim*. Each instance doesn't yet have any place to store data so the next line in **Matrix::build()** calls the **Vector::build()** function for each **Vector** in the array in turn allocating memory for it of size equal to the number of columns. Since *M* is a pointer to the **Vector** array, it can use normal subscripting to get a particular Vector. To get the i'th **Vector** you write M[i]. Then to build space for the elements of this **Vector**, the **build()** function belonging to it is used so that it can access that **Vector**'s private data array. That is all done by the statement

```
M[i].build(cols);
```

where the member selection operator (.) has been used.

This **Matrix::build()** function is very succinct but does a lot of work. Study this function carefully because has been possible to express it in a few lines only because it uses a substantial amount of code hidden in the **Vector** class.

Let's now look at the overloaded constructors.

Matrix::Matrix()

The default constructor which does nothing but clear the data members.

Matrix::Matrix(int,int)

This constructor creates an empty Matrix but with the dimensions given.

The next three constructors are used to instantiate a **Matrix** from data which may be presented in one of three different ways.

Matrix::Matrix(int*,int,int)

Here data is presented in the form of a simple 1-D array together with the number of rows and columns. This is just about the simplest way in which data can be presented. From an integer array data is copied into the internal data member *M*. What is passed to the constructor is a pointer to the array called *ptr*. Then one by one, using the for loop, the integers are copied using dereferencing and post-incrementing *(ptr++). This means "get what you are pointing to and afterwards move along one integer". A simple instruction like this inside a loop is all that's necessary to walk along an array. Look however at what is on the left hand side of that assignment. The integer fetched is assigned to *M*[i][j]. Now *M* is a pointer to an array of **Vectors** so *M*[i] means the i'th **Vector**. But the second index is only possible because we overloaded the [] operator for indexing **Vectors**. There are two different overloaded []'s here. *M*[i][j] looks simple and tells us immediately what is meant: the element in the i'th row and j'th column of the Matrix, and looks just like a 2-D array. But it isn't at all; *M* is a pointer to an array of **Vectors** in each of which is a pointer to an array of integers floating somewhere in free memory. That's definitely not a 2-D array, but it has been made to look like one from our use of the overloading of the [] operator.

Matrix::Matrix(int**,int,int)

This one takes an array of pointers together with the dimensions. It copies data from a pointer array called *ptr*. This is an array of pointers, each of which points to an array of integers. Data is copied as before but this time it is possible to use *ptr*[i][j] in the loop because *ptr*[i] is the i'th pointer and *ptr*[i][j] is the j'th element in the 1-D array of that pointer.

Matrix::Matrix(Vector*,int,int)

The last constructor instantiates from an array of **Vector**s named *m*. Inside the loop we have the copying of data in the form $M[i]=m[i]$. There is a lot going on here but once again it has been made to look very simple. The assignment here is of the **Vector** $m[i]$ and this is only possible because the assignment operator (=) and subscripting ([]) has been overloaded for **Vectors**.

Here in these constructors, several of the overloaded operators defined for the Vector and Matrix classes have been used to make the statements look simple and natural.

Matrix::Matrix(Matrix&)

This last constructor is the copy constructor. It takes a reference to a Matrix and uses it to make a new instance. The action is all in the line:

```
(*this)[i]=src[i]
```

where the source is copied. The expression on the left hand side illustrates the use of **this** and **Matrix** subscripting. **this** is a pointer to the instance which is calling the overloaded operator so ***this** is a self reference to the current **Matrix** object. (*this)[i] therefore means the i'th **Vector** of the object being copied to. Since ***this** is a **Matrix**, the subscripting is **Matrix** subscripting and therefore the overloaded [] operator is being used, but it looks just like any subscripting operator.

Matrix::~Matrix()

Here is the destructor. The destructor has to delete *M* when an instance goes out of scope and release the memory it points to. But since *M* is a pointer to an array of **Vectors**, their destructors will also be called one by one at this point and they will release the space occupied by the actual data array. Destroying a **Matrix** is a big job.

Matrix& Matrix::operator=(Matrix&)

This is the overloaded assignment operator which enables us to copy one **Matrix** instance into another which already exists. It also uses **Matrix** subscripting and overloaded **Vector** assignment.

Vector& Matrix::operator[](int)

Here is the important overloaded subscripting which selects a row of the **Matrix**; it returns a row of *M* which is a **Vector**.

Vector Matrix::operator()(int)

There is often a need to select a column of the **Matrix** and call it a **Vector**. That's what this function does. To do so it has to instantiate a Vector and fill it with the elements of the **Matrix** column. A copy of the vector is returned using the **Vector** copy constructor.

The two functions which give public access to the private data members *rows* and *cols* are given inline in the class declaration.

void Matrix::norm(int)

This is used to normalise (reduce) the data elements when they have been scaled up to allow sufficient accuracy for graphics arithmetic, especially of trigonometric functions. It come as a consequence of the need to do fast arithmetic and therefore use integers for data elements. This function is later needed to normalise products to the right size.

void Matrix::show()

It displays the elements of a Matrix on the monitor.

5.8 Nonmember Functions

There are several functions which describe the interactions instances of the **Vectors and Matrix** objects. They are not member functions and so are available to any part of the program. They are binary functions i.e. they have two operands and mostly involving overloaded operators. They are mathematical type operations as one might see in an equation and are not included as class member functions so as to give the operands equal status in the expression. This will allow the operator to lie between the operands as in the mathematical expression. They are listed below.

Vector operator+(Vector&,Vector&)

The sum of two 3-D **Vectors**. The access functions are used to get the private data members *V* and their components are added. A copy is returned via the **Vector** copy constructor.

Vector operator-(Vector&,Vector&)

The difference of two Vectors. Like the sum.

Vector cross(Vector&,Vector&)

The cross product of two **Vectors**. A **Vector** is returned. An overloaded operator is not used for this function. Instead it is left as a function with the name cross.

int operator*(Vector&,Vector&)

The scalar or dot product of two Vectors. An integer is returned.

Vector operator*(Matrix&,Vector&)

Another overloading of the * operator. Here it represents the multiplication of a **Matrix** and a **Vector**. A **Vector** is returned. Note how it first constructs an empty **Vector** and then fills the elements using the **Vector** dot product. Once again this all happens in a loop in the line

```
T[i]=A[i]*B;
```

Here A[i] is the **Vector** which is the i'th row of the **Matrix** A using the overloaded **Matrix** subscripting and A[i]*B is the dot product of that **Vector** with the input **Vector**. The line is short because we have already done all the work in the operator overloading.

Matrix operator*(Matrix&,Matrix&)

The last function. Here is a product of two **Matrix** objects. This is a *tour de force* for our overloaded operators. Each row **Vector** of the first **Matrix** is multiplied by each column **Vector** of the second **Matrix**. The action occurs on the line

```
prod[i][j]=A[i]*B(j);
```

where the row **Vector** A[i] has a dot product with the column **Vector** B(j) and the result assigned to the (i-j)'th element of the **Matrix** product *prod* using both **Matrix** and **Vector** subscripting. The are five different overloaded operators at work here, all defined by us.

That ends our implementations of the **Vector** and **Matrix** classes. You might be thinking that it was a lot of work when 1-D and 2-D arrays are standard features of the language. What they have given us are two new data types which we can use whenever there is the need. We don't have to worry where their data will be kept nor whether they will upset any existing data structures. They exist as the **Vector** and **Matrix** abstract data types ready to use; just like **int** or **float**, but more complicated and specially designed to suit our needs.

5.9 Example Program

The example program here illustrates the use of the **Vector** and **Matrix** classes. It appears to be quite a short program but a lot is going on. If you run it from the IDE you will have to switch to the user screen to see the output. The example program is in the file VEC_MAT.CPP. It needs a project file which includes the files VEC_MAT.CPP and DEFN_00.CPP. Here is a description.

First an array of 5 integers is created and then an array of 10 integers. These arrays are used to instantiate the **Vectors** *vec5* and *vec10*. These **Vectors** are then displayed.

Then   *vec5* is added to itself as if it were a 3-component **Vector** and the sum displayed. The result is bound to be wrong since *vec5* has 5 components; only the first 3 are worked out! However, there isn't a crash, an answer is delivered.

Following this *vec5* is subtracted from *vec5* as if it were a 3 component **Vector**. Once again the answer is wrong but the program doesn't crash. It gives a **Vector** with all three components 0.

Then a 2 x 5 **Matrix** *mat2x5* is instantiated and displayed.

Finally the 2 x 5 **Matrix** is multiplied using the overloaded operator with the **Vector** *vec5* to give a *product* **Vector**, which is then displayed. The *product* **Vector** has the components 30 and 80 which is correct.

Try some combinations yourself. Maybe you can crash the program! If you can, fix it! The code works fine in all the later programs in the book.

```
// VEC_MAT.CPP
// examples of the Vector and matrix classes

#include "C:\TC\3D\DECL_00.H"

int main(){

    int arry5[]={0,1,2,3,4};                // short array
    int arry10[]={0,1,2,3,4,5,6,7,8,9};     // long   array
    Vector vec5(arry5,5);                   // short Vector
    Vector vec10(arry10,10);                // long Vector

    vec5.show();                            // display short
    vec10.show();                           // display long

    Vector sum=vec5+vec5;                   // add two 3D Vectors!
    sum.show();                             // display sum

    Vector difference=vec5-vec5;            // subtract two 3D Vectors!
    difference.show();                      // display difference

    Matrix mat2x5(arry10,2,5);              // 2 rows, 5 columns
    mat2x5.show();                          // display Matrix

    Vector product=mat2x5*vec5;             // Matrix times Vector
    product.show();                         // display Matrix

    return 0;
}
```

```
// DECL_00.H
// Vector and Matrix classes

// 1. A vector class

class Vector{
private:
    int *V;                         // integer array
    int dim;                        // array size
public:
    Vector();                       // default constructor
    Vector(int);                    // construct to dimension
    Vector(int, int, int);          // construc from three components
    Vector(int*, int);              // construct from an array
    Vector(Vector&);                // copy constructor - make a copy
    ~Vector();                      // destructor
    void build(int);                // get memory on heap
    Vector& operator=(Vector&);     // Vector assignment
    int& operator [](int);          // subscripting: this element
    int* getV(){return V;};         // public access to V
    int getdim(){return dim;};      // public access to dim
    void show();                    // display Vector
};


// 2. A Matrix class

class Matrix{
protected:
    Vector *M;                      // Vector array
    int rows,cols;                  // range from 0,0 to rows,cols
public:
    Matrix();                       // default constructor
    Matrix(int,int);                // construct to dimensions
    Matrix(int*,int,int);           // construct from an array
    Matrix(int**,int,int);          // construct from a pointer array
    Matrix(Vector*,int,int);        // construct from a Vector array
    Matrix(Matrix&);                // copy constructor
    ~Matrix();                      // delete rows Vectors
    void build(int,int);            // get memory
    Matrix& operator=(Matrix&);     // matrix assignment
    Vector& operator [](int);       // subscripting:this row
    Vector operator ()(int);        // subscripting:this column
    Vector* getM(){return M;}       // public access to M
    int getrows(){return rows;}     // public access to rows
    int getcols(){return cols;}     // public access to cols
    void norm(int);                 // normalise a 3 x 3
    void show();                    // display Matrix
};


// Non-member functions, mostly overloaded operators

    Vector operator +(Vector&, Vector&);  // add two Vectors
    Vector operator -(Vector&, Vector&);  // subtract two Vectors
    Vector cross(Vector&, Vector&);       // cross product
    int operator *(Vector&, Vector&);     // scalar product
    Vector operator *(Matrix&, Vector&);  // Matrix times Vector
    Matrix operator *(Matrix&, Matrix&);  // multiply two Matrices
```

```
// DEFN_00.CPP
// member functions for the Vector and Matrix classes

#include "C:\TC\3D\decl_00.h"
#include <stdio.h>
#include <stdlib.h>
#include <iostream.h>

// Implementation of class Vector
// default constructor ....................................
Vector::Vector(){
    dim=0;V=NULL;
}

// construct to size ......................................
Vector::Vector(int size){
    build(size);
}

// construct from 3 components ............................
Vector::Vector(int nx ,int ny, int nz){
    build(3);
    *V=nx;*(V+1)=ny;*(V+2)=nz;
}

// construct from an array ................................
Vector::Vector(int *src,int size){
    build(size);
    memcpy(V,src,dim*sizeof(int));
}

// copy constructor .......................................
Vector::Vector(Vector& src){
    build(src.dim);
    memcpy(V,src.V,dim*sizeof(int));
}

// destructor .............................................
Vector::~Vector(){delete []V;}

// allocate free memory ...................................
void Vector::build(int n){
    dim=n;
    if(!(V=new int[dim])){           // failure shuts down normally
        printf("\n Unable to allocate memory for new");
        exit(1);                     // failure
    }
}

// assignment operator ....................................
Vector& Vector::operator =(Vector& src){// make sure same size!!!
    dim=src.dim;
    memcpy(V,src.V,dim*sizeof(int));
    return *this;
}

// subscripting operator ..................................
int& Vector::operator [](int index){
    return *(V+index);
}
```

```
// display Vector ...................................................
void Vector::show(){
    cout<<"\n";
    for(int i=0;i<dim;i++){
        cout<<" "<<*(V+i);
    }
    cout<<"\n";
}

// Implementation of class Matrix
// default constructor ..............................................
Matrix::Matrix(){
    rows=0;cols=0;M=NULL;
}

//   construct to dimensions ........................................
Matrix::Matrix(int row,int col){
    build(row,col);
}

// from an integer array ............................................
Matrix::Matrix(int *ptr,int row,int col){
    build(row,col);
    for(int i=0;i<rows;i++){
        for(int j=0;j<cols;j++){
            M[i][j]=*(ptr++);
        }
    }
}

// construct from a pointer array ...................................
Matrix::Matrix(int **ptr,int row,int col){
    build(row,col);
    for(int i=0;i<row;i++){
        for (int j=0;j<col;j++){
        M[i][j]=ptr[i][j];
        }
    }
}

// construct from a Vector array ....................................
Matrix::Matrix(Vector *m,int row,int col){
    build(row,col);
    for(int i=0;i<rows;i++){
        M[i]=m[i];                       // Vector assignment
    }
}

// copy constructor .................................................
Matrix::Matrix(Matrix& src){
    build(src.rows,src.cols);
    for(int i=0;i<rows;i++){
        (*this)[i]=src[i];               // overloaded Vector =
    }                                    //   +Matrix subscripting
}

// destructor .......................................................
Matrix::~Matrix(){delete []M;}
```

```cpp
// allocate free memory ....................................
void Matrix::build(int row,int col){
    rows=row; cols=col;
    M=new Vector[rows];          //set up an array of (row) vectors
    for (int i=0;i<row;i++)
    M[i].build(cols);            //each vector is an array of integers
}

// assignment operator ....................................
Matrix& Matrix::operator =(Matrix& src){
    rows=src.rows;cols=src.cols;        // should be same
    for(int i=0;i<rows;i++){
        (*this)[i]=src[i];              // overloaded Vector =
    }                                   // + Matrix subscripting
    return *this;
}

// get a row Vector from the Matrix ....................................
Vector& Matrix::operator [](int row){
    return M[row];                      // a Vector
}

// get a column Vector from the Matrix ....................................
Vector Matrix::operator ()(int col){
    Vector Col(rows);                   // construct a Vector
    for(int i=0;i<rows;i++){
        Col[i]=M[i][col];
    }                                   // a Vector
        return Col;
}

// normalise a Matrix ....................................
void Matrix::norm(int scale){
    int i,j;
    for(i=0;i<rows;i++){
        for(j=0;j<cols;j++){
            M[i][j]/=scale;
        }
    }
}

// display a Matrix ....................................
void Matrix::show(){
    cout<<"\n";
    for(int i=0;i<rows;i++){
        for(int j=0;j<cols;j++){
            cout<<" "<<M[i][j];
        }
    }
    cout<<"\n";
}
```

```
// Non-member functions
// add two 3D Vectors ...............................................
Vector operator +(Vector &A,Vector &B){
    int *a=A.getV(); int *b=B.getV();
    int x=a[0]+b[0];//temporary
    int y=a[1]+b[1];
    int z=a[2]+b[2];
    return Vector(x,y,z);                        // construct it
}


//   subtract two 3D Vectors .......................................
Vector operator -(Vector &A,Vector &B){
    int *a=A.getV(); int *b=B.getV();
    return Vector(a[0]-b[0],a[1]-b[1],a[2]-b[2]);
}

// scalar product of two Vectors ...................................
int operator *(Vector &A,Vector &B){
    long prod=0;                                 // could be big
    for(int i=0;i<A.getdim();i++){
        prod+=A[i]*B[i];                         // hope it gets smaller
    }
    return (int)prod;
}

// cross product of two 3D Vectors .................................
Vector cross (Vector &A,Vector &B){
    int *a=A.getV(); int *b=B.getV();
    int x=int((long)a[1]*(long)b[2]-(long)a[2]*(long)b[1]);
    int y=int((long)a[2]*(long)b[0]-(long)a[0]*(long)b[2]);
    int z=int((long)a[0]*(long)b[1]-(long)a[1]*(long)b[0]);
    return Vector(x,y,z);                        // construct
}

// multiply a Vector by a Matrix ...................................
Vector operator *(Matrix &A, Vector &B){
    int ra=A.getrows();
    Vector T(ra);                                // construct empty Vector
    for(int i=0;i<ra;i++){                       // for all T elements
        T[i]=A[i]*B;                             // dot product
    }
    return T;
}

// multiply two Matrices ...........................................
Matrix operator *(Matrix &A, Matrix &B){
    int ra=A.getrows(); int cb=B.getcols();
    Matrix prod(ra,cb);                          // construct empty Matrix
    for(int i=0;i<ra;i++){                       // fill up the elements
        for(int j=0;j<cb;j++)
            prod[i][j]=A[i]*B(j);
    }
    return prod;                                 // here's the answer
}
```

6

Modelling a 3-D World

One of the most fascinating aspects of computers is the way they can be used to build life-like models. The great attraction of realistic computer games and, at the more serious end, simulators stems from the way the computer screen can be made to look like a window onto an invented universe – a Virtual Reality. Some famous scientists, impressed with the similarity to the process of creation, have even gone so far as to consider theories of reality based on a real Universe built up from 'bits' of information. Whatever the fundamental significance of it all, the fact remains that computers offer a new dimension for human expression and experience. Simply put, they provide the possibility to create alternative realities where the laws of Nature may or not apply. All sorts of strange and exotic situations can be invented and investigated. For human beings, who relate most easily to objects and situations met in everyday life (and dreams), what appears on the computer screen should look familiar. Great effort has gone into constructing models of this kind. In a simulator which is supposed to accurately depict reality, the emphasis is on models which obey the laws of Nature precisely.

In this chapter we will look at a way of modelling which provides a very fast and reasonably accurate picture of real objects. For the most part, but not completely, this involves polyhedral structures with polygonal faces as the building blocks, the so-called 'vector' graphics. Spheres and other objects with a high degree of symmetry can also be drawn quickly. Actually, to set the record straight, vector graphics originally meant something else. It was a name given to a mode of display where points on the monitor were joined directly by an electron beam that could be switch quickly from one part of the screen to another. This did not require much memory devoted to the screen and gave very fast 'wire-frame' pictures. The displays on monitors today do not use this technique. Instead, the image is built up from horizontal raster scans from one side of the image to the other. It is called raster scan (or scan conversion) graphics. The speed with which an outline can be filled by raster scans makes it a very useful technique. However the name vector graphics has become commonly used to describe the graphics modelling technique itself, not the display technology. The adjective "vector" here really refers to the extensive use made of vector geometry in the programs.

One other important technique is the Block Image Transfer (BLIT) type of graphics, in which SPRITES play an important role. In such graphics, blocks of memory are manipulated as a whole, which is very useful since, once laid out in RAM, scan conversion need not be done a second time. The block of bytes is simply moved to the screen area. Some very clever and fast things can be done this way, particularly with sprites, but the relationships between the parts of the image are essentially determined by how the block is initially laid out in RAM although transforms of bit-maps are possible. Sprite graphics is not discussed any further in this book.

Having said that, it is likely that the next generation of popular computers will have hardware implementation of all the common graphics functions including the 'vector' graphics we are about to discuss. It is very probable that soon all graphics functions will be done by very fast hardware 'geometry engines'.

6.1 3-D Modelling

"Real-time" 3-D modelling has to be very fast. This is because humans can spot the flicker of the picture if it changes more slowly than about once every 50 milliseconds. The programs in this book are not the world's fastest. This is mainly because they are written in C++. Had they been written in assembler they would have been faster but not by a very large factor. But rest assured there is a real bonus in doing it in C++. In the first place the code is portable, i.e. it can run on any machine that has a C++ compiler although it may be necessary to alter the basic screen drawing routines from those supplied by Turbo C++. With the popularity of the language it is certain that every popular platform will have a C++ compiler. In the second place it is not possible to maintain and extend large programs reliably in assembler. There is too much microscopic detail to remember. In the third place consider that you are preparing for the future; hardware speed is not likely to be the bottle-neck in the future where many of the basic graphics functions will be implemented in hardware. Today's machines, like the PC, are just passing that point. It's more important to get the programming right and wait a little while for the machines to arrive. I'm sure that will happen in the next few years. Fourthly, and finally, even the largest program "PC City" in the last chapter runs tolerably well on a '486 running at 33 MHz. The graphics in the earlier chapters run OK on a '386 running at 25 Mhz.

In order to work in real time, the viewer has to be able to enter new data through the keyboard, joy-stick or mouse and see its effects immediately. The solid 3-D structures which can be transformed and drawn on this time scale most easily are polyhedra. Polyhedra are very good graphics building blocks or 'primitives' for several very good reasons:

❑ they are completely defined by their vertices,

❑ the faces are polygons with straight edges,

❑ in any transformation only the vertices need to be recalculated,

❑ a transformed polygon is also a polygon

❑ polygons can quickly be filled in to look 'solid' using raster scans.

What all this means really is that it's very hard to draw and shade in curved surfaces which don't have high symmetry (like circles) and the only 3-D objects without curved surfaces are polyhedra.

In fact computer graphics does not have a monopoly on the use of polyhedra as basic building blocks. The real world uses them extensively; many houses are made from bricks, which are six-sided polyhedra.

6.2 Frames of Reference

All of the above statements concerning polyhedra can be translated into a definite mathematical framework called vector algebra, which is a very elegant and precise formulation of the mathematics of lines and planes. It becomes even move useful when presented in matrix form and it is this approach which usually appears in text books on computer graphics. You can see why we invested much effort in developing the **Vector** and **Matrix** classes. For someone with little knowledge of advanced mathematics this looks very intimidating; actually it's not. Many secondary school syllabuses handle simple rotations using 2 x 2 matrices, and it really isn't much more complicated than that. For those of us who do not wish to blaze new trails in the world of mathematics it is simply a case of understanding the general method and taking the results on trust. After all, once you've seen the transforms working you can use them in your programs and forget about them. There's no need to re-invent the wheel. None-the-less, we have invented the **Vector** and **Matrix** classes ready to go.

For the moment though, in order to see the problem laid out in its entirety, let's consider all the various stages of transforms, as shown in figure 6.1 that a graphics primitive goes through before it finally gets projected on the screen.

6.2.1 The Object Frame

An object which exists inside the computer has quite a complicated life before it is seen on the screen. Most of this complication arises from the various transforms required to make it 'lifelike'. But whatever they are (rotations, translations or even something more exotic), the object must preserve its original identity, i.e. its relative dimensions. What this means is that since no calculation can be absolutely precise and, with the picture being recalculated several times each second, if the original definition were not continually referenced, it would not be long before accumulative errors would make it unrecognisable (this problem crops up in all our calculations which, for speed, are done in the limited accuracy allowed by 16 bit integers). Therefore it is necessary to constantly refer back to the original data which define the object. We call this place, in which the object is defined, the object frame (there is nothing sacrosanct about this name, other people have invented other names). Of course, it doesn't 'exist' in any real sense, it's just that the numbers which fix the positions of the vertices are coordinates measured from some origin. This origin is where the object frame is said to be located. The object frame can be positioned so as to reflect the symmetry of the object. For example, the natural object frame of a cube could be a Cartesian (x,y,z) coordinate system centred at the centre of symmetry (centre of gravity) of the cube, with the sides of the cube parallel to the x, y and z axes of the coordinate system as shown in Figure 6.1.

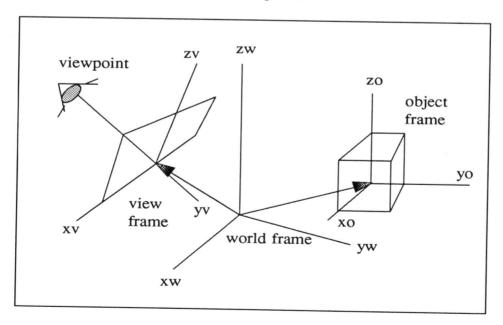

Figure 6.1 Frames of reference

There may be several object frames combined together, particularly when a complex object is made up of several simpler objects. The process of sticking together simple objects (primitives) to make a complex one involves just the kind of transforms we have been talking about. These transforms are sometimes referred to as instance transforms (not to be confused with instances of a class).

6.2.2 The World frame

Having constructed a complex object – which can be thought of as an 'actor' in the scenario we are about to create – it is necessary to place it in the arena with all other 'actors'. This common space, inhabited by all objects is called the world frame. It is the place where the Laws of Nature play a role. For example, objects which are not subject to any force either remain at rest or move at constant velocity. That's Newton's First Law. Since this world is our creation, we do not have to stick to these laws, if we wish. This is the place where collisions are tested for. We will call the transform which moves the object into its final position in the world frame the object-to-world transform. It may consist of some combination of rotation and translation.

6.2.3 The View Frame

Everyone in the real world has a different view of it, and the same thing applies to the world we are creating inside the computer. The only difference is that there is only one screen and therefore only one viewer. The view of the world depends on where the observer is standing and looking.

The view of the world seen by the observer is most easily represented by the view frame. This is a set of x, y, and z-axes which follow the gaze of the observer. In our convention the z-axis points vertically up and the y-axis points into the screen. In this picture, an object which is straight ahead at a distance of 100 will have the coordinates (0,100,0) in the view frame and if the observer rotates to the left by 90 degrees it will have view frame coordinates (100,0,0). In general the view frame's position in the world frame will be changing continuously. In a flight simulator, for example, the view frame is the view from the cockpit.

It might appear at first sight that there is an unnecessary duplication of points of view in all these frames of reference. However they define a natural hierarchy within which the overall picture can be constructed to make it easy to take account of the relative motions of the observer and graphics primitives.

One thing in particular is worth noting. Rotating the view frame to the left or moving the scene to the right results in the same relative motion and gives the same picture on the screen. This suggests that there is a simple connection between two motions. In the language of mathematics, one is said to be the inverse of the other. We will now look in detail at this subject.

6.2.4 The Screen

Finally there is the screen on which an image is projected. Remember that because of double buffering, or page switching, there are always two screens to reduce flicker: a hidden one to draw on (active screen) and a finished one to display (visual screen). It is mapped out following the way RAM is allocated to the screen. This results in the origin (the point with screen coordinates (0,0)) being right at the top left hand corner of the screen. To get from the view frame to the screen we must make a 'projection' onto a plane, called the view plane, of the objects which we wish to display. This is called a perspective transform and must preserve the ordering in space, so that objects which are farther away look smaller. It is done by tracing "rays" from objects to the view point, which is the location of the observer's eye. The intersection of these rays with the view plane defines the outlines as they will appear on the screen.

The transform to the screen coordinate system is almost the last stage, but not quite; the screen has limits. It may turn out that parts of the picture lie outside the screen RAM; that part of memory allocated to the screen. If no attempt is made to restrict points to appear on the visible screen then the program will attempt to plot them outside screen RAM, which could lead to a system crash. For this reason, unless it is absolutely certain that no point to be displayed will ever lie outside the screen RAM, only part of what is visible on the view plane will reach the screen. This is "windowing". What is not visible must be "clipped" away. The outline which defines the window on the display is called a view port. Fortunately for us, the Turbo C++ screen routines take care of these clipping details.

There is even a need to clip in three dimensions in the view frame itself. Objects which are a long way away from the observer should not be displayed, and no time should be wasted worrying about them. It is a consequence of having a finite drawing resolution on the screen that small objects become badly distorted. Ultimately all very distant objects will end up as single pixels and the horizon could have a cluster of dots all over it. Sets of parallel lines will ultimately converge to a single line which will then never diminish in intensity. To stop all of this it makes sense to clip out altogether objects which are more than a certain distance from the origin of the view frame.

6.3 Geometric and Coordinate Transforms

There are two types of transform used widely in computer graphics: geometric and coordinate transforms. What is confusing is that they are really two aspects of the same thing and it is possible to achieve the same end result by either method. However in order to stay sane it helps greatly to think of them as different, choosing one or the other depending on the problem. Many clever shortcuts become possible once the distinction and connection between them is understood.

Imagine that you are sitting in a swivel chair positioned at the centre of circular carpet in a room with black featureless walls. Since there is no external reference point (apart from remembering what actually happened) it is not possible to distinguish between rotating the chair to the right on a stationary carpet, or keeping the chair fixed and rotating the carpet to the left. The observer on the chair sees the same relative movement of chair and carpet and his view of the carpet pattern is the same in both cases. But we must be careful to establish a scheme of rotation of either the chair or the carpet which are consistent. Let us decide that left rotations are positive and right rotations are negative. Then we can see that a positive rotation of the chair (the observer) is equivalent to a negative rotation of the carpet (the object): they are said to be the *inverse* of each other.

Now we come to the formal definitions. Rotating the observer is called a coordinate transform and rotating the object is called a geometric transform. There are many times in computer graphics when we wish to do both of these. When an object is moved in the world frame, it is subject to a geometric transform. When we wish to see the world from a different point of view a coordinate transform must be done. When the observer is controlling his viewpoint orientation by means of the keyboard it is useful to exploit the connection between the two transforms.

6.3.1 Coordinate Systems and Frames of Reference

To some extent these terms are used interchangeably. For the most part the positions and vertices of objects are determined in Cartesian coordinates by a set of three x, y and z axes at right angles. The position of the zero of this set of axes is called the origin of the coordinate system. The whole constitutes a frame of reference to track subsequent motion of the various objects. As we have seen, there are two types of movement: a coordinate transform (when the observer moves) and a geometric transform (when an object moves). When the object moves it is easiest to keep track of what is going on by following the motion of the frame of reference attached to the object itself. We have called this the object frame. In the main text the object-to-world transform was made by selected rotations and a displacement of this object frame. Now we can see exactly how this works.

Imagine a set of axes permanently attached to the object so that when it moves they also move. For simplicity, we consider a rotation by an angle γ about the z axis, as shown in Figure 6.2. A transform matrix is now needed to relate the coordinates after the rotation (x1,y1,z1,) to those before (x,y,z). The beauty of this scheme is that we can construct this matrix by observing what happens to the base vectors. The base vectors are the unit vectors (of size 1) pointing like sign posts along the x,y and z axes. The base vectors before the rotation are **i**, **j**, and **k** and after the rotation are **i1**, **j1** and **k1**.

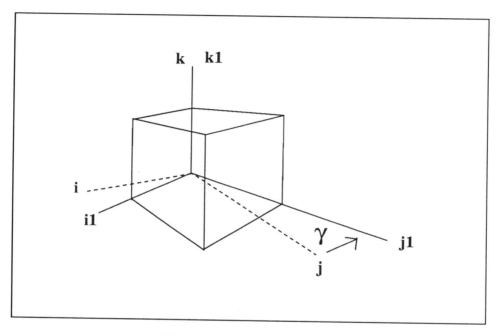

Figure 6.2 Rotation of an object

Looking at the Figure we can see the relations between these:

$$\mathbf{i1} = \cos\gamma \,.\mathbf{i} + \sin\gamma \,.\mathbf{j}$$

$$\mathbf{j1} = -\sin\gamma \,.\mathbf{i} + \cos\gamma \,.\mathbf{j}$$

$$\mathbf{k1} = \mathbf{k}$$

leading to a transform matrix for the base vectors:

$$\begin{pmatrix} \cos\gamma & \sin\gamma & 0 \\ -\sin\gamma & \cos\gamma & 0 \\ 0 & 0 & 1 \end{pmatrix}$$

Now this matrix as it stands cannot be used to transform the coordinates (x,y,z) to $(x1,y1,z1)$, but its inverse can. Fortunately, the inverse of a pure rotation is simply obtained by switching (transposing) the rows and columns. In technical language, the inverse of a rotation is its transpose. Doing this yields the matrix:

$$\begin{pmatrix} \cos\gamma & -\sin\gamma & 0 \\ \sin\theta & \cos\gamma & 0 \\ 0 & 0 & 1 \end{pmatrix}$$

so that, for example, in a rotation of γ by 90 degrees, the point $(0,1,0)$ becomes the point $(-1,0,0)$ and the point $(1,0,0)$ becomes $(0,1,0)$. So we have found a way of rotating an object to a new orientation: perform that reorientation on the object base vectors and express the result in terms of the original base vectors; then transpose the matrix to produce the coordinate transform matrix.

Can the original matrix be used for anything? Yes. As it stands, before it is transposed, it is a coordinate transform. If we were to leave the object stationary and just rotate the frame of reference, it gives us the transform to calculate what the object coordinates appear to be in the new rotated frame. This is shown in Figure 6.3.

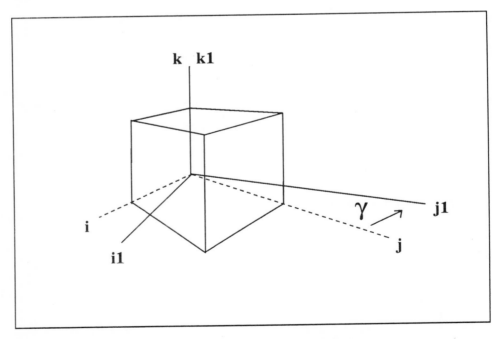

Figure 6.3 Rotation of a frame of reference

Hence in the rotation of γ of 90 degrees, the vertex (0,1,0) appears to be at (1,0,0), and the vertex (1,0,0) appears to be at (0,-1,0) when seen from the rotated frame. Note that in both of these rotations, of the object and reference frame respectively, the sense of the rotation was positive.

Now we can see the qualitative discussion concerning the observer on the swivel chair and the carpet expressed mathematically. The transform which calculates the coordinates of the object after its positive rotation is:

$$\begin{pmatrix} \cos\gamma & -\sin\gamma & 0 \\ \sin\gamma & \cos\gamma & 0 \\ 0 & 0 & 1 \end{pmatrix}$$

and the transform which calculates the new apparent coordinates of the stationary object after the reference frame has been moved in a positive direction is:

$$\begin{pmatrix} \cos\gamma & \sin\gamma & 0 \\ -\sin\gamma & \cos\gamma & 0 \\ 0 & 0 & 1 \end{pmatrix}$$

They are different when both involve a positive rotation but become the same if the reference frame (the chair) is rotated negatively. Then, the angle γ is negative and, because $\sin(-\gamma) = -\sin\gamma$ but $\cos(-\gamma) = \cos\gamma$, the terms involving $\sin\gamma$ change sign but those involving $\cos\gamma$ don't.

This is only restating the fact that rotating the reference frame one way gives the same relative motion as rotating the object the other way.

6.4 Data Structures

6.4.1 Lists

Finding ways of efficiently storing and accessing data is very important in computer graphics, particularly where speed matters. The important thing is to store data in a form such that is easy to get at for the problem in hand. It may not always be in the best form for all applications all the time, and some manipulation may be required along the way.

In vector graphics where primitives are modelled by polyhedral structures with polygonal faces, what is most important are lists of vertices (corners) and the straight line edges joining them. Figure 6.4 illustrates a house modelled in this way. There is more than one way of setting up a data list to describe this structure, but the one we will most commonly use has at its centre the list of connections which describe the surfaces uniquely: the edge list. One thing to avoid is having to repeat the actual coordinates of the vertices more than once. It is better to give each vertex a number and instead refer to this. When the x, y and z-coordinates of a vertex are required they can be drawn from the list of coordinates by a dereferenced pointer, providing the position in the list is simply related to the vertex number. To make this point clear, here are the lists which are needed to draw the house. There will be other lists as well, containing other attributes such as the colour of each surface and so on, but they are not shown here. The house is not very complicated, but sufficiently so to show how long the lists might become for a really complex object.

First the actual coordinates, in whatever scale is being used, are given for x, y and z in the order of vertex numbers:

x coordinates: 0,100,100,0,100,0,0,100,150,150,0,50,50,0

y coordinates: 50,50,50,50,-50,-50,-50,-50,0,0,50,50,50,50

z coordinates: -100,-100,100,100,100,100,-100,-100,-100,100,-10,-10,10,10

After this the ordered list of vertex numbers going clockwise round the exterior face makes up the edge list.

edge list: 7,8,9,2,1,1,2,3,4,4,3,10,5,6,6,5,8,7,5,10,9,8,2,9,10,3

                      1,4,6,7,11,12,13,14

if the base is included.

Then the number of edges in each surface is given, where the entry has the same position as the number (circled) of the surface as shown in the figure:

edge numbers: 5, 4, 5, 4, 4, 4, 4, 4

Finally the number of polygons in the house as a whole must be specified. Each plane face qualifies: four walls, two sloping roofs, one floor, one door, so we have:

polygon number: 8

There is only one entry here but if there were other buildings it would be a list.

These data and others would be used to define the house in the object frame. Following the transformation to the world frame some of the lists, the edge list, the edge numbers and the surface number would all be unchanged but the coordinates in the world frame would be different. It is clear that there is ample scope here for the

Vector and **Matrix** abstract data types we have defined. Lists such as the edge list and edge numbers can be described by integer arrays.

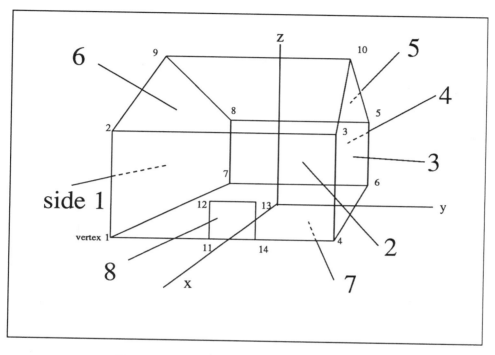

Figure 6.4 A house modelled as a polygon mesh

6.5 Summary

What should be one's attitude towards these very mathematical aspects of 3-D graphics? If you are mathematically inclined, then it makes sense to try to understand what's going on in detail. This gives you the power to write your own transforms and explore some of the very interesting effects that can be produced. If you are not mathematically inclined then just regard the mathematical transforms as software "black boxes" to be "plugged in" as required. The transforms in this book are based on the **Matrix** class to allow you to do this. You will see later several examples of instances of a **Transform** class changing the data structures. This is particularly evident in the program ROTATE.CPP where Transforms are constructed that produce rotations in three dimensions.

7

Drawing on the Screen

In this chapter we look at drawing on the screen. A very important aspect of this will be filling in polygonal shapes quickly. Fortunately Turbo C++ supplies library routines to do this.

7.1 The Screen

The monitor screen is a rectangular end of a cathode ray tube on which an electron beam writes. To make this look like a picture the beam moves very quickly from left to right and top to bottom in a series of 'raster' scans; the picture is made up of closely spaced horizontal lines each made up of units called pixels. There isn't really a solid picture at all, it just looks that way from a distance. To see this for yourself, inspect the monitor screen closely with a magnifying glass. Figure 7.1 shows a small filled polygon magnified so that the otherwise straight lines joining the vertices become jagged staircases. The strange visual effects you can get when the sharp features of an image interact with the pixels on the screen is called aliasing. Advanced graphics systems have hardware which counteracts this effect (anti-aliasing).

Memory, on the other hand, is laid out as a contiguous line of bytes, which are the smallest elements the microprocessor can directly address and of these, the smallest resolvable unit is the bit (8 bits = 1 byte). It is on these that the image is initially written by the graphics routine. There are many ways in which this pattern of bits can appear on the visible screen and exactly what scheme is used depends on the graphics adapter in your machine. The programs in this book have been written to run in medium resolution VGA (Video Graphics Array) which has a resolution of 640 pixels across (the x direction) and 350 down (the y direction), can simultaneously show 16 colours and supports screen buffering through the two video pages. This mode allows us to produce fast real-time pictures with a reasonable colour range. Other modes may be higher resolution and more colourful but are too slow. Within this scheme, we can implement shading using different fill patterns for the polygons whilst still retaining the full range of colours or use slightly different colours.

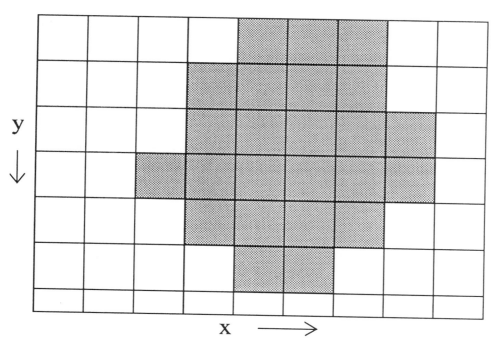

Figure 7.1: Pixels in a small polygon.

7.2 Screen Buffering

Screen buffering (or double buffering or page switching) is an important aspect of displaying flicker-free images. What it amounts to is having two chunks of Video RAM available: one to draw on and the other to display. The one currently being drawn is called the active page and the one being displayed on the screen is called the visual page. They aren't both visible at once; at any given instant you can only see the visual page. They are switched back and forth so that whilst a picture is being drawn on the active page the visual page, which holds the last complete picture, is displayed on the monitor. Then when the new picture is completed on the active page the page names are switched, it becomes the new visual page and is put on display. The old visual page then becomes the new active page and is erased ready for drawing the next picture. It helps to think of each new picture as a frame, in the movie sense, so that the real-time graphics evolves like an interactive movie. In medium resolution VGA there is sufficient memory available on the graphics adaptor to hold two pages for this, and there are library functions to switch between the pages.

7.3 The Colour Palette and Colour Planes

Colour is usually implemented in a strange way on a computer display usually to save memory and make the reading of it as fast as possible. The scheme is called colour indirection and it works in the following way. At any given instant it is possible to display 16 colours on the screen. This is not the total number of colours which can be shown however but the colours currently set in a special register called the colour palette. Many more different colours can be selected but to do so requires changing the settings in the colour palette. If you change the colours in the colour palette all the colours on the screen change, not just those in the pixel you're interested in. Let's see how this comes about.

It is very expensive to hold colour information. Consider the mode we will work in: medium resolution VGA. With a screen resolution of 640 x 350 that is a total number of 224000 pixels and if each pixel is mapped to a bit in memory that is 28000 bytes or 27 Kbytes just to write to every pixel. All this will do is enable us to set the pixels to 1 or 0 and is really nothing more than the minimal memory for a monochrome display. We might think of this as a single colour plane.

What now if we require a possible 16 colours? This can be done by having 4 colour planes notionally lying on top of each other so that a screen pixel is now represented by the same bit in each colour plane (sometimes it's not as simple as this but the idea is the same). In each plane the bit can be 0 or 1 giving a total of $2^4=16$ possible combinations. Now we have our 16 colours. But it doesn't end there. There are certainly 16 colours, but what 16 colours? That's where the palette comes in.

The palette is a list of 16 colours with each colour being specified by three RGB (red, green, blue) colour codes. You can change the entries in the palette with several of the Turbo C++ library routines, such as **setrgbpalette()** or **setpalette()** to use standard colours. The entries are generated in medium VGA from three colours red, green and blue with each colour increasing in intensity from 0 to 255 and therefore being covered by a byte. However only the top 6 bits of the byte can be used which means that the values go up in intervals of 4. Since there are 64 such numbers in the range 0 to 255, there is 64 possible values of red, green and blue and therefore a total of

262144 different possible colours. That's a lot more than 16! Since you can change the palette you can select which 16 of these are available for display at any given moment. When you want a change, change one of the entries in the palette. But remember, it will change every occurrence of that colour on the screen.

Lets' summarise how it works. The number, in the range 0 – 15, generated by the colour planes is an index into the palette. If for a given pixel the bit is set in the first plane, cleared in the second plane, set in the third and cleared in the fourth, the total value is 5 and that pixel will display the colour of the fifth palette entry. Figure 7.2 shows the connection between the bit planes and the colour palette.

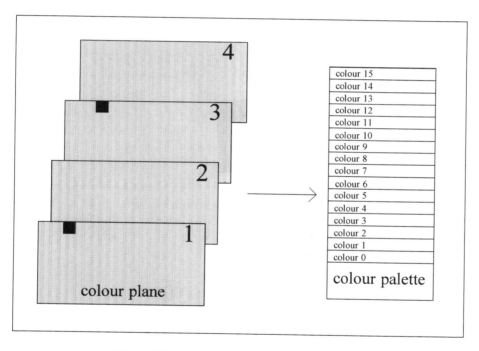

Figure 7.2: Colour planes and colour palette.

There is, of course, a default setting of the colour palette which gives the following colours (see next page):

Name	Value
Black	0
Blue	1
Green	2
Cyan	3
Red	4
Magenta	5
Brown	6
Light Grey	7
Dark Grey	8
Light Blue	9
Light Green	10
Light Cyan	11
Light Red	12
Light Magenta	13
Yellow	14
White	15

For the graphics in this book we will use these default colours.

7.4 Shading

In order to bring realism to the computer graphics we will wish to implement illumination from a light source. The side of 3-D structure that faces the light should be brighter than that which faces away. This is one of many possible "rendering" tricks to make things look real. Having seen how it is possible to set the colours in the palette, you will realise that we could set up 15 (colour 0 is the background) different shades of one colour and do it that way.

An alternative which shows another aspect of drawing offered by the Turbo C++ library routines is to change the fill pattern of the polygon. Look back at Figure 7.1. See how the polygon in that picture is filled with solid lines. It is possible to deviate from that and choose a user-defined fill pattern of bits which can range from all 1's, the full colour, to all 0's, the background. By setting up 16 fill patterns in this range it is possible to simulate levels of intensity of each of the 15 colours. The disadvantage is that the pattern is not fine enough to avoid a grainy appearance, and is implemented as a static pattern which can look strange. The advantage is the full range of colours. Anyway, this is an educational book and you are encouraged to try your own ideas. The programs will use the fill pattern technique.

7.4.1 The Fill patterns

The fill patterns for the shading are in the file SHADES.H They are in the form of sixteen 4-word bit-maps. A word is two bytes in this compiler so it is convenient to list the patterns as 4 pairs characters since a character is a byte. You can see from the file that each shading pattern is an array of characters and there are 16 arrays: 0 to 15. The arrays start off with nearly all 0's in the binary equivalent of the numbers and at the highest shade are all 1's, which is full brightness. Finally these array names, which are pointer constants are placed in a pointer array called *shadings*. It is *shadings* which appears in the other listings and is passed as a parameter to the **Screen** Class which we will discuss shortly.

7.5 Windowing

If a picture is larger than the limits of the screen then there is a problem with what happens to the excess. Unless some provision is made for this possibility, the program will attempt to write to addresses outside of the section of RAM reserved for the screen. Fortunately the Turbo C++ library functions take care of all of this in setting up the screen, as we will see. Confining a picture in this way is called windowing because of the obvious analogy to someone looking out of a window and what remains visible is called the viewport. The viewport is a window onto the internal world of the computer. This viewport could be the maximum screen size or something smaller (one obvious way to make graphics fast is to keep the picture small so that not much has to be drawn). All this will be handled by the constructor of the **Screen** class.

7.6 Language Features

There are two new language features in this section which have been delayed until they can be illustrated by example. They are the **enum** (enumeration) data type and **friends** of a class.

7.6.1 Enumerations

An enumeration is a way of specifying a series of integer constants which, by default starts at zero. An example of this is

```
enum {first, second};// first = 0, second = 1
```

in which first has the value 0 and second the value 1. An enumeration can be named in which case it becomes a type and can create instances

```
enum flag{on, off};    // enum type
flag sort;             // sort can be "on" of "off"
```

An instance can be created immediately

```
enum {on,off}flag;
```

and be assigned values

```
flag=on:               // value 1
flag=off;              // value 0
```

The enumeration in the **Screen** class is used in exactly this last way, as a flag, which can be on or off.

7.6.2 Friends of a Class

The encapsulation of data accorded to private members of a class is there to provide a degree of "data hiding", since in the simplest case only member functions of the class have access to them. But the security this provides sometimes forces artificial constraints on the programming style. The **friend** is a device to circumvent this privacy in a controlled way without throwing open the class to the general public.

Functions are usually friends of a class but entire classes can also be friends. If class **A** is a friend of class **B**, then **A** has access to all the private members of **B**. Friends have to be explicitly declared as such inside the class declaration. There are two new classes declared in the examples at the end of this chapter: the **Screen** class and the **Polygon** class. **Polygon** is declared a friend of **Screen** so that it has access to all of **Screen**'s members, especially the list of shadings. Look at the listings to see exactly how it is done.

7.7 A Screen Class

In keeping with our plan to use abstract data types, the screen on which the picture is displayed has been abstracted into a **Screen** class. There will only be one instance of the class but that does not matter. **Screen** will encapsulate our idea of a screen.

What do we want from a **Screen**? It must take care of the final stage of displaying the graphics. It must set up the screen hardware, know what the shading patterns are and take care of screen buffering. The member data and functions are chosen to do this. Refer to file DECL_01.H for the Screen interface and DEFN_01.CPP for the implementation. Here is a listing of the members. Note that the **Polygon** class is forward-declared but not expanded in the first line, so that it will be recognised by the **Screen** class and can be included as a **Screen** class member. Without that forward declaration the word Polygon would have no meaning for the **Screen** class. The full interface for the **Polygon** class comes after the **Screen** class.

char** Screen::pfill

The data member which is a pointer to the shading pointer array.

enum Screen::page_config

The flag to switch screen pages. An enumeration. It recognises *draw_active*=0 and *draw_visual*=1. It works together with the other nameless enumeration which recognises *draw*=0 and *show*=1, in order to toggle the video page for graphics display. These enum types are really labels for 1 and 0.

Screen::Screen(char**)

The only defined constructor. This copies the pointer to the shading array in the external data into the internal data member *pfill* and initialises the screen. Initialising the screen means putting the system into VGA graphics mode at medium resolution and loading the desired graphics driver file from the .BGI directory on the hard disk. This is done in the constructor by the library function **initgraph()**. Then the default settings (like the palette) are restored and the viewport dimensions set. Which page to make active first is specified and a linestyle set. The linestyle determines the type of border line around filled polygons. Initially we want there to be no line. Later in the graphics, on occasion for effect, this may be changed.

Screen::~Screen

The destructor which is responsible for closing down the graphics system and restoring things to the way they were using the library function **closegraph()**. A true destructor job.

void Screen::swap_screen()

The member function to swap the screens. The switch-case statement is used to detect the current configuration and then switch it. The **clearviewport()** library function is used to clear the new active page before drawing the next frame. It's fairly slow and accounts for a substantial fraction of the time spent drawing polygons.

friend class Polygon

A friend class. We can keep the data members private to **Screen** whilst still accessing them with a friend. In this case the entire **Polygon** class is a friend. Every function in class **Polygon** has access to **Screen**'s data.

7.8 A Polygon Class

The polygon is the simplest building block in our graphics. The solid structures which will appear on the screen are made of polygons connected together into polyhedra. The Polygon class is very simple. It contains data to describe a polygon and has member functions, which are library functions, to draw the polygon.

int* Polygon::vtx_array

The list of vertices in order (x,y) of the screen coordinates going round the polygon clockwise. The last one is not a repeat of the first one, so the function joins up the last to the first vertex. The screen coordinates are x left to right and y top to bottom. So the screen origin is in the top left hand corner with the y axis inverted from what you might expect, as usual with computer display coordinates.

int Polygon::edge_no

The number of edges in the polygon also equal to the number of vertices.

int Polygon::pcolour

The palette colour.

int Polygon::pshade

The index into the shade list.

Polygon::Polygon(int*,int,int,int)

The constructor to load up data. To show an important way of copying data into the internal data members whilst the constructor is invoked. This is an important way of initialising a class member which itself requires a constructor. If it isn't done this way, the constructor for the member will be called twice, once to construct the enclosing class with a default constructor and again to initialise it with the copy constructor which is a waste of time.

Note that although all the data members are initialised, the body of the constructor is empty.

void Polygon::putcolour(int,int)

The inline function which sets the colour and shade on the fly.

void Polygon::paint(Screen&)

Paint the polygon, but with access to the shading patterns owned by the Screen instance. This function uses the shade number as an index to select the appropriate shading bit pattern form the *pfill* pointer. The actual drawing is done by the library function **fillpoly**().

7.9 The Example Program

Here at last is a graphics example program. The listing is in the file POLYDRAW.CPP. It is a program to illustrate the use of the Screen and Polygon classes to draw, colour and shade a polygon. There's not much to it but it shows how the polygon painting occurs and that is the important basis for all the graphics programming that follows.

7.8.1 POLYDRAW.H

First of all header files for the **Screen** and **Polygon** classes are included and the file for the shadings. The main program instantiates a Screen object named screen with the shading patterns passed to the constructor. We think of the shadings as belonging to the screen rather than the polygon, since they are a display feature. Then the polygon vertex array is set up and a **Polygon** called *poly* instantiated. Finally the full range of colours in the default palette is scrolled through and for every one of those the shading patterns are scrolled. The program itself within the loop is very simple and says clearly what it is doing: swap the active and visual screens, put the *poly* colour and paint it. The program has a return value of 0 to show there were no errors.

7.8.2 POLYDRAW.PRJ

This is the project file to produce an executable .exe file. It should contain the following files

```
POLYDRAW.CPP
DEFN_00.CPP
```

With the project opened, and the above files added, select **Run|run** from the menu.

```
// POLYDRAW.CPP
// A polygon is painted in different colours and shadings

#include "C:\TC\3D\DECL_01.H"// header for Screen and Polygon classes
#include "C:\TC\3D\SHADES.H" // list of shadings - make your own


int main(void)
{
    // instatiate a screen with a pointer to the sading patterns
    Screen screen(shadings);

    // then a polygon with 5 sides
    int edge_no=5;
    int arry_ptr[]={20,20,300,10,600,170,500,300,40,200};//vertices
    Polygon poly(arry_ptr,edge_no);                      // instantiate it

    for(int i=0;i<16;i++){                  //scroll through 16 colours
        for(int new_shade=0;new_shade<16;new_shade++){// 16 shades
            screen.swap_screen();          // swap screens
            poly.putcolour(i,new_shade);// next colour and shade
            poly.paint(screen);            //draw it
        }
    }
    return 0; // safe return
}
```

```
// DECL_01.H
// The Screen and Polygon class declarations

class Polygon;//forward declaration for Polygon::paint(Screen)

// A Screen class to set up the screens and implement screen buffering

class Screen{
    char** pfill;                                // shadings array
    enum {draw_active,draw_visual}page_config;   // video pages
    enum {draw,show};                            // video labels
public:

    Screen(char**);                  // constructor with shadings
    ~Screen();                       // destructor to close display
    void swap_screen();              // swap the screens
    friend class Polygon;            // needs access to shading list
};


// A Polygon class which holds the vertices of a polygon and
// paints it on the screen

class Polygon{
    int *vtx_array;          // vertex list
    int edge_no;             // number of edges
    int pcolour;             // colour
    int pshade;              // shade
public:

    // constructor initialises data members directly
    Polygon(int *arry,int no,int colour=0,int shade=15):\
    vtx_array(arry),edge_no(no),pcolour(colour),pshade(shade){}

    // set the colour - minimum shade is the default
    void putcolour(int colour,int shade=15)
        {pcolour=colour;pshade=shade;}

    void paint(Screen&);            // draw polygon
};
```

```
// DEFN_01.CPP
// Definition of the Screen and Polygon class functions

#include <graphics.h>
#include "C:\TC\3D\DECL_01.H"


// member functions or the Screen class

// the Screen constructor to set up the screen when it's instantiated
Screen::Screen(char** fillpat){

    pfill=fillpat;                              // shadings table
    int graphdriver=VGA,graphmode=VGAMED;//640x350 resolution;2 pages
    initgraph(&graphdriver,&graphmode,"\\tc\\bgi");//set display
    graphdefaults();                            //default values

    // the viewport and clipping
    setviewport(50,50,getmaxx()-50,getmaxy()-30,1);

    page_config=draw_active;              // set sreen buffering
    setlinestyle(4,0,1);                  // no polygon outline
}


// the destructor ...........................................
Screen::~Screen(){closegraph();}         // close display


// screen buffering ..........................................
void Screen::swap_screen(){

switch(page_config){                      // flip the screens
        case draw_active:   setactivepage(draw);//draw here
                    setvisualpage(show);          //display this
                    clearviewport();              //erase old
                    page_config=draw_visual; break;//next time

        case draw_visual:   setactivepage(show);
                    setvisualpage(draw);
                    clearviewport();
                    page_config=draw_active;break;
    }
}


// The member function of the Polygon class

// paint a polygon ..........................................
void Polygon::paint(Screen& scrn){               // draw polygon
    setfillpattern(scrn.pfill[pshade],pcolour); // shade and colour
    fillpoly(edge_no,vtx_array);               // do it!
}
```

```
// SHADES.H
// 16 fill patterns for shading


char shade0[]={16,0,0,2,128,0,0,8}; // 4 word bitmap
char shade1[]={2,128,16,1,68,16,1,72};
char shade2[]={132,32,130,8,65,8,130,16};
char shade3[]={136,34,136,34,136,34,136,34};
char shade4[]={68,145,34,137,36,145,68,145};
char shade5[]={146,73,164,73,146,73,146,73};
char shade6[]={73,170,85,146,101,146,73,170};
char shade7[]={85,170,85,170,85,170,85,170};
char shade8[]={85,170,85,170,85,170,85,170};
char shade9[]={182,85,170,109,154,109,182,85,};
char shade10[]={109,182,91,182,109,182,109,182};
char shade11[]={187,110,221,118,219,110,187,110};
char shade12[]={119,221,119,221,119,221,119,221};
char shade13[]={123,223,125,247,190,247,125,239};
char shade14[]={253,127,239,254,187,239,254,183};
char shade15[]={255,255,255,255,255,255,255,255};


// make a pointer array
char *shadings[]={shade0,shade1,shade2,shade3,
                  shade4,shade5,shade6,shade7,
                  shade8,shade9,shade10,shade11,
                  shade12,shade13,shade14,shade15};
```

8

Getting Things into

Perspective

It is a curious thing that distant objects look smaller than ones which are close. They aren't smaller, but they do subtend a smaller angle at the eye. For any scene to look real therefore, the size of graphics primitives must diminish as they recede into the distance. All of this is done by the eye and the brain. Simulating the same effect on the computer screen is what the perspective transform is all about.

In parallel with this is our need to avoid lists of data describing polygonal structures floating around in global space. We wish to represent graphics primitives as an abstract data type i.e. as a class. In doing this we meet another of the powerful tools in C++ which encourages data abstraction and code reuse – inheritance.

First let us discuss the perspective transform.

8.1 The Perspective Transform

The perspective transform is a set of mathematical operations which project an image of an object from the world reference frame onto the screen. This has a similarity to the way in which a shadow is formed, except that in that case the shadow falls behind the object and is larger, whereas in the perspective projection it is between the viewpoint and screen and smaller. This is shown in Figure 8.1.

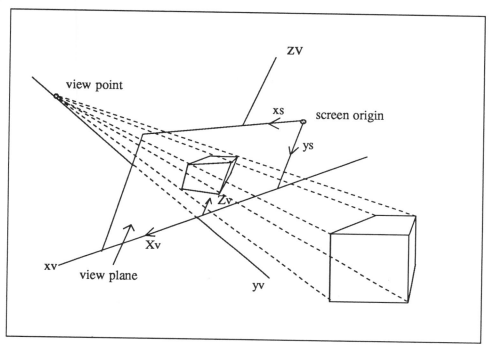

Figure 8.1 Perspective projection of a cube

Figure 8.1 shows an object, in this case a cube, defined inside the computer in the world frame and projected onto the screen. The screen lies in the xv-zv plane of the view frame and the projected image is defined by the points where the 'rays' from the view point (also called the centre of projection, at –d along the yv axis) pierce the view plane. The viewport is the area of the view plane which is visible on the screen. That's really all there is to it. The view point plays a very important role in this scheme and could be placed anywhere. Placing it along the –y axis makes the algebra simple and centres the projection about the view frame origin. This is a very simple type of projection; draughtsmen use many other kinds. But it works fine and the algebra associated with it is minimal.

To make life simple, take the case where the viewport entirely fills the monitor screen. Let's look at how a very simple object projected onto the screen. This is shown in Figure 8.2. As part of the transform it is also necessary to adjust to the screen coordinate system, where the origin is at the top left-hand corner. There are three coordinate systems shown in the diagram: the view frame (xv,yv,zv), the screen frame (xs,ys), and the projected coordinates (Xv,Zv). This projected coordinate system is an intermediate one, introduced for convenience and centred at the view frame origin.

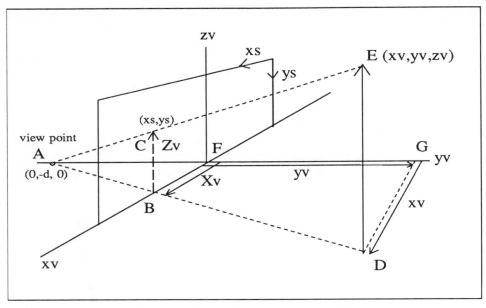

Figure 8.2 Perspective projection of a line

From the similar triangles ABC and ADE and the similar triangles ABF and ADG we get the results:

$$Xv/xv = d/(yv+d) \text{ and } Zv/zv = d/(yv+d)$$

or

$$Xv = xv.d/(yv+d) \text{ and } Zv = zv.d/(yv+d).$$

It only remains to choose where to centre the projection on the visible screen. If it is to be centred half-way across at the bottom then in screen coordinates

$$xs = Xv+Wx/2 \text{ and } ys = Wy-Zv$$

where Wx and Wy are the width and height of the screen in the current resolution which is medium resolution VGA with Wx=640 and Wy=350. In what follows we shall only consider this resolution since it gives two screen pages for buffering and is reasonably fast, though a conversion from one resolution to another is straightforward. The perspective transform becomes, for display in screen coordinates:

$$xs = 320+xv.d/(yv+d); ys = 350-zv.d/(yv+d)$$

These transforms can be worked out using straightforward algebra. The only thing to look out for is that the denominator doesn't ever become zero because this will cause a 'divide by zero' exception. The program can be set up to watch out for this.

8.2 Inheritance

There is a now a need to encapsulate the data required to describe a graphics primitive. The data will move through the program and although certain parts of it will be changed as various transformations take place, particularly the vertex coordinates, most of it, for example the vertex connections will remain constant. We need a way of holding the data but allowing it to change and have new data members added as it proceeds through the graphics pipeline. A good way to do this is through inheritance.

Inheritance is deriving one class, the derived class, from another, called the base class. The derived class is a descendant of the base class, which is usually simpler, with the derived class being more complex. The derived class inherits the members of the base class and adds some new ones, possibly both data and functions. In this chapter we will invent a **Prim** class to hold the basic data of a structure and from it derive a **ViewPrim** class to take care of the perspective projection and display. Later on we will need another class to hold information required to simulate illumination and hidden surface removal. This class, **DefPrim**, is also derived from the **Prim** class. Deriving one class from another is an example of code reuse since all the members of the base class can be immediately available in the derived class without having to rewrite them. Instances of the **Prim** class occur in the next chapter. If the base class were never instantiated, it could be what is called an abstract class. The use of such classes is to provide an interface to the data type without giving any information away as to how the type is implemented. The user is meant to derive classes from the abstract base and add his own data and functions. Many commercial libraries of classes work his way. **Virtual functions** (and **pure virtual functions in abstract base classes**) also play a role in inheritance from base classes where functions with the same names can appear in derived classes. But we will not pursue those topics any further. They are topics beyond the scope of this book.

When a (derived) class inherits from a base class it can do so in one of three ways given by the following keywords: **public, protected** and **private**. These three are access specifiers. **Protected** is also a category of class member in addition to its use in inheritance. Protected members are only accessible to members and friends of a class and to members and friends of a derived class. Here's how the inheritance status affects the status of class members which are inherited:

❑ **public**

This makes public members of the base class become public members of the derived class, protected members of the base class become protected members of the derived class, but keeps the private members of the base class private to the base class and therefore inaccessible to the derived class and anyone else.

❑ **protected**

This makes public members of the base class protected members of the derived class, protected members of the base class protected members of the derived class, but keeps private members of the base class private to the base class and therefore inaccessible to the derived class.

❑ **private**

This makes public members of the base class private members of the derived class, protected members of the base class private members of the derived class but keeps private members of the base class private to the base class and therefore inaccessible to the derived class.

You can see that private really means what it says and you must not take the word lightly. Of course, if you wish to gain access to a private data member you can always put in a friend function as a Trojan Horse or include a public access member function.

8.3 The Prim and ViewPrim classes

The graphics primitive in this chapter is one that we use repeatedly throughout the remainder of the book to illustrate various aspects of computer graphics. It is the word PC-CITY. It is not held as bitmapped text but as a large piece of geometry, each letter being a flat polygon. It's easiest to think of it as a large sign. To illustrate the graphics we will do various manipulations with PC-CITY. In later chapters it will be rotated, illuminated with a light to show shading and finally end up as the name of a city in an artificial world you can fly around. In this chapter it will be used to illustrate the perspective transform.

We now need a class for large data structures of which PC-CITY will be an instance.

8.3.1 The Prim Class

As the name implies, this is the simplest class to hold the idea of a graphics primitive. It does very little except contain all the lists of vertex coordinates, edge list connections etc., which go to make a polygonal structure. Its task is to encapsulate the data and through its constructors provide ways of generating instances. The class interface is shown in the file DECL_02.H and the implementation in DEFN_02.CPP. It is a base class from which other primitive classes are derived. The derived classes can use the base class members since they are all public in the base class and publicly inherited in derived classes. Public access has made the data wide open here, with loss of privacy, because speed is required for the data to be utilised frequently in successive parts of the programs. Access functions would slow this down and make the code bulkier. Of course, making friends of those functions requiring access would also solve the problem but that would require excessive forward declaration. In a more robust system such publicity would not be acceptable. In the interests of simplicity, we will forgo the data hiding here.

Matrix* Prim::m

Here are the x, y and z coordinates of the vertices of the primitive. Lo and behold they are held in a **Matrix**. But only a pointer to the **Matrix** is held as a data member here. The data is actually quite remote. *m* is a pointer to a **Matrix** and the **Matrix** holds a pointer to an array of **Vector**s and the **Vector**s hold a pointer to an array of integers on the heap, which is the data. It's miles away. By only holding pointers to data the class itself is quite small.

int* Matrix::edge_lst

A pointer to the list of vertex connections of every polygon, in an array.

int* Matrix::nedges

A pointer to the list of numbers of edges in each polygon in the entire structure.

int* Matrix::colors

A pointer to the list of colours of each polygon.

int Matrix::nvxt

The number of vertices in total.

int Matrix::nedgelst

The length of the list of edge connections.

int Matrix::npoly

The number of polygons.

void build()int**,int*,int*,int*)

Prim has its own build function to open space in free memory and copy in data. The data for the vertex coordinates is used to construct a **Matrix**, so in turn the **Matrix** constructor is called which, of course, calls the **Vector** constructor. There are therefore calls to three overloaded **build**() functions of all these classes.

Prim::Prim()

The default constructor. It initialises all variables to zero.

Prim::Prim(int**,int*,int*,int*,int,int,int)

This constructs from data. The coordinates x, y and z are addressed from a pointer array. Others from arrays of integers.

Prim::Prim(Matrix&,Prim&)

This constructs from a **Matrix** and a **Prim** and therefore can instantiate from new coordinates but old connections and colours etc. This is clearly useful to catch the output of a transform.

Prim::Prim(Prim&)

The copy constructor. To construct a new **Prim** from an old one.

Prim::~Prim()

The destructor releases the space in free memory taken by the arrays. The last statement deletes the **Matrix** pointed to by m which, of course, calls the **Matrix** destructor which calls the **Vector** destructors.

That's the end of the **Prim** class; just a simple encapsulation of data but using the **Matrix** data type to hold the vertex coordinates.

8.3.2 The ViewPrim Class

The **ViewPrim** class is publicly derived from the **Prim** class and so has access to all the data members of **Prim, which it inherits**. The **ViewPrim** class is still a primitive but it has the ability to project itself on the screen using the perspective transform and then show itself. It also has data arrays of the projected vertices. Here are the class members.

int* ViewPrim::scrnx

The array of screen x coordinates of the perspective projected view frame coordinates.

int* ViewPrim::scrny

The array of screen y coordinates of the perspective projected view frame coordinates.

int ViewPrim::ViewPoint

The position of the focal point for the perspective projection

int ViewPrim::Yoffset

A data member to adjust the position of the screen origin along the viewframe y axis.

int* ViewPrim::shades

A list of the shades of the polygons. This is used to hold the result of the illumination by a light source.

ViewPrim::ViewPrim(int**,int*,int*,int*,int*,int,int,int)

The constructor from data. Notice how it immediately passes data to the constructor of the base class, even before the body of the constructor has been opened. **Prim**'s constructor takes care of setting up its data members and they belong to **ViewPrim** because **ViewPrim** is derived from **Prim**. **ViewPrim** is a **Prim**! The body of **ViewPrim**'s constructor takes care of the new data members.

ViewPrim::ViewPrim(Prim&)

Construct from a **Prim** and initialise the shadings to index 15 which is full brightness.

ViewPrim::ViewPrim(ViewPrim&)

The copy constructor.

ViewPrim::~ViewPrim()

The destructor which will also call the base class destructor.

void ViewPrim::project()

The function to do the perspective projection and calculate the screen coordinates of the vertices. It first checks for a zero in the denominator of the perspective projection and, if true, to avoid an overflow error sets the denominator to 1. Then the perspective transform is calculated and the arrays *screenx* and *screeny* filled.

void ViewPrim::show(Screen&)

The final and most important function which draws everything on the screen. It goes through each polygon and first checks its shade. If the shade is greater than 15 the polygon isn't drawn. This is a hook for later eliminating hidden surfaces from being displayed. Hidden surfaces are those which face away from the observer and therefore can't be seen. Finally each polygon must find its screen coordinates for final drawing and then instantiate a **Polygon** instance called *poly* which will do the drawing. Note the statements inside the loop that finds the screen coordinates of the vertices and puts them in the array *arry[]* which has x, y pairs in order:

```
arry[j++]=*(sx+*(e_lst));
arry[j++]=*(sy+*(e_lst++));
```

There's a lot of indirection going on here and extra parenthesis has been used to separate the parts. What it says is "get the next vertex number for this polygon (pointed to by e_lst) and use it as an index into the screen coordinates lists pointed to by sx and sy". We could have used subscripting instead but it has left as a straight pointer indirection exercise.

That's the end of the ViewPrim class.

8.4 Example program

The example program shows a view of PC-CITY sloping forwards in the view frame. When the perspective transform is done (together with windowing and everything else) it appears on the screen like the opening logo in a movie, where the words diminish into the distance. Figure 8.3 shows the connections of the polygon mesh that goes to make up PC-CITY.

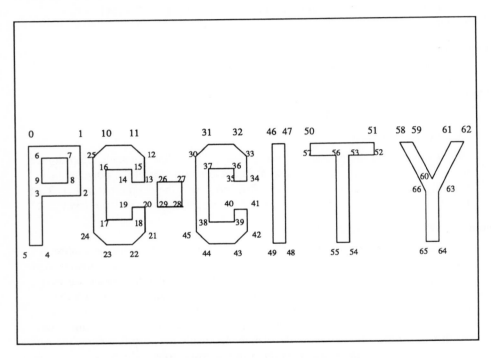

Figure 8.3: Vertex numbers of PC-CITY.

You can look at the coordinates in the data file PC_CITY.H and change them if you wish to see how it looks in different orientations. If you want, you can change the data altogether to draw something different, but first read carefully how the data is laid out. This is explained more fully below in the data file. Be careful to join up the characters and label the vertices properly.

8.4.1 PERSPECT.CPP

This is the main program. Its function is to load up the data, draw the picture and terminate with a key press. It first instantiates the usual **Screen** instance, *screen*, and then the **ViewPrim** *PC_CITY*. Then forever, (for(;;)), or until a key is pressed, the loop is executed where *PC_CITY* is first projected and then displayed. The standard library function **kbhit**() checks for a keypress and if so breaks out of the loop and quits the program.

8.4.2 PC_CITY.H

This is discussed next because it contains lists of the data. Understanding how these are used is essential to understanding how the program works. Since we start off with an object drawn in 3-D in the view frame, each of its vertices must be fixed by three coordinates (xv,yv,zv). The lists of these are held in arrays x_c, y_c and z_c. There is a scheme to identify each vertex in these lists. Each vertex has a number as shown in Figure 8.3. To find its coordinates simply read in from the start counting the first coordinate as number zero. The number of vertices in each polygon is given at nedges_c.

More data than this is required to actually draw the picture. The connections between the vertices are specified in edglst_c. For each polygon there is a list of connections in this table. The overall object is split into 8 polygons, with the hole in the "P" being done as an additional polygon with the background colour. For looping in the program, it is necessary to know the number of edges in the list associated with each polygon. This is given in the array *nedges_c*.

Arranged in this way all the information required to draw the object is readily available. To colour in the polygons a list of individual colours is held in the array *colors_c*, and to shade them the array *shades_c* is used. To supplement these lists the total number of vertices is given as *nvtx_c*, the total number in the edge list as *nedgc_c* and the number of polygons as *npoly_c*.

Finally the x, y and z arrays are used to construct a pointer array called r_c. These data will be used by constructors in for **Prim** and **ViewPrim**.

You can change these lists to draw anything you wish. Just remember it is a 3-D object in the view frame and coordinates are easiest to determine from views along the different axes. It must also be placed in front of the view plane.

8.4.3 SHADES.H

This file contains the bit patterns for the 16 shadings for filling in polygons. Each pattern is a bit block of dimensions four by sixteen bits. Since a **char** is 8 bits, it is convenient to arrange the pattern as 8 successive characters, which amounts to the same thing. The sixteen patterns, which go from dark to light, are held in a pointer array called *shadings*.

8.4.4 PERSPECT.PRJ

This is the project file you need to make. It must contain

```
PERSPECT.CPP
DEFN_00.CPP
DEFN_01.CPP
DEFN_02.CPP
```

Run it directly from the **Run** menu.

```
// PERSPECT_CPP
// draw a "PC-CITY" in perspective

#include "C:\TC\3D\DECL_00.h"      //header file for Vector and Matrix
#include "C:\TC\3D\DECL_01.h"      //header file for Screen and Polygon
#include "C:\TC\3D\DECL_02.h"      //header file for Prim and ViewPrim
#include "C:\TC\3D\SHADES.H"       // shading patterns
#include "C:\TC\3D\PC_CITY.H"      //   "PC-CITY"
#include <conio.h>                 // to read the keyboard


int main()
{
    Screen screen(shadings);          //a Screen

                                      // instantiate from data
    ViewPrim PC_CITY(r_c,edglst_c,nedges_c,colors_c,
                 shades_c,nvtx_c,nedgc_c,npoly_c);


        PC_CITY.project();        // perspective
        PC_CITY.show(screen);     // display on screen

    for(;;){                      // until a key is pressed
            if(kbhit() ){         // if a key is pressed

                if (getch() == 0) // eat the keypress
                    getch();      // and 2nd bit for extended keys
                break;            // terminate program
            }

    }
    return 0;                     // safe return to caller
}
```

```
//DECL_02.H
//Declarations of the Prim and ViewPrim classes


class Prim{
public:
    Matrix *m;                        // pointer to a Matrix
    int *edge_lst,*nedges,*colors;// pointers to arrays
    int nvtx,nedgelst,npoly;       // integers

    Prim(){m=0;edge_lst=nedges=colors=0;nvtx=nedgelst=npoly=0;}//default
    Prim(int**,int*,int*,int*,int,int,int); // construct from data
    Prim(Matrix&,Prim&);                      // new x,y,z old connections
    Prim(Prim&);                              // copy an existing one
    ~Prim();
    void build(int**,int*,int*,int*);        // open space

};



class ViewPrim:public Prim{        // publicly derived from Prim
public:
    int *scrnx;int *scrny;          // arrays of screen vertices
    int ViewPoint,YOffset,*shades;// focal point,
                                    // displace screen, shading list

    ViewPrim(int**,int*,int*,int*,int*,int,int,int);// from data
    ViewPrim(Prim&);                // construct from a Prim
    ViewPrim(ViewPrim&);            // copy constructor
    ~ViewPrim();
    void project();                 // do the perspective transform
    void show(Screen&);             // make it visible
};
```

```
//DEFN_02.CPP
// Implementation of the Prim and ViewPrim classes
#include "C:\TC\3D\DECL_00.H"
#include "C:\TC\3D\DECL_01.H"
#include "C:\TC\3D\DECL_02.H"
#include <mem.h>

// Construct a Prim from data ...................................
Prim::Prim(int **ar,int *eg_l,int* ngs,int* cls,
           int nvx,int neg,int npol){
    nvtx=nvx;nedgelst=neg;npoly=npol;
    build(ar,eg_l,ngs,cls);
}

// construct a Prim from new coords ............................
Prim::Prim(Matrix& srcM,Prim& srcP){
    m=new Matrix(srcM);                    //copy the Matrix
    nvtx=srcP.nvtx;nedgelst=srcP.nedgelst;npoly=srcP.npoly;
    edge_lst=new int[nedgelst];
    memcpy(edge_lst,srcP.edge_lst,nedgelst*sizeof(int));
    nedges=new int[npoly];
    memcpy(nedges,srcP.nedges,npoly*sizeof(int));
    colors=new int[npoly];
    memcpy(colors,srcP.colors,npoly*sizeof(int));
}

// copy constructor ...........................................
Prim::Prim(Prim& src){
    // copy the coords - use the Matrix copy constructor
    m=new Matrix(*(src.m));
    nvtx=src.nvtx;nedgelst=src.nedgelst;npoly=src.npoly;
    edge_lst=new int[nedgelst];
    memcpy(edge_lst,src.edge_lst,nedgelst*sizeof(int));
    nedges=new int[npoly];
    memcpy(nedges,src.nedges,npoly*sizeof(int));
    colors=new int[npoly];
    memcpy(colors,src.colors,npoly*sizeof(int));
}

// destructor .................................................
Prim::~Prim(){                             // destructor
    delete []edge_lst;delete []nedges;
    delete []colors;delete m;
}

// allocate free memory .......................................
void Prim::build(int **r,int *e_l,int *ng,int *cs){
    edge_lst=new int[nedgelst];
    memcpy(edge_lst,e_l,nedgelst*sizeof(int));
    nedges=new int[npoly];
    memcpy(nedges,ng,npoly*sizeof(int));
    colors=new int[npoly];
    memcpy(colors,cs,npoly*sizeof(int));
    m=new Matrix(r,3,nvtx);
}
```

```
// The ViewPrim class
// construct with data to the base class constructor ...............
ViewPrim::ViewPrim(int **ar,int *eg_l,int* ngs,int* cls,
                   int* shds,int nvx,int neg,int npol)
                   :Prim(ar,eg_l,ngs,cls,nvx,neg,npol){
    scrnx=new int[nvtx];scrny=new int[nvtx];
    ViewPoint=200;YOffset=0;
    shades=new int[npol];
    memcpy(shades,shds,npol*sizeof(int));
}

// copy constructor from a Prim ...................................
ViewPrim::ViewPrim(Prim& src)
    :Prim(src){              // use the base class copy constructor
    scrnx=new int[nvtx];scrny=new int[nvtx];
    ViewPoint=200;YOffset=0;
    shades=new int[npoly];
    int i=npoly;
    while(i--){                     // set the shades to 15 as default
        shades[i]=15;
    }
}

// copy constructor - from a Viewprim ............................
ViewPrim::ViewPrim(ViewPrim& src)
    :Prim(src){                     // use base class constructor

    scrnx=new int[nvtx];scrny=new int[nvtx];
    memcpy(scrnx,src.scrnx,npoly*sizeof(int));
    memcpy(scrny,src.scrny,npoly*sizeof(int));
    shades=new int[src.npoly];
    memcpy(shades,src.shades,npoly*sizeof(int));
    ViewPoint=200;YOffset=0;
}

// destructor .....................................................
ViewPrim::~ViewPrim(){           // will also call base destructor
    delete []scrnx; delete []scrny;
    delete []shades;
}

// perspective projection .........................................
void ViewPrim::project(){
    Vector vx=(*m)[0];Vector vy=(*m)[1];Vector vz=(*m)[2];
    int n=nvtx;int *sx=scrnx;int *sy=scrny;float vpoint=ViewPoint;
    float offy=YOffset;
    int i=0;float denom;
    while(n--){                     // for all vertices
        if((denom=(float)(vy[i])+offy+vpoint)==0.0){//check 0
            denom=1.0;
        }
        *(sx++)=int(320+(float)(vx[i])*(vpoint)/denom);// vertices
        *(sy++)=int(250-(float)(vz[i])*(vpoint)/denom);
        i++;
    }
}
```

```cpp
// display the polygon on the screen ..............................
void ViewPrim::show(Screen &scrn){
    int *sx=scrnx;int *sy=scrny;
    int *e_lst=edge_lst;int *e_num=nedges;
    int *colr=colors;int *shade=shades;int n=npoly;

    while(n--){                     // for all the faces
        if(*shade>15){              // if this face is invisible
            e_lst+=*(e_num++);      // update the list pointer
            colr++;shade++;         // and the colour and the shade
        }
        else{                       // face visible so show it
            int arry[40],i=*e_num,j=0;
            while(i--){                         // for all vertices
                arry[j++]=*(sx+*(e_lst));       // the next vertex x
                arry[j++]=*(sy+*(e_lst++));     // and y; ready for next
            }
            Polygon poly(arry,*(e_num++));      // a Polygon
            poly.putcolour(*(colr++),*(shade++));//colour and shade
            poly.paint(scrn);                   // show it
        }
    }
}
```

```
//PC_CITY.H

// the "PC-CITY" logo

// vertices x array
int x_c[]={-255,-195,-195,-240,-240,-255,-240,-210,-210,-240,
    -165,-135,-120,-120,-135,-135,-165,-165,-135,-135,-120,-120,
    -135,-165,-180,-180,-105,-75,-75,-105,-60,-45,-15,0,0,-15,-15,
    -45,-45,-15,-15,0,0,-15,-45,-60,30,45,45,30,75,150,150,120,
    120,105,105,75,180,195,218,240,255,225,225,210,210};

// vertices y array
int y_c[]={80,80,40,40,0,0,70,70,50,50,80,80,70,50,50,60,60,20,20,
    30,30,10,0,0,10,70,50,50,30,30,70,80,80,70,50,50,60,60,20,20,
    30,30,10,0,0,10,80,80,0,0,80,80,70,70,0,0,70,70,80,80,50,80,
    80,40,0,0,40};

// vertices z array
int z_c[]={160,160,100,100,40,40,145,145,115,115,160,160,145,115,
    115,130,130,70,70,85,85,55,40,40,55,145,115,115,85,85,145,160,
    160,145,115,115,130,130,70,70,85,85,55,40,40,55,160,160,40,40,
    160,160,145,145,40,40,145,145,160,160,115,160,160,100,40,40,
    100};

// connections of the vertices
int edglst_c[]={0,1,2,3,4,5,6,7,8,9,10,11,12,13,14,15,16,17,18,19,
    20,21,22,23,24,25,26,27,28,29,30,31,32,33,34,35,36,37,38,39,40,
    41,42,43,44,45,46,47,48,49,50,51,52,53,54,55,56,57,58,59,60,61,
    62,63,64,65,66};


int nedges_c[]={6,4,16,4,16,4,8,9};// number edges in each polygon
int colors_c[]={13,0,13,13,13,13,13,13};// colours
int shades_c[]={15,15,15,15,15,15,15,15};// shades-default is bright
int nvtx_c=67;                          // number of vertices
int nedgc_c=67;                         // number of edges
int npoly_c=8;                          // number of polygons

// set up an array of pointers
int *r_c[]={x_c,y_c,z_c};
```

9

Simple Rotations

What we wish to do in this chapter is rotate an object in three dimensions. In our world model this is part of what can happen when an object is moved from its object frame to the world frame or when it undergoes individual motion in the world frame. In addition, in general, there will be an associated translation as it is moved to its current location. It is also what the observer does when she moves around the world. In a complex world with several different objects, each one would have different translations and rotations to bring them all together to make the world picture.

Let's take a simple world with just one object to start with. We already have a good example to work on – the "PC-CITY" sign, which was used to illustrate the perspective transform. The data is already entered and ready to go. What we would like to see is PC-CITY rotating in the centre of the screen. That's what we'll do next.

First a brief discussion again of the two types of transforms which are really different views of the same thing but which have different uses in computer graphics: geometric and coordinate transforms. We have already discussed these in Chapter 6 "Modelling a 3-D World". Here is a further brief discussion emphasising the points we wish to use in the rotational transforms.

9.1 Geometric and Coordinate Transforms Revisited

As has already been said, there are two types of transform used widely in computer graphics: geometric and coordinate transforms. Geometric transforms are concerned with moving and rotating graphics primitives – the visible objects in a scene. Coordinate transforms are more subtle; they are concerned with changing the observer's view. A spinning top is a good example of an object undergoing geometric rotation about the vertical, z, axis. An aeroplane doing a loop-the-loop is a geometric transform about the x axis.

As has been said, if you move your head to the left (coordinate transform) it's equivalent to moving the scenery to the right (geometric transform). The two are said to be the inverse of each other – whichever you're concerned with you can get the other by going backwards. In this section simple rotations about the x, y and z axes are presented but orientated towards what we wish to do in the last chapter, 12, where an observer can move freely around a Virtual Reality world. In that situation we will wish to rotate the observer's view about the z axis (vertical) so he can turn his head from side to side and then about his x axis so he can look up and down. With these two motions, in that order, it is possible to head in any direction in the world whilst keeping the horizon horizontal. A further rotation about the y axis then allows the possibility of tilting the head from side to side, although that is omitted in Chapter 12 to keep the horizon horizontal. Right now we will implement the three rotations in that order as coordinate transforms, but remember they are exactly the same as the observer keeping his gaze fixed whilst rotating the objects in the scene in the opposite directions about his z, x and y axes in order.

The transforms we are about to discuss are illustrated in Figures 9.1 and 9.2.

9.2.1 Rotation about the z axis

We can illustrate this as a coordinate transform as shown in Figure 9.1.(1). Here the set of axes that the observer calls his reference frame are rotated by angle γ about the z axis. This is alternatively illustrated in Figure 9.2(1) by a point P with coordinates (x,y,z) being rotated about the z-axis by an angle $-\gamma$ to arrive at the point P' with coordinates x', y' and z'. Representing the points by vectors clearly shows the rotation. Notice how the sense of the rotation in the coordinate transform is defined in Figure 9.1(1); it is clockwise when looking along the positive z-axis from behind the x-y plane. Thinking of it in terms of the equivalent geometric transform in figure 9.2(1) the coordinates of P are changed to those of P'.

Writing this as straightforward algebra of the relation between P' and P gives

$$x' = x.\cos\gamma + y.\sin\gamma + 0.z$$

$$y' = -x.\sin\gamma + y.\cos\gamma + 0.z$$

$$z' = z$$

z is unchanged by this rotation.

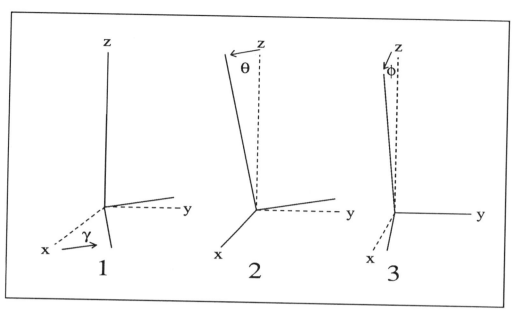

Figure 9.1: Coordinate rotational transforms about the Z,X and Y axes.

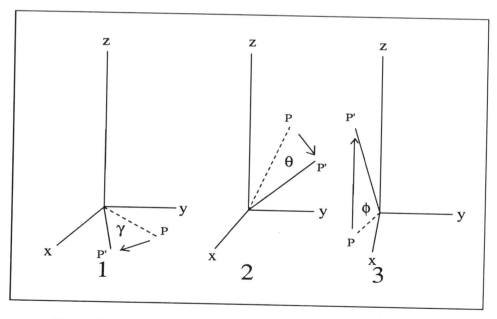

Figure 9.2: Geometric rotational transforms about the Z,X and Y axes.

As a matrix transformation of the vector to P to give the vector to P', this is:

$$\begin{pmatrix} x' \\ y' \\ z' \end{pmatrix} = \begin{pmatrix} \cos\gamma & \sin\gamma & 0 \\ -\sin\gamma & \cos\gamma & 0 \\ 0 & 0 & 1 \end{pmatrix} \begin{pmatrix} x \\ y \\ z \end{pmatrix}$$

For conciseness, the matrix is abbreviated to $R'(\gamma)$ and the transform is then abbreviated to

$P' = R'(\gamma).P$

9.2.2 Rotation about the x axis

The coordinate transform is shown in Figure 9.1(2) and the equivalent geometric transform in Figure 9.2(2). In this case the point P is rotated about x-axis by an angle $-\theta$. As before, the coordinate rotation $R'(\theta)$ is clockwise looking along the positive y-axis from behind the x-z plane. Expressed as a matrix product, the transform is:

$$\begin{pmatrix} x' \\ y' \\ z' \end{pmatrix} = \begin{pmatrix} 1 & 0 & 0 \\ 0 & \cos\theta & \sin\theta \\ 0 & -\sin\theta & \cos\theta \end{pmatrix} \begin{pmatrix} x \\ y \\ z \end{pmatrix}$$

9.2.3 Rotation about the y axis

The coordinate transform is shown in Figure 9.1(3) and the geometric transform in figure 9.2(3). In Figure 9.2(3) the point P is rotated about the y axis by an angle $(-\phi)$. The rotation of the coordinate system, $R'(\phi)$, is clockwise looking along the z axis from behind the x-y plane and given by the matrix:

$$\begin{pmatrix} x' \\ y' \\ z' \end{pmatrix} = \begin{pmatrix} \cos\phi & 0 & -\sin\phi \\ 0 & y & 0 \\ \sin\phi & 0 & \cos\phi \end{pmatrix} \begin{pmatrix} x \\ y \\ z \end{pmatrix}$$

9.2.4 Composite Rotations

When all three types of rotation are done simultaneously things become a good deal more complicated. This is because the order of rotation matters; rotating first by γ, second by θ and third by ϕ does not end up with P in the same place as with any other order. This may seem to be a surprising result. In mathematical jargon, three dimensional rotations are said to be non-commutative. To illustrate the point look at Figure 9.3.

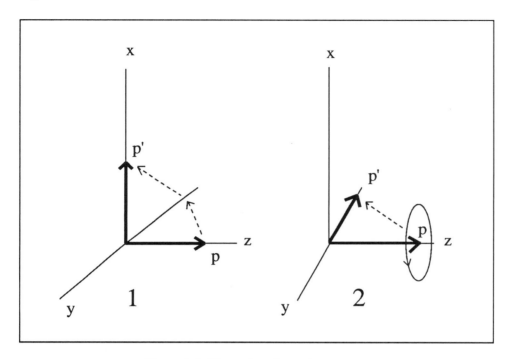

Figure 9.3: The order of rotation matters.

This has two parts to it. In part 1 a vector which lies along the z axis to start with is first rotated about the x axis by 90° and then about the z axis by 90°. It ends up pointing along the x axis. In part 2 the order of rotations is reversed. Consequently the first rotation does nothing and the second leaves it pointing along the −y axis. Clearly, changing the order of rotation alters the end result.

A consequence of this is that keeping count of the individual rotations θ, ϕ and γ separately provides insufficient information to get to the final position. The order of rotation must also be given, which is what we do. As long as this order is fixed, there is no problem. To have a consistent scheme, we rotate first by γ, second by θ and third by ϕ. In shorthand the overall transform when all these rotations take place in this order is:

$$P' = R'(\phi).R'(\theta).R'(\gamma).P$$

Notice how the first rotation appears next to the original point P, and later rotations appear farther to the left. This is the order of matrix multiplication with column vectors.

There is no need to perform the matrix products on the vector separately. Their product can be found beforehand to produce one resultant matrix, which can the be multiplied by the vector in one single operation. This combined (concatenated) rotation is denoted by

$$\begin{pmatrix} \cos\phi.\cos\gamma-\sin\theta.\sin\phi.\sin\gamma & \cos\phi.\sin\gamma+\sin\theta.\sin\phi.\cos\gamma & -\cos\theta.\sin\phi \\ -\cos\theta.\sin\gamma & \cos\theta.\cos\gamma & \sin\theta \\ \sin\phi.\cos\gamma+\sin\theta.\cos\phi.\sin\gamma & \sin\phi\sin\gamma - \sin\theta.\cos\phi.\cos\gamma & \cos\theta.\cos\phi \end{pmatrix}$$

9.3 A Class for Rotation

We now need to develop a class for the transforms. Since the rotational transform is a matrix we can derive a new class from the **Matrix** class with the specific task to handle rotations. The class interface is given in DECL_03.H and the implementation in DEFN_03.CPP.

9.4.1 The Rotator Class

The **Rotator** class is descended publicly from **Matrix** and therefore possesses all the members of **Matrix**. **Rotator** is different from previous classes in that it is a function abstraction. Its main task is to rotate a data structure; it is a class which does something rather than being something, although it does carry its own data in the form of the three rotation angles. In addition it has a member function to increment the angles. The actual rotational transformation itself is done through overloaded nonmember operators on **Prim** and **Matrix.** There is less work to do here than one might imagine, largely as a result of the investment of code in the **Matrix** class; we are reaping the benefits of earlier efforts. Here are the class members.

int Rotator::theta

   The angle of rotation about the x axis.

int Rotator::phi

   The angle of rotation about the y axis.

int Rotator::gamma

   The angle of rotation about the z axis.

void Rotator::setup()

A function to set up the Matrix; it is called by the constructor. Here we have a slight problem. Since a **Matrix** holds its data internally as integer type, how are we to hold the products of sines and cosines for the matrix elements which are all less than 1? The answer is to calculate them as floating point type and then scale them by a factor, 32 in this case, to generate a sizeable integer number by a cast. There is a loss in accuracy in doing this but it is not very noticeable. To use floating point throughout would be nice but would slow the calculations down by a substantial factor.

This function does an explicit cast to **float** on the angles before calculating their sines and cosines. Then the appropriate products of these which make up the combined rotation, above, are determined and put into the **Vector** array pointed to by the data member M, which has been inherited from **Matrix**. A scale factor of 32 is used before the elements are cast back to **int** and entered as data with **Vector** subscripting.

Rotator::Rotator()

The default constructor. It initialises the angles, builds an empty Matrix and fills it using **setup()**.

void Rotator::angl_inc(int,int,int)

It increments the angles by the amounts given and recalculates the matrix elements by calling **setup()**. The angles are kept within the limits 0-360 degrees.

9.5 A class for Translation

We also require a class for translating graphics primitives. Very often, before a rotation, it is necessary to move a primitive to the origin so that the rotation occurs about the centre of the primitive. If that were not done, the primitive would swing round in a big arc. After the rotation it is necessary to replace the primitive back at its original location. These movements both require translations.

9.5.1 The Translator Class

The **Translator** class is also very simple but that is because it does not have to do much. The most important feature of the class will be a nonmember overloaded operator to translate (relocate) a **Prim**. The **Translator** class is also a function abstraction since it is seen as an operation on something else. Here are the class members.

int Translator::x

Increment the x coordinates by this amount.

int Translator::y

Increment the y coordinates by this amount.

int Translator::z

Increment the z coordinates by this amount.

Translator::Translator(int xx=0,int yy=0,intzz=0){x=xx;y=yy;z=zz;}

An inline constructor which takes default values of 0 for the displacements if parameters are not specified.

int Translator::getx(){return x;}

Inline access function for x.

int Translator::gety(){return y;}

Inline access function for y.

int Translator::getz(){return z;}

Inline access function for z.

Its most important operation is to move a **ViewPrim** which it does in a nonmember overloaded operator function.

9.5 Nonmember Functions

These important overloaded operator functions allow an algebra to be created between **Rotator**s and **Translator**s and the types on which they operate.

Matrix operator*(Rotator&,Matrix&)

An overloaded * operator which adjusts the vertex coordinates of the Matrix to return a new matrix. It does so by creating a temporary **Matrix** called *prod* and then fills the elements. The entire operation is done on a single line inside two **for** loops. This line represents a lot of code but appears concise because of the effort already made in setting up **Matrix** and **Vector** types and their overloaded subscripting and product operators. The result is copied as a return value.

ViewPrim operator*(Rotator&,Prim&)

A second overloaded * operator to express the rotation of a **Prim**. We are now thinking of a **Prim** as a data type and the **Rotator** as another data type, just as you would in mathematics. Of course, both of these are combinations of data and functions but the overloaded * enables us to express the manipulation of the internal data members of **Prim** by **Rotator** as a single operation. The implementation of the operator shows that it rotates the **Matrix** in the **Prim** using the operator defined above and uses the appropriate **ViewPrim** constructor to make a new one. It would be possible to shorten the code at the end, but that would make it less readable to a learner.

void operator>>(Translator&,ViewPrim&)

The overloaded operator >> which moves a graphics primitive by increasing the vertices of the **ViewPrim** that represents it, by amounts equal to the data members of the **Translator**.

9.6 Example Program

This is a program to show "PC-CITY" rotating about in the world frame. Here are the files.

9.6.1 ROTATE.CPP

This is the main program. It first instantiates a screen, followed by the **Prim** called *PC-CITY*, then a **Rotator** called *transform* and finally a Translator called *displace*. In the following loop **while(!kbhit())** is used to test for a key press. As long as there is not one the loop is executed and the rotation done.

In the loop the *transform*, rotates *PC-CITY*. Then *PC-CITY* is repositioned at a suitable distance from the screen with *displace* and projected and shown. The effect to the observer is of a continuously rotating "PC-CITY".

Change the rotation increments in **angl_inc()** and *displace* and see what you get. If you have already set up you own polygon structure for the perspective projection, see how it looks in rotation.

9.6.2 ROTATE.PRJ

This is the project file you will need.

```
ROTATE.CPP
DEFN_00.cpp
DEFN_01.CPP
DEFN_02.CPP
DEFN_03.CPP
```

```
//ROTATE.CPP
// rotate the logo

#include "C:\TC\3D\DECL_00.H"
#include "C:\TC\3D\DECL_01.H"
#include "C:\TC\3D\DECL_02.H"
#include "C:\TC\3D\DECL_03.H"
#include "C:\TC\3D\SHADES.H"
#include "C:\TC\3D\PC_CITY.H"
#include <conio.h>


int main(void){

    Screen screen(shadings);

    Prim PC_CITY(r_c,edglst_c,nedges_c,colors_c,
              nvtx_c,nedgc_c,npoly_c);        //instantiate PC-CITY

    Rotator transform(0,0,0);
    Translator displace(0,200,200);           // 200 in and up

    while(!kbhit()){

            screen.swap_screen();
            transform.angl_inc(5,2,10);       // increment angles
            ViewPrim PC=transform*PC_CITY;    // rotate logo
            displace>>PC;                     // in position
            PC.project();
            PC.show(screen);

    }
    if(getch()==0)getch();                    // clear key buffer
    return 0;
}
```

```
// DECL_03.H
// Rotation and displacement classes

// Rotator class

class Rotator:public Matrix{        // descendant of Matrix
int theta, phi, gamma;              // rotation angles
public:
    Rotator(int,int,int);           // construct from angles
    void set_up();                  // make the transform
    void angl_inc(int,int,int);     // increment angles Matrix
    int get_theta(){return theta;}  // public access
    int get_phi(){return phi;}
    int get_gamma(){return gamma;}
};


// Translator class

class Translator{                   // displace a ViewPrim
    int x,y,z;                      // by this much
public:
    Translator(int xx=0,int yy=0,int zz=0){x=xx;y=yy;z=zz;}
    int getx(){return x;}           // public access
    int gety(){return y;}
    int getz(){return z;}
};


// Nonmember functions

Matrix operator *(Rotator&,Matrix&);// rotate a Matrix
ViewPrim operator *(Rotator&,Prim&);// rotate a Prim
void operator >>(Translator&,ViewPrim&);// move a ViewPrim
```

```
// DEFN_03.CPP
// Implementation of the Rotator and Translator classes

#include <math.h>
#include "C:\TC\3D\DECL_00.H"
#include "C:\TC\3D\DECL_01.H"
#include "C:\TC\3D\DECL_02.H"
#include "C:\TC\3D\DECL_03.H"

// construct a 3 x 3 rotation Matrix .............................
Rotator::Rotator(int t,int p,int g):Matrix(3,3){
    theta=t;phi=p;gamma=g;                         //use base constructor
    set_up();                                      // make the matrix
}

// make the matrix elements .....................................
void Rotator::set_up(){
    float f=0.01756,e=32.0;                        // convert to radians
    // sines and cosines
    float st=sin(f*float(theta));float ct=cos(f*float(theta));
    float sp=sin(f*float(phi));float cp=cos(f*float(phi));
    float sg=sin(f*float(gamma));float cg=cos(f*float(gamma));

    M[0][0]=(int)((cp*cg-st*sp*sg)*e);             // all elements
    M[0][1]=(int)((cp*sg+st*sp*cg)*e);             // scaled by 32
    M[0][2]=int(-ct*sp*e);                         // are integers

    M[1][0]=(int)(-ct*sg*e);
    M[1][1]=(int)(ct*cg*e);
    M[1][2]=(int)(st*e);

    M[2][0]=(int)((sp*cg+st*cp*sg)*e);
    M[2][1]=(int)((sp*sg-st*cp*cg)*e);
    M[2][2]=(int)(ct*cp*e);
}

// increment the angles .........................................
void Rotator::angl_inc(int inct,int incp,int incg){
    theta+=inct;phi+=incp;gamma+=incg;
    while(theta>360)theta-=360;                    //less than 360
    while(theta<0)theta+=360;                      //greater than 0
    while(phi>360)phi-=360;
    while(phi<0)phi+=360;
    while(gamma>360)gamma-=360;
    while(gamma<0)gamma+=360;
    set_up();                                      // make matrix
}

// rotate a Matrix ..............................................
Matrix operator *(Rotator &A, Matrix &B){
    int ra=A.getrows(); int cb=B.getcols();
    Matrix prod(ra,cb);                            // empty product matrix
    for(int i=0;i<ra;i++){                         // fill up the elements
        for(int j=0;j<cb;j++){
            prod[i][j]=(A[i]*B(j))/32;             // multiply a row by a column
        }
    }                                              // and normalise
    return prod;                                   // copy result
}
```

```
// rotate a Prim ...........................................................
ViewPrim operator *(Rotator& rot,Prim& src){
    Matrix temp=*(src.m);                    // copy source Matrix
    Matrix prod=rot*temp;                    // rotate it
    Prim tempP(prod,src);                    // make from new coords
    ViewPrim tempV(tempP);                   // then a ViewPrim
    return tempV;                            // copy result
}

// move a ViewPrim ..........................................................
void operator>>(Translator& T,ViewPrim& D){
int x=T.getx(),y=T.gety(),z=T.getz();
    for(int n=0;n<=D.nvtx-1;n++){
      (*(D.m))[0][n]+=x;// adjust x's        // add to all x, y and z
      (*(D.m))[1][n]+=y;// adjust y's
      (*(D.m))[2][n]+=z;// adjust y's
    }
}
```

10

Hidden Surfaces and

Illumination

A computer is a fast number-cruncher, but it doesn't know anything about the real world. When it comes to conveying simple everyday experiences like not being able to see through solid opaque objects, the computer is a real loser. It seems obvious to us that the rear sides of opaque objects are not visible and that an opaque object will obscure those behind it. Making the computer show this simple fact of life is hard work. It is called the hidden surface problem and it is the basis of some very time-consuming algorithms in computer graphics.

For any micro without dedicated graphics hardware, this becomes a severe problem since the burden of computation falls on the main processor, and of necessity therefore, any strategy we adopt to deal with hidden surfaces cannot be too time consuming. As a consequence, the geometry of the objects themselves cannot be so complex as to require a time consuming hidden surface algorithm. The simplest solution is to require that all polyhedra be convex, i.e. each surface polygon looks outward and not towards another polygon. It is possible to deal with simple polyhedra which are not convex but we shall only consider ones which are convex. It is always possible to construct complex objects out of several convex polyhedra and the strategy then is to draw the furthest ones first and the nearest ones last. This is the so called 'painter' algorithm by which objects in the background are naturally obscured by those in the foreground. More of this later.

The procedure for deciding whether a surface is visible, combines naturally with the calculation to decide how brightly it is illuminated by a distant light source, a necessary attribute if the object is to look real. Surfaces which face towards the light source must be brighter than those which face away. We shall combine both of these into a single algorithm in this chapter.

10.1 Hidden Surface Removal

In the simple strategy for convex polyhedra adopted here, deciding whether a surface is visible requires a vector algebra which is minimised by pre-calculating normal vectors. The procedure is straightforward: a polygonal surface is visible if it faces the view point. The problem is how to convert the word "faces" into a mathematical expression. This is done in the following way.

Each surface has associated with it a vector which points out at right angles from the surface so that the polyhedron as a whole looks like a porcupine. All such vectors have the same length, which is chosen to be unity. They are called **surface normal unit vectors**. The only difference between two unit vectors is their direction, which reflects the different directions in which the surfaces face as shown in Figure 10.1.

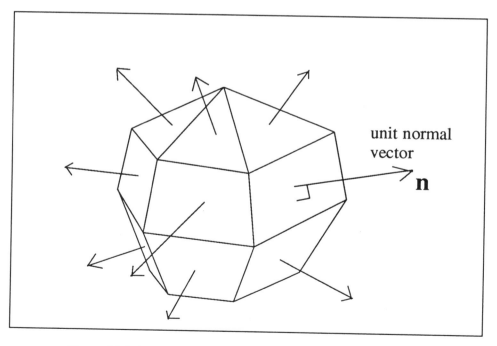

unit normal vector **n**

Figure 10.1 A convex polyhedron showing surface normal vectors

To see whether a surface is visible from the view point now consists of testing whether its unit vector is in the same or opposite direction to a vector, the **view vector**, drawn from the viewpoint to the surface. There is a basic vector product which performs this test. It is called the scalar or dot product. We have met this in the **Vector** class. In the language of mathematics, where the view vector is **V** and the surface normal vector is **n,** the scalar product will yield a positive result if the surface is hidden and a negative result if it is visible:

hidden: scalar product **V.n** is positive

visible: scalar product **V.n** is negative.

The scalar product itself is really nothing more than the distance from the view point to the surface times the cosine of the angle between the view vector and the surface normal. The sign of the product naturally follows therefore from the fact that the cosine of an angle less than 90º is positive whereas the cosine of an angle between 90º and 180º is negative. Figure 10.2 shows the directions of the vectors for a visible and a hidden surface. In the classes that will be described shortly the surface normal unit vector is calculated when the primitive is instantiated, as an object of another class, **DefPrim**, derived from **Prim**, and then transformed with rotations along with the vertices as its position changes in the World frame.

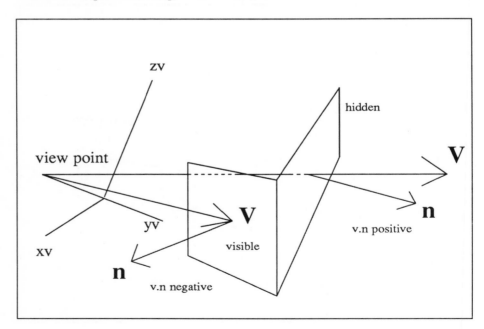

Figure 10.2 Visible and hidden surfaces

We choose to use the scalar product here because the normal unit vectors, once calculated, can also be used to determine the level of illumination of each surface.

10.2 Calculating the Surface Normal Unit Vector

The particular vector product which allows us to calculate the normal vector is called a cross product. It is more difficult to understand than the scalar product but it's precisely what we want. We have already discussed these vector products in Chapter 5. A vector product is illustrated in Figure 10.3. for a single polygon.

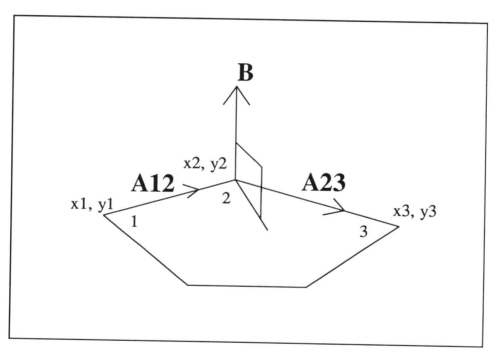

Figure 10.3 The vector product of two vectors

Going round the perimeter of the polygon, the first two edges we meet are from vertices 1 to 2 and 2 to 3. Let us call the vectors associated with these edges **A**12 and **A**23. The normal vector **B** is then calculated as the cross product between them:

B = **A**23 x **A**12.

This shorthand notation is all fairly meaningless until translated into a set of mathematical operations. The x, y and z components of A12 and A23 are:

A12x = x2-x1, A12y = y2-y1, A12z = z2-z1

A23x = x3-x2, A23y = y3-y2, A23z = z3-z2

and the components of **B** are:

Bx = A12z.A23y-A12y.A23z

By = A12x.A23z-A12z.A23x

Bz = A12y.A23z-A12x.A23y

These multiplications constitute the bulk of the calculation.

There is one final step. What we want is the unit vector. The vector **B** is in the right direction but its size is too large. To get the unit vector, each of the components must be divided by the magnitude of **B**. This provides an additional chore because the magnitude of **B** is calculated from:

$B = \sqrt{(Bx^2+By^2+Bz^2)}$

Once the magnitude B has been calculated, the components of the unit vector are

bx = Bx/B, by = By/B, bz = Bz/B.

After this the line-of-sight vector (view vector) from the view point to the first vertex of the surface in the edge list is then found and the scalar product taken with the normal vector. On the basis of this test, the surface is either flagged as hidden or else its level of illumination calculated. We discuss illumination next.

10.3 Illumination and Colour

It is possible to employ the most elaborate computations to construct geometrically accurate 3-D models, and yet the attributes which make them look real may be very subtle and less obvious. In sprite graphics, the shadow on the ground which follows the motion of a projectile is a small but essential clue to its altitude. In 3-D, one of the easiest and dramatic improvements to add realism to a model is illumination by a light source. Facets which face the light source are more brightly illuminated than those which face away. As the object changes its orientation, so the changes in illumination give additional visual clues to its shape and structure. This is what we shall try to simulate next. There are limitations to what can be achieved on the PC, not so much a consequence of software constraints, but mainly resulting from the way colour is implemented in the colour palette. The way in which illumination is determined is very similar to the way visibility is tested for, but in this case an actual number must be generated, depending on the angle of the surface to the light source.

The direction of the beam of light emanating from a light source is specified by a vector, called the illumination vector. It would be possible to simulate a diverging or converging beam by having this vector change its direction across the field of illumination, but for simplicity the beam is taken to be parallel. Consequently a single vector is sufficient to define to direction of the beam. Likewise, the intensity of the light is taken to be constant everywhere. These approximations are valid for a distant light source such as the Sun, but the difference for a near light source is hardly noticeable. This illumination vector is also a unit vector, (i.e. it has a magnitude of unity).

Because we have already calculated the surface normal unit vectors, everything is set up to find the level of illumination of each facet on the surface. It is nothing more than the scalar product of the illumination vector and the normal vectors. This is a realistic calculation since the level of illumination does depend on the cosine of the angle between the two vectors.

There is one minor modification we will use in the calculation. Consider how the earth is illuminated by the Sun: the side which faces the Sun is brightly lit but the side which faces away would be pitch black if it weren't for the reflected light of the Moon (forgetting the light from the stars). In a room a single light source is sufficient to illuminate everything, though much of this is back-reflected light from the walls and all the objects in the room. This is the basis of the Radiosity method of illumination calculation which is used in very advanced graphics to simulate realism to a high degree. We can incorporate a very rudimentary version of this into our method, using the scalar product to set an illumination level even where it is negative, so there is some illumination even on the dark side of objects.

Here then is the method in outline: for each surface, take the scalar product of the illumination unit vector with the normal unit vector; since both vectors are 1 in magnitude, this will yield a result between +1 (minimum illumination) and −1 (maximum illumination). If you're confused by the sign, remember in our geometry the illumination vector points away from the light source. This result can then be used to index as many different shading patterns as are required. In these programs the scalar product will be reduced to lie in the range 0-15 so as to fit in with the 16 different shadings we have already established for the screen.

10.4 The DefPrim and Illuminator Classes

DefPrim is another class derived from **Prim**. **DefPrim** is a **Prim** with scaled surface unit normal vectors. We need the unit normals for each polygon for both a test for visibility and the calculation of surface illumination. It makes sense to calculate the surface unit normals in the constructor when a **DefPrim** is instantiated so as to save time in the program loop.

You can think of the **Illuminator** class as a kind of lamp. It shines on the **DefPrim** to produce a **ViewPrim** which, of course, is needed to put an image on the screen. Here are the classes in detail. The interfaces are in DECL_04.H and the full implementations in DEFN_04.CPP.

10.4.1 The DefPrim Class

The **DefPrim** class is a **Prim** with surface normals. It is a full definition of a graphics primitive. It is publicly descended from the **Prim** class. Here are the members.

Matrix* DefPrim::Normals

> Where would the surface unit normal vectors be stored? In a **Matrix**! Each vector has three components, so *Normals* is a pointer to a **Matrix** with three rows.

void DefPrim::Normbuild()

> This is the function that opens space in free memory for the **Matrix** which is pointed to by *Normals*. There is nothing new here since the **Matrix** has three rows and as many columns as there are polygons.

void DefPrim::NormCalc()

> This is where all the work is done. **NormCalc()** fills up the **Vectors** of *m*, the data member inherited from **Prim**. The unit normal vectors are calculated as floating point because to start with their magnitude is less than or equal to unity. If such a variable were an integer, then the only possible values it could have would be 0 or 1. In **float** form it is a fraction and there is no loss of accuracy. However a **Matrix** can only hold integer variables so first the **floats** are converted multiplied by 32, a suitable scaling factor, and then there is a cast to **int** type. The factor of 32 gives reasonable accuracy and is small enough for most dimensions to ensure that integer variables do not overflow. It is necessary not to forget that this scaling factor may have to be removed if we really wish *Normals* to point to a **Matrix** of unit vectors.

Defprim::Defprim(){Normals=0;}

> The default constructor which initialises the normals pointer to zero.

DefPrim::DefPrim(int**,int*,int*,int*,int,int,int)

> Construct from data. The coordinates are accessed from a pointer array and the other lists from integer arrays or as simply integers.

DefPrim::DefPrim(Matrix&,Prim&)

> Construct from old connections and new coordinates.

DefPrim::DefPrim(DefPrim&)

> The copy constructor.

DefPrim::~DefPrim()

> The destructor, whose main task is to delete the memory on the free store pointed to by *Normals*.

10.4.2 The Illuminator Class

The **Illuminator** class is an abstract data type which represents a light source, like a lamp it shines light in a particular direction. The vector which specifies the direction of the light beam is given by its three components in the constructor. The constructor copies them into the internal data members. The most useful functions associated with the illuminator class is not a member function. It is the overloaded operator < to shine light on a defprim to produce a ViewPrim. Here are the member functions

float Illuminator::illx

> The x component of the light unit vector.

float Illuminator::illy

> The y component of the light unit vector.

float Illuminator::illz

> The z component of the light unit vector.

Illuminator::Iluminator(float,float,float)

> The constructor to copy the components of the light source vector.

10.4.3 Nonmember functions

These are an overloaded * operator to rotate a **DefPrim**, an overloaded < operator to illuminate a **DefPrim** and an overloaded >> operator to displace a **DefPrim**.

DefPrim operator*(Rotator&,DefPrim&)

> Rotate a **Defprim**. A **DefPrim** has two **Matrices**: one for the coordinates and one

for *Normals*. When a **DefPrim** is rotated, it is the components of these **Matrices** which are actually changed. The **Matrix** multiplications are spelled out in detail, including lines which could be removed in more terse code, to be clear. A rotated **DefPrim** is returned.

ViewPrim operator<(Illuminator&,DefPrim&)

Shine light on a **DefPrim**. An overloaded operator, <, of just the right shape to symbolise the beam of light from a lamp. This is quite a complicated function. Instances of the **Vector** data type are used to access the components of the normals and coordinates **Matrices**. Then a line-of-sight vector (*los*) is constructed to test for visibility. There are in fact two options here. The first is for a *los* from the viewpoint to a vertex on a polygon and the second is for an los which has components looking down at 45 degrees in the y-z plane. The reason for these two is cosmetic: the demos in the next chapter look better with the second option but the big demo in the last chapter, EXPLORE.CPP, works correctly with the first option. The first option is actually the correct one but the second gives a translucent and attractive look to the demos RIPPLE.CPP, FLATFISH.CPP and FLATWORM.CPP in the next chapter.

Also these demos use a grid of rectangles which are modulated at the vertices and are not exactly planar, for which the *los* from the viewpoint fails at glancing angles. The *los* from the viewpoint is turned on with the preprocessor directive

```
# define LOS 1
```

at the top of the header file DECL_04.H. The other alternative is turned on with

```
# define LOS 0
```

There is then a scalar product of the line-of-sight vector (*los*) with each of the surface normals to establish whether a given polygon is visible. Remember, it is visible if the scalar product is negative. If it is not visible the shade of the polygon is set to 256, which will fail the test to be drawn in **ViewPrim::show**(). Otherwise the shade is calculated from the scalar product of the illumination vector with the unit surface normal vector, the answer is scaled to lie within 0 and 15 to allow for 16 shades and then entered into the shading list of a temporary **ViewPrim** which is then returned from the function via the copy constructor.

void operator>>(Translator&,DefPrim&)

Move a **DefPrim** along a bit. This is the overloaded operator to displace a **DefPrim**. The increments held as data members in the **Translator** are added to the x, y and z components of the **Matrix** of the coordinates.

10.5 Example Program

The example program for this chapter is ILLHIDE.CPP. It illustrates the dual aspects of drawing a polygonal structure: hidden surface removal and illumination of each surface with a light source. It shows the polygonal structure PC-CITY in rotation with hidden surface removal and illumination. The program is set up with rotation about the z axis but this can be altered as desired. The monolith is coloured in light magenta but can be also be changed as desired by altering the values in the colours list.

The program starts with the instantiation of several objects: a **Screen** as usual, a **DefPrim** to hold the PC-CITY structure data, a **Translator** called *displace* to position it and an **Illuminator** called *light* to illuminate it.

While no key is pressed the loop is executed which flips the video pages, rotates the polygon structure a little, moves it into position and shines a light on it. Then the results are projected on the screen and shown.

10.6 Project File

The project file for this example is:

```
ILL_HIDE.CPP
DEFN_00.CPP
DEFN_01.CPP
DEFN_02.CPP
DEFN_03.CPP
DEFN_04.CPP
```

```
// ILLHIDE.CPP
// Illumination and Hidden Surface Removal

#include "C:\TC\3D\DECL_00.h"
#include "C:\TC\3D\DECL_01.h"
#include "C:\TC\3D\DECL_02.h"
#include "C:\TC\3D\DECL_03.h"
#include "C:\TC\3D\DECL_04.h"
#include "C:\TC\3D\SHADES.H"
#include "C:\TC\3D\PC_CITY.H"

#include <graphics.h>
#include <stdlib.h>
#include <stdio.h>
#include <conio.h>


int main(void){

    Screen screen(shadings);

    DefPrim PC_CITY(r_c,edglst_c,nedges_c,colors_c
                  ,nvtx_c,nedgc_c,npoly_c);     // make a Defprim

    Rotator transform(0,0,0);                    // Rotator
    Translator displace(0,200,0);                // Translator
    Illuminator light(1,0,0);                    // Illuminator

    while(!kbhit()){                             // if no keys pressed

            screen.swap_screen();                // screen flip
            transform.angl_inc(0,0,10);          // next angle
            DefPrim temp=transform*PC_CITY;      // rotate it
            displace>>temp;                      // move into place

            ViewPrim CITY=light<temp;            // illuminate it
            CITY.project();                      // project it
            CITY.show(screen);                   // display it

    }
    return 0;
}
```

```
// DECL_04.H
// Declarations of the DefPrim and Illumination Classes

#define LOS 1 // set to 1 for los from viewpoint, otherwise set to 0


//The DefPrim class

class DefPrim:public Prim{              // publicly descended
public:                                 // from Prim
        Matrix *Normals;                // normal components

        DefPrim(){Normals=0;}           // default
        DefPrim(int**,int*,int*,int*,int,int,int);//from data
        DefPrim(Matrix&,Prim&);         // from new coordinates
        DefPrim(DefPrim&);              // copy constructor
        ~DefPrim();
        void NormBuild();               // open space
        void NormCalc();                // make normals
};


// The Illuminator class

class Illuminator{                      // shine a light
  public:
     float illx,illy,illz;              // from this direction
     Illuminator(float,float,float);    // direction unit vectors
};



// Non-member functions
DefPrim operator*(Rotator&,DefPrim&);    // rotate a DefPrim
ViewPrim operator<(Illuminator&,DefPrim&);// light up a DefPrim
void operator>>(Translator&,DefPrim&);   //move a defprim
```

```
// DEFN_04.CPP
// Implementation of the DefPrim and Illuminator classes

#include "C:\TC\3d\DECL_00.H"
#include "C:\TC\3d\DECL_01.H"
#include "C:\TC\3d\DECL_02.H"
#include "C:\TC\3d\DECL_03.H"
#include "C:\TC\3d\DECL_04.H"
#include <math.h>
#include <mem.h>


// Defprim

// construct from data ...........................................
DefPrim::DefPrim(int **ar,int *eg_l,int* ngs,int* cls,int nvx,
              int neg,int npol):Prim(ar,eg_l,ngs,cls,nvx,neg,npol){
        NormBuild(); // set up the arrays for the normals
        NormCalc();  // fill them
}

// construct from new normals ....................................
DefPrim::DefPrim(Matrix& nrm,Prim &src):Prim(src){//make from normals
              Normals=new Matrix(nrm);// and Prim
}

// copy constructor ..............................................
DefPrim::DefPrim(DefPrim& src):Prim(src){// copy constructor
              Normals=new Matrix(*(src.Normals));
}

//destructor ....................................................
DefPrim::~DefPrim(){
      delete Normals;
}

// allocate free memory ..........................................
void DefPrim::NormBuild(){       // open space for normals
    Normals=new Matrix(3,npoly);//set up 3*npoly matrix
}

// calculate normals .............................................
void DefPrim::NormCalc(){        //calculate unit normal vector
    Vector x=(*m)[0],y=(*m)[1],z=(*m)[2];//the vertex coords
    // where to put the result
    Vector &nx=(*Normals)[0],&ny=(*Normals)[1],&nz=(*Normals)[2];
    int n=npoly;             // this many polygons
    int *ElstPtr=edge_lst;   // list of edge connections
    int *NedgePtr=nedges;    // how many edges per polygon
    // where the answers go:
    int i=0;// array index
        while(n--){              // for each polygon
            int Dx21=x[ElstPtr[1]]-x[ElstPtr[0]];//x2-x1 overloaded
            int Dy21=y[ElstPtr[1]]-y[ElstPtr[0]];//y2-y1 subscripting
            int Dz21=z[ElstPtr[1]]-z[ElstPtr[0]];// z2-z1
            int Dx32=x[ElstPtr[2]]-x[ElstPtr[1]];// x3-x2
            int Dy32=y[ElstPtr[2]]-y[ElstPtr[1]];// y3-y2
            int Dz32=z[ElstPtr[2]]-z[ElstPtr[1]];// z3-z2
```

```
// the normal vector is
// i          j          k          giving Bx=Dz21*Dy32-Dy21*Dz32
// Dx32       Dy32       Dz32              By=Dx21*Dz32-Dz21*Dx32
// Dx21       Dy21       Dz21              Bz=Dy21*Dx32-Dx21*Dy32

        float Bx=Dz21*Dy32-Dy21*Dz32;       // the normal components
        float By=Dx21*Dz32-Dz21*Dx32;
        float Bz=Dy21*Dx32-Dx21*Dy32;
        float B=sqrt(Bx*Bx+By*By+Bz*Bz);
        // the magnitude
        if(B==0.0)B=1.0;// avoid divide by zero error
        int e=32;// scale by x32 to store as int in a Vector
    nx[i]=(int)(e*Bx/B);ny[i]=(int)(e*By/B);nz[i]=(int)(e*Bz/B);
        i++;
        ElstPtr+=*(NedgePtr++);// adjust the pointers to lists
    }
}


// Illuminator
// constructor ...........................................................
Illuminator::Illuminator(float lightx=0,float lighty=0,
        float lightz=0){illx=lightx;illy=lighty;illz=lightz;
}


// nonmember functions

// rotate a defprim ......................................................
DefPrim operator*(Rotator &rot,DefPrim &src){// rotate a DefPrim
    // rotate all vectors
    Matrix tempM=*(src.m);                    // get vertices
    Matrix prodM=rot*tempM;                   // rotate vertices
    Matrix tempNormals=*(src.Normals);        // get normals
    Matrix prodNormals=rot*tempNormals;       // rotate normals
    // make the DefPrim
    Prim tempP(prodM,src);                    // Prim from Matrix and source
    DefPrim tempD(prodNormals,tempP);// from Matrix and Prim
    return tempD;
}
```

```cpp
// Find visibility and illumination ...............................
ViewPrim operator<(Illuminator& Ill,DefPrim& DPrim){
// remember the normals are still x 32 too big
    int n=DPrim.npoly;
    int *ElstPtr=DPrim.edge_lst;       // list of edge connections
    int *NedgePtr=DPrim.nedges;
    Vector x=(*(DPrim.m))[0];
    Vector y=(*(DPrim.m))[1];
    Vector z=(*(DPrim.m))[2];          //polygon coords
    Vector nx=(*(DPrim.Normals))[0];// normals
    Vector ny=(*(DPrim.Normals))[1];// remember they're
    Vector nz=(*(DPrim.Normals))[2];// x32 too big
    float Ix=Ill.illx,Iy=Ill.illy,Iz=Ill.illz;//illum. vectors<1
    int i=0;                           // counter
    int *shades=new int[n];            //temp store for shades
    int j=n;
    while(j--){                        // for all the polygons

// These sections of code will be selectively included by the
//  preprocessor depending on whether LOS is 1 or 0 in DECL_04.H
  /*****************************************************************/
// 1.Line-of-sight vector for everything for everything except
// RIPPLE.CPP, FLATFISH.CPP and FLATWORM.CPP
#if LOS     // if LOS = 1
    float losx=x[*(ElstPtr)];      // the first vertices
    float losy=y[*(ElstPtr)]+200;// taken for line-of-sight vector
    float losz=z[*(ElstPtr)];
    float los=sqrt(losx*losx+losy*losy+losz*losz);
    losx/=los;losy/=los;losz/=los;
/*****************************************************************/
// 2.Line-of-sight vec. for RIPPLE.CPP, FLATFISH.CPP and FLATWORM.CPP
#else       // if LOS = 0
    float losx=0;
    float losy=0.70;
    float losz=-0.70;
#endif
/*****************************************************************/

    shades[i]=256;                  // set shade to hidden temporarily
    float Nxi=((float)nx[i])/32;// get down by 32
    float Nyi=((float)ny[i])/32;
    float Nzi=((float)nz[i])/32;
    float vis=Nxi*losx+Nyi*losy+Nzi*losz;
    if(vis<=0)shades[i]=8+int((8)*(Ix*Nxi+Iy*Nyi+Iz*Nzi));

    i++;ElstPtr+=*(NedgePtr++);//update edge list and no. pointers
    }               // now all the shades are set in the temporary array

    // construct a new ViewPrim
    ViewPrim Temp((Prim)DPrim);
    memcpy(Temp.shades,shades,n*sizeof(int));//copy the shades
    delete []shades;
    return Temp;// here's the result - needs a copy constructor
}
```

```
// Move a DefPrim ...............................................
void operator>>(Translator& T,DefPrim& D){

int x=T.getx();int y=T.gety();int z=T.getz();
    //add x,y and z to all D's vertices
    for(int n=0;n<=D.nvtx-1;n++){

      (*(D.m))[0][n]+=x;                // adjust x
      (*(D.m))[1][n]+=y;                // adjust y
      (*(D.m))[2][n]+=z;                // adjust z

    }
}
```

11

A Ripple Tank

This chapter is devoted to a scientific simulation program which builds on what we have done so far. It is called a Ripple Tank, but actually it's far more than that. It is a way of visualising time varying mathematical functions in 3-D and has a much wider application than the title might suggest. However it is certainly true that there is a well-known Physics demonstration to show the propagation and interference of waves on the surface of a fluid and it is called the ripple tank. Our ripple tank will show the motion of a travelling wave across a surface with the user having choice of wave direction, wavelength, amplitude and frequency. In addition there are several other parameters which can be selected depending on how fast the simulation is to operate and how detailed it is drawn. To start with let's discuss what we would like to see.

11.1 Waves

Anyone who has looked at the surface of water has seen waves. The surface is never still and, depending on what disturbance is applied, waves will propagate across the surface. If a stone is dropped in the middle, a set of circular waves will propagate out. If there are boundaries at the edge which reflect the waves then the net disturbance will be the combination of the initial wave and the reflected waves from the boundary. For a continuing disturbance, this will give rise to standing waves like the pattern on a skipping rope.

It is not our intention here to investigate all the various types of waves on the surface of a fluid but, rather, to provide a test-bed to look at time varying waveforms. These waves need not look like anything that has ever been seen before. The user has the option of building in whatever function desired. We will design the device. It is called a Ripple Tank and to illustrate its operation we will show travelling sinusoidal waves across a diagonal i.e. 2-D waves (the displacement in the z-direction is the 3rd dimension) with a 2-D wave vector. The equation for the displacement, away from the equilibrium position, zdisp, of the z coordinate of a given point depends on the x and y coordinates of that point in the following way

$$zdisp = A.sin(2\pi ft - kx.x - ky.y)$$

where f is the frequency, t is time, kx is the wave vector in the x direction, ky is the wave vector in the y direction, and A is the amplitude of the wave. That sounds very technical but it is in fact not as bad as it seems. The wave vector is 2π divided by the wavelength and the product $2\pi ft$ is the part of the phase of which increases with each iteration of the program. The wavelength is the distance over which the undulation of the grid surface repeats itself, so a small wavelength means the undulations are closely spaced while a large wavelength means they are widely spaced. The fact that there are two wave vectors, kx and ky, means that the wave moves across the grid at an angle and has different wavelengths in the x and y directions which are not necessarily the same. This sounds complicated but you will understand by seeing it in action.

11.2 A Polygon Mesh

In this case we definitely need a polygon mesh. In the previous chapters a polygon mesh was taken to mean a polygonal structure made out of polygonal surfaces. The structure could be any shape. We want it to be a flat grid. Figure 11.1 shows the undisturbed grid. In fact we will invent a **Grid** class to encapsulate our idea of a grid mesh. Undisturbed, the grid is a 2-D array of connected squares in the x-y plane. When a wave passes the vertices have a displacement in the z-direction so that the grid is seen as an undulating surface. In the more general case it is the visualisation of a time dependent mathematical function. We will watch a sinusoidal wave propagate across the grid.

11.3 The Grid and Wave Classes

In the previous structures we have used, the data was laid out in a series of arrays. This is a clumsy way to describe a regular grid which we recognise will be a set of connected identical rectangles. The **Grid** class is our perception of a grid. A **Grid** is a regular mesh of polygons positioned somewhere in front of the screen with a certain number of elements in the x-direction and a number, not necessarily the same, in the y-direction of the viewframe. It must be possible to generate such a structure from just the dimensions and the size of a mesh element. Here is the **Grid** class; it is a mesh of rectangles.

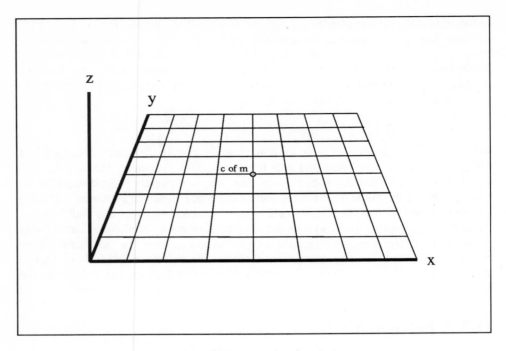

Figure 11.1: Layout of a grid.

11.3.1 The Grid Class

int Grid::cofmx

The x location of the centre.

int Grid::cofmy

The y location of the centre.

int Grid::cofmz

The z location of the centre.

int Grid::dimx

The x width of a mesh element.

int Grid::dimy

The y width of a mesh element.

int Grid::nx

The number of elements in $\frac{1}{2}$ the y direction

int Grid::ny

The number of elements in $1/2$ the y direction

int Grid::color

The colour of all elements.

Prim* Grid::layout

The complete data for the grid held in a Prim on the free store.

void Grid::build()

Here's where all the work is done. The raw information is converted to a **Prim** by calling this function in the constructor. The calculations are complicated since the list of edge connections must be made up in cyclic order going round the individual meshes. Figure 11.2 shows the ordering of the vertex numbers in terms of the data members *nx* and *ny*.

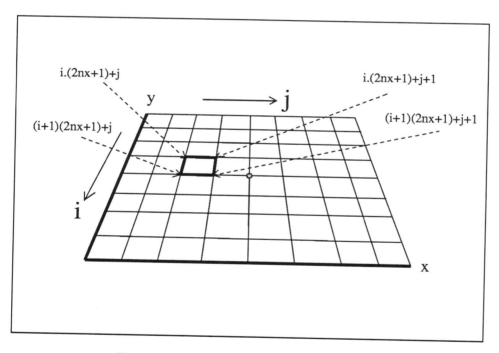

Figure 11.2: Vertex numbers of a mesh element.

We will do the vertex labelling in the following way. The number of elements in the x direction is equal to (2*nx) and the number in the y direction is (2*ny). This gives (2*nx+1) vertices in the x direction and (2*ny+1) in the y direction with

(2*nx+1)*(2*ny+1) vertices altogether although the total number of polygons is 4*nx*ny. You can see this from Figure 11.2 where both *nx* and *ny* are shown as 4. The x coordinates of these vertices range from (cofmx-nx*dimx) to (cofmx+nx*dimx) and the y coordinates range from (cofmy-ny*dimy) to (cofmy+ny*dimy). The first part of **build()** consists of selecting the vertices in order and putting them into the coordinates arrays.

Following this the edge connection list has to be constructed. This is more difficult since a mesh element will have sides spanning two adjacent rows of vertices. It turns out there is a simple formula for determining the vertex labels going round an element clockwise. If we make the grid with equal numbers of elements, 2*nx, in both directions and write s=(2*nx+1) then on any given element given by the grid indices i,j the vertex labels are, going round clockwise, (i*s+j), (i*s+j+1), ((i+1)*s+j) and ((i+1)*s+j). This is exactly how they should be entered in the edge connection list. An array is built up with these values.

Finally these temporary arrays are used to instantiate a **Prim** in free memory (on the heap) and the pointer to it returned to the data member *layout*.

Grid::Grid(int,int,int,int,int,int,int,int)

The constructor from data. The data is, in order, the x, y, and z coordinates of the grid centre, the dimensions of a mesh element in the x and y directions, half the number of elements in each x and y direction and the common colour of each element. The constructor copies these data to the data members and then calls **build()**.

Grid::~Grid()

The destructor which releases the memory occupied by the **Prim** pointed to by *layout*.

Prim* Grid::Layout()

The access function to get *layout*.

11.3.2 The Wave Class

The **Wave** class is a function abstraction. It is more than a function since it takes data in its constructor which is internally incremented on the tick of the clock so as to allow the function member of the class to change its effect with time. For variety, and to give an interesting appearance to the relevant statement in the example program, the waving effect is implemented in a function member. The **Wave** class holds the notion of a mathematical function to be imposed on a the data array inside a **Grid**. It will have the effect of changing the z coordinates of the **Grid** depending on the x and y coordinates. In this case it does what it suggests; it imposes a travelling wave which moves diagonally across the grid. Here are the class members.

float Wave::phase

The current phase of the wave. The phase is an angle between 0 and 360 degrees. The greater the phase, the further the wave is in its cycle. The phase in this case is the argument of the sine function and depends on both the time through the $2\pi ft$ term and space through the k.x term. That is why the wave moves across the grid; if it only varied in time the grid would just vibrate up and down, and if it only varied in space it would be a frozen undulation. We can change the time dependent part each time the **while** loop executes and that will give the appearance of a travelling wave.

float Wave::phase_inc

This is the amount by which the phase is incremented on each iteration of the **while** loop, which acts as a tick of the clock and simulates the passing of time. In this program the "tick time" is determined by how long it takes each **while** and so the speed of the wave will be machine dependent: it will run faster on a machine with a higher clock frequency.

float Wave::kx

The wave vector in the x direction. Non-physicists shouldn't be frightened by this; it's just 2π (6.284) divided by the wavelength (the distance over which the wave repeats) in the x direction.

float Wave::ky

The wave vector in the y direction. Non-scientists shouldn't be frightened by this either; it's just 2π (6.284) divided by the wavelength (the distance over which the wave repeats) in the y direction.

float Wave::Amp

The amplitude of the wave i.e. the maximum displacement of the wave, either at a peak or a trough, away from the flat grid.

Wave::Wave(float,float,float,float)

The constructor. It sets the phase to zero and copies data to the data members.

DefPrim Wave::modulate (Prim*)

Here's where all the work is done. This member function takes a copy of the **Prim** pointer held by the **Grid** instance and modulates the data it points to. The first thing it does is call the other function member **clock_tick()** to advance the phase and simulate the passing of time.

The using double dereferencing it makes temporary **Vector** instances of the x, y and z coordinates arrays and then calculates the net phase angle for this vertex according to the formula

angle = phase – kx.x – ky.y

and uses it to sine modulate the z coordinate:

z = cofmz + Amp.sin(angle)

The modulated z values are stored in an array and together with the x and y arrays are used to return a **Defprim** via the copy constructor, taking care to **delete** the array used to hold the modulated z's.

void Wave::clock_tick()

The member function which increments the phase angle but checks that it doesn't go outside the range 0 to 360. There are two sets of phase units at work here. Most people like to think of phase in terms of angular degrees, so that 360 degrees makes a full cycle. In the mathematical functions that Turbo C++ makes available, the angle is in radians. There is no great difficulty here if you remember that 2π (= 6.283) radians equals 360 degrees. For this reason this function makes sure that the phase remains within the principal range of 360 degrees. There isn't really much of a problem here since the **sine**() function itself keeps the angle in range, but this way we know there won't be any unpleasant surprises.

11.4 Example Programs

There are three example programs in this section which illustrate the sinusoidal modulation of a mesh of polygons. They are RIPPLE.CPP, FLATFISH.CPP and FLATWORM.CPP. They all use the same basic program, but with changes of parameters it can be made to look like a wave moving across the surface of a liquid, a swimming ray-like flat fish or a similar swimming flat worm.

Remember to set LOS=0 in the file DECL_04.H for just these programs. The line-of-sight-vector recommended will give a translucent appearance to the pictures and will allow them to be seen from below without the removal of otherwise hidden surfaces. Also there is an error in the detecting of visibility of the squares which make up the grid due to the fact that opposite vertices are displaced differently and are no longer planar. This can cause the omission of oblique squares. This could be avoided by using triangles. Remember to set LOS=1 in DECL_04.H before trying to run the Virtual Reality world in Chapter 12.

11.4.1 RIPPLE.CPP

This is the main program to show the ripple tank. It begins by instantiating the *screen* and then alters the linestyle, which shows as a border round the filled polygons, to a dotted line. This border adds to the translucent appearance of the simulations. Then a **Grid** object called *surface* is instantiated. *surface* has its centre at –20 on the x axis, 0 on the y axis and 80 in the air on the z axis and consists of 64 mesh square elements in a 8x8 grid. The dimensions of each element are 25 x 25. Each element has the colour blue which is palette colour number 1.

Then, a **Wave** object called *ripple* is instantiated. It has an increment of phase each tick of 0.5 radians which, since there are 6.28 radians in a full cycle, means that it will go through a full cycle in just over 13 iterations. Since the phase increment is given in radians, a wave vector component in the x direction of –0.03 means the wavelength is 2*3.142/0.03 = 209.43 or just about the full width of the grid. This is a wave moving in the –ve x direction. Similarly it also has a wave vector in the y direction of –0.03 which means it is moving in the –ve y direction with the same wavelength. It has an amplitude of 12.0 which means at its maximum it is 12 units above the equilibrium position and at its minimum it is 12 units below the equilibrium. The peak-to-trough difference is 24 units.

Next, a **Rotator** object called *transform* is instantiated and finally an **Illuminator** *light*.

In the main loop which, as usual continues until a key is pressed, the following takes place. First the screen is paged and transform is incremented. Then by virtue of the member function of the **Wave** class it is possible to effect the modulation of the **Grid** with the statement

```
DefPrim tempR=ripple.modulate(surface.Layout());
```

This does exactly what it says: it modulates the *surface layout* with a *ripple*. This is an example of the satisfying appearance of OOP; it allows a line of programming to look like a line of text.

Then the waved *surface* is rotated into view with *transform*, then it is illuminated, projected and finally shown.

This is compiled from RIPPLE.PRJ which should contain the following files:

```
RIPPLE.CPP
DEFN_00.CPP
DEFN_01.CPP
DEFN_02.CPP
DEFN_03.CPP
DEFN_04.CPP
DEFN_05.CPP
```

11.4.2 Flatfish

This is identical to RIPPLE.CPP except that it has a different colour, magenta, and **Grid** components and rotates as it goes. The sinusoidal modulation gives the illusion of a Ray-like fish, swimming. It is included for fun. FLATFISH.PRJ contains the same files as RIPPLE.PRJ except that RIPPLE.CPP is replaced by FLATFISH.CPP.

11.4.3 Flatworm

This is also identical to FLATFISH except that the colour is red and the data members of the Grid are different to make it look more worm-like. As its moves around it looks like a burrowing flat worm. The project is the same as FLATFISH.PRJ except that FLATFISH.CPP is replaced by FLATWORM.CPP.

11.5 Visualization of Mathematical Functions

The Ripple Tank is just a name for a device to visualise time-varying mathematical functions. There is no reason to stick with the sinusoidal wave. You can replace the two lines in **modulate**() which begin *float angle....* and *new_z[i]....* with any function you like. Here is another function to try. It is a peaked function which fluctuates up and down:

    angle=phase-sqrt ((kx*x[i])*(kx*x[i])+(ky*y[i])*(ky*y[i]));

There is one general point to watch out for. It is that for the integer variables we have used for speed, the range spans -32768 to +32767 and any number which falls outside this will become remainder. That will lead to peculiar results and perhaps polygons with dramatically incorrect vertex coordinates. The effect on the screen will be of large irregular and fragmented images which take a long time to draw.

```
// RIPPLE.CPP
// A Ripple Tank

#include "C:\TC\3D\DECL_00.h"
#include "C:\TC\3D\DECL_01.h"
#include "C:\TC\3D\DECL_02.h"
#include "C:\TC\3D\DECL_03.h"
#include "C:\TC\3D\DECL_04.h"
#include "C:\TC\3D\DECL_05.H"
#include "C:\TC\3D\CREATURES.CPP"
#include "C:\TC\3D\SHADES.H"
#include <graphics.h>
#include <conio.h>

// change to LOS=0 in DECL_04.H

int main(void){

    Screen screen(shadings);
    setlinestyle(4,0x0404,1);               //grid has dotted outline
    Grid surface(-20,0,80,25,25,4,4,1);     //8x8 squares 25x25,blue

    Wave ripple(.5,-.03,-.03,12.0);//0.5 radian phase inc. per cycle,
    // wavelength = 209, amplitude = 12.

    Rotator transform(-40,0,0);             // tilt view down 40 degrees
    Illuminator light(-0.71,-0.71,0);       // light from above and side

    while(!kbhit()){                        //while no keys are pressed

            screen.swap_screen();
            transform.angl_inc(0,0,0);

            // impose the ripple on the layout
            DefPrim tempR=ripple.modulate(surface.Layout());

            DefPrim TempR=transform*tempR;// rotate into view
            ViewPrim nextR=light<TempR;   // illuminate it
            nextR.project();              // project it
            nextR.show(screen);           // display it

    }
    if(getch()==0)getch();                  // clear key buffer
    return 0;
}
```

```
// FLATWORM.CPP
// A swimming orange flat worm.

#include "C:\TC\3D\DECL_00.h"
#include "C:\TC\3D\DECL_01.h"
#include "C:\TC\3D\DECL_02.h"
#include "C:\TC\3D\DECL_03.h"
#include "C:\TC\3D\DECL_04.h"
#include "C:\TC\3D\DECL_05.H"
#include "C:\TC\3D\CREATURES.CPP"
#include "C:\TC\3D\SHADES.H"
#include <graphics.h>
#include <conio.h>

// change to los=0 in DECL_04.H
// so the worm can be seen from below

int main(void){

    Screen screen(shadings);
    setlinestyle(4,0x0404,1);
    Grid surface(0,30,30,20,20,4,4,4); // colour red
    Wave ripple(.5,-.05,-.05,10);
    Rotator transform(0,0,0);
    Illuminator light(-0.65,-0.65,0.4);

    while(!kbhit()){

            screen.swap_screen();
            transform.angl_inc(0,0,2);
            DefPrim tempR=ripple.modulate(surface.Layout());
            DefPrim TempR=transform*tempR;
            ViewPrim nextR=light<TempR;
            nextR.project();
            nextR.show(screen);

    }
    if(getch()==0)getch();
    return 0;
}
```

```
// flatfish.cpp
// A swimming Ray fish

#include "C:\TC\3D\DECL_00.h"
#include "C:\TC\3D\DECL_01.h"
#include "C:\TC\3D\DECL_02.h"
#include "C:\TC\3D\DECL_03.h"
#include "C:\TC\3D\DECL_04.h"
#include "C:\TC\3D\DECL_05.H"
#include "C:\TC\3D\CREATURES.CPP"
#include "C:\TC\3D\SHADES.H"
#include <graphics.h>
#include <conio.h>

// change LOS=0 in DECL_04.H
// so the fish can be seen from below

int main(void){

    Screen screen(shadings);
    setlinestyle(4,0x0404,1);
    Grid surface(0,50,50,20,20,4,4,5); // a grid in magenta
    Wave ripple(.5,-.034,-.034,12);
    Rotator transform(0,0,0);
    Illuminator light(-0.65,-0.65,0.4);

    while(!kbhit()){
            screen.swap_screen();
            transform.angl_inc(0,0,2);
            DefPrim tempR=ripple.modulate(surface.Layout());
            DefPrim TempR=transform*tempR;
            ViewPrim nextR=light<TempR;
            nextR.project();
            nextR.show(screen);
    }
    if(getch()==0)getch();
    return 0;
}
```

```
// DECL_05.CPP
// Grid and Wave classes


// The Grid class

class Grid{                             // a representation of a grid
    int cofmx, cofmy, cofmz;            // centred here
    int dimx, dimy;                     // element dimensions
    int nx,ny,;              // number of elements in each 1/2 direction
    int color;                          // their color
    Prim* layout;                       // here's the layout
public:

    //position x, y and z,mesh size,number of meshes x and y, colour
    Grid(int,int,int,int,int,int,int,int);

    ~Grid();                            // delete layout
    void build();                       // build layout
    Prim* Layout(){return layout;}      // public access
};



// The Wave class

class Wave{


    float phase,phase_inc;  // phase angle, its increment each cycle
    float kx,ky,Amp;        // wavevector x and y components, amplitude
public:
    Wave(float,float,float,float);   // make from data
    DefPrim modulate(Prim*);         // modulate a layout
    void clock_tick();               // increment the phase
};
```

```
// DEFN_05.CPP
// Implementation of the Grid and a Wave classes.

#include "C:\TC\3D\DECL_00.H"
#include "C:\TC\3D\DECL_01.H"
#include "C:\TC\3D\DECL_02.H"
#include "C:\TC\3D\DECL_03.H"
#include "C:\TC\3D\DECL_04.H"
#include "C:\TC\3D\DECL_05.H"
#include <math.h>


// The Grid class

// construct from data ..................................................
Grid::Grid(int cx,int cy,int cz,int dx,int dy,  //construct from data
           int nnx,int nny,int col){             //2*nx=num on a side
        cofmx=cx;cofmy=cy;cofmz=cz;
        dimx=dx;dimy=dy;nx=nnx;ny=nny;color=col;
        build();                     // make a DefPrim - make up the arrays
}

// allocate free memory .................................................
void Grid::build(){
    // build a flat grid in the x-y plane      //build a Prim
    int npoly=2*nx*2*ny;                        // number of polygons
// fill up the array of edge numbers
    int* nedgs=new int[npoly];                  // num edges in each poly
    int* eptr=nedgs;
    for(int ecount=npoly;ecount>0;ecount--) *(eptr++)=4;// all 4 sided
// fill up the array of colours
    int* colors=new int[npoly];
    int* cptr=colors;
    for(int ccount=npoly;ccount>0;ccount--) *(cptr++)=color;
// fill up vertex arrays
    int nvtx=(2*nx+1)*(2*ny+1);                 // num vertices
    int* xarray=new int[nvtx];                  //temp store for x's
    int* yarray=new int[nvtx];                  // y's
    int* zarray=new int[nvtx];                  // z's
    int* r[]={xarray,yarray,zarray};            //for DefPrim constructor
    //there are 2*nx+1 vertices in each row and 2*ny+1 in each column
    // the grid is in the x-y plane; the ranges of x and y are:
    // cx-nx*dimx < x <cx+nx*dimx ; cy+ny*dimy > y >cy-ny*dimy
    int *ptrx=xarray,*ptry=yarray,*ptrz=zarray;
    int vindex=0;// vertex index
    for(int county=-ny;county<=ny;county++){
        for(int countx=-nx;countx<=nx;countx++){// fill x,y,z arrays
            ptrx[vindex]=cofmx+countx*dimx; //     x array
            ptry[vindex]=cofmy-county*dimy; //     y
            ptrz[vindex]=cofmz;             // all z are cofmz
            vindex++;
        }
    }

//fill up array of edge connections
    int nedglst=4*npoly;                        // 4 sides per poly
    int *edglst=new int[nedglst];               // empty list
    //let s=2*nx+1
    //the vertex numbers around a square at grid location i,j are
    // i*s+j,i*s+j+1,(i+1)*s+j,(i+1)*s+j+1
```

```
        int *elstptr=edglst;
        int s=2*nx+1;
        for(int i=0;i<=2*ny-1;i++){              //for each row
            for(int j=0;j<=2*nx-1;j++){          //for each column
                *(elstptr++)=i*s+j;              // write the vertex numbers
                *(elstptr++)=i*s+j+1;
                *(elstptr++)=(i+1)*s+j+1;
                *(elstptr++)=(i+1)*s+j;
            }
        }// everything is done, now make the Prim
        layout=new Prim(r,edglst,nedgs,colors,nvtx,nedglst,npoly);
        delete xarray;delete yarray;delete zarray;//burn the evidence
        delete nedgs;delete colors;delete edglst;
}

// destructor .............................................................
Grid::~Grid(){
    delete layout;                               // kill the Prim
}


// The Wave class

// constructor
Wave::Wave(float ph,float Kx, float Ky,float A){
    phase=0;
    phase_inc=ph;kx=Kx;ky=Ky;Amp=A;
}


// modulate the z coordinates ............................................
DefPrim Wave::modulate(Prim *gp){
    clock_tick();// advance the phase
// modulate z coordinates by Asin(wt-k.r)
// or any other function you care to put in
    Vector x=(*(gp->m))[0],y=(*(gp->m))[1],z=(*(gp->m))[2];// data
    int nvtx=gp->nvtx;                           // this many vertices
    int* new_z=new int[nvtx];                    // output
    int i=0,counter=nvtx;                        // counters
    while(counter--){                            // for all the vertices
        float angle=phase-kx*x[i]-ky*y[i];
        new_z[i]=z[i]+(int)(Amp*(sin(angle)));
        i++;
    } // x and y remain same
    // construct a new Defprim
    int *xx=x.getV(),*yy=y.getV();               // x and y arrays and new_z
    int* r[]={xx,yy,new_z};                      // array of pointers
    // make a new DefPrim
    DefPrim tempD(r,gp->edge_lst,gp->nedges,gp->colors,nvtx
                ,gp->nedgelst,gp->npoly);
    delete new_z;                                //clean up
    return tempD;                                // here it is
}

// advance the phase each cycle ..........................................
void Wave::clock_tick(){
    phase+=phase_inc;                            // advance the phase
    while(phase>6.283)phase-=6.283;              //going up
    while(phase<0.0)phase+=6.283;                //going down
}
```

12

A Virtual Reality

This is a popular name for a world inside the computer.

In this chapter we will construct a 3-D world inside the computer. It will have roads, buildings, a sky and horizon and you will be able to drive around it. You can design your own buildings if you wish. Objects will be sorted for display so that those in the foreground will be drawn after those in the distance and illumination will make objects change their shade when you move around them. We will meet many new objects and several new kinds of abstract data types, in particular a Control Abstraction in the form of a sorted list iterator. This chapter contains a lot of new ideas. At the end you will see that OOP has enabled us to encapsulate data and functions into meaningful data types which give a good representation of the world we are trying to model.

12.1 Introduction

The transition from a single graphics primitive to a scene containing several brings a host of new problems. Drawing one object on the screen is relatively simple; there is just one primitive type to keep track of. The scene of many objects introduces a new level of complexity. Instead of the single primitive there is now the list of visible primitives from which single primitives must be selected in turn. In addition these primitives must coexist in the World reference frame together with the observer which is ourselves. There are many new details to take care of. For example, in the complex scene of many objects, spatial relationships must be preserved; objects in the foreground must not be obscured by those in the distance which is a spatial relation derived from the position and view of the observer. Some form of depth sorting is required that orders objects for drawing on the basis of their distance from the observer. Just as important is a sound strategy for ignoring all objects outside the immediate environment of the observer. In a world consisting of hundreds of objects of different types spread out over a landscape, it would be pointlessly time consuming to attempt to draw them all. As in real life, the observer need only be concerned with those that are close by and affect current decisions. We examine these aspects of the multi-object World in turn.

12.2 Databases

If you wish to keep track of many separate documents you have to have a filing system from which you can retrieve important data as required efficiently and quickly. The computer Operating System itself uses such a filing system to hold programs and other data. In the case of a world populated by graphics objects some kind of filing system is also required though a more appropriate name is a database. There are several databases we need to construct to describe the complex World. There will be a database listing the distribution of all the occupants of the World, i.e. what is where. This will contain such attributes as the location and type of each object in the complex world and will contain the essential information to draw any view seen by the observer. Exactly how this database is laid out in memory is very important in determining the speed with which it can be accessed for graphics. This is a map of the World.

Yet again there will be a list of the attributes of each type of object which will have to be referenced from the map when an instance of each type is drawn. Another database, which will be constructed towards the final stage of the program, will be a sorted list of those objects which are visible in the vicinity of the observer. It has to be sorted to ensure objects are drawn in the right order and objects closest are drawn last.

To explain what the map is, consider the choices available in listing the objects in the World. Objects could be entered in a database in order of increasing x, y or z coordinate in the world or indeed at random with no spatial order whatsoever. Objects could be listed according to their type, colour or any one of their attributes. Of all the possibilities there will be those that provide fast access to those objects which need to be drawn, i.e. those in the immediate vicinity of the observer. It is clear that some kind of ordering in position is needed to achieve this, but what kind? The position of an object in the World is specified by its three World coordinates xw, yw and zw. It is clear that ordering the database in any one single coordinate xw or yw or zw alone will not provide an immediate picture of where each object is in relation to its neighbours.

What is needed is a database where the objects are arranged in 2-D order as they are laid out on the ground. This is difficult to visualise until it is realised that what is being described is nothing more than a map. The similarity to an ordinary route map is fairly exact for the world we will construct which consists of objects sitting on a surface, just like the surface of the Earth. The advantage of a map of this kind, (which is a 2-D array) is that all the objects that lie in a particular region are immediately obvious in their spatial relations.

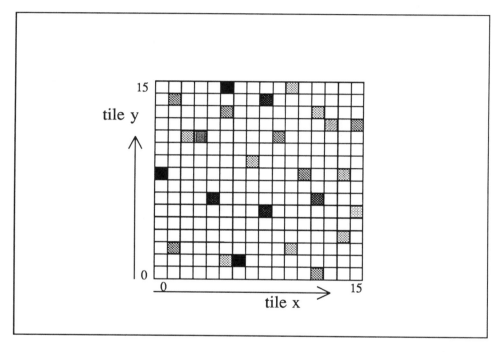

Figure 12.1 Layout of world 'tiles'

What is done is shown in Figure 12.1. The world space is divided into a 16*16 array of "tiles" (just like on the bathroom wall) each one of which has the dimensions 256 units wide and 256 units long. The map is a shorthand description of the World; by glancing at it you can see what lies where. Each tile is a unit of space to be considered for display. It can contain a collection of objects but in the example program it contains just one, for simplicity. Of course, this is not a very extensive world, but there is nothing in the method which limits it to these dimensions; it could be as big as you like and the individual tiles as small as you like. But, "wrap" occurs so that when the observer strays off any edge he reappears on the opposite side; in this way the world is effectively "infinite", like a sphere. For our purposes a 16*16 tile world is sufficient to illustrate the method. Each tile defines a region of space which, for the purposes of display, is a single entity. To construct the view seen by the observer, all one has to do is find one's position on the tile grid, select the nearest-neighbour tiles, find which ones are in front and draw the objects placed on them with the farthest ones being drawn first.

How can this 2-D array be laid out in the 1-D contiguous RAM? There is nothing new here. The screen itself is a 2-D world which is represented in memory as a 1-D database. The pixel is analogous to a tile and the four bits which specify its colour are analogous to the data list specifying the attributes of the object on the tile. An arrangement of information in this way, where each element is linked to its adjacent ones is called a linked list. In this case, the links are permanent and fixed by the physical position in the array. The world database is thus a linear array of 256 integers, each one holding the attributes of one tile in the 16*16 tile world. It is held in the file MAP.H. The identifier of the array is in fact *map* and every 16th byte starts a new tile in the y direction. The tile position in the list, modulo 16, represents the sixteen y values. In this model, the world is flat and z does not vary.

There is very little information needed for the attributes, since the position in space is automatically included by the tile's position in the list. The attribute of each tile is given in hexadecimal and only the low byte is used. In fact it could have been an array of characters, but integers were chosen to give room for increasing the amount of information. The higher nybbles are left clear to give you the option of including extra information for each tile, for example additional objects on the tile. The lowest nybble gives the type of object which is to sit on the tile and the highest nybble gives the background colour. At present only nine are possible (listed in *CREATURE.H*), but in principle there is no limit. Seeing how it is done, you can add as many as you wish.

12.2 Classes for Data Storage and Retrieval

As mentioned above, once the visible objects in the near vicinity to the observer have been identified there is the problem of ordering them for drawing so that the more distant ones are drawn first. This is commonly known as the painter's algorithm, since in painting a picture the last brush stroke overlays earlier ones. Figure 12.2 shows the observer looking into the screen on a scene of objects with the clear need to display them in the order 1, 2, 3, 4, 5, 6 so the ones closest are drawn last and aren't obscured by more distant ones.

There are many well known algorithms for sorting data in order. Most of the more exotic varieties have been developed to handle large databases with a large number of entries or records. In our case it is necessary to handle the information of a small number of tiles which are visible to the observer: typically half the number in the inspected immediate environment and these are to be ordered in depth order. To do this we will use an abstraction called **Sorted_List** which is a list sorted in some kind of order. This leads to another interesting abstract data type called a control abstraction. It is called this because the abstract data type is not visual, nor is it a really a function abstraction. It is a special operation consisting of the traversal of a data structure. It is in fact called an iterator since it walks along the sorted list gathering information and keeping count of its place in the list. The class we will invent for it is called class **Iterator**. **Sorted_List** is a list of instances of the class **Node**, each **Node** holding a **RECORD** of the data and pointing to the next **Node** in the chain. There are several new ideas here so we will go through them in detail.

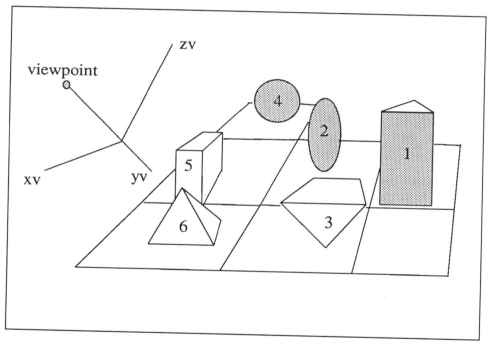

Figure 12.2: Depth ordering of sorted list

Note that at this stage we are referring to the attributes and other accumulated data about the objects to be drawn as records. A record is a set of data where each data type is confined to specific parts or "fields". This is how data for visible objects is carried around in the example programs. A record is constructed containing all the relevant data to draw in the tile and its contents and when the sorted list is built up the records are inserted in order of distance from the observer with the farthest objects at the top, or head, of the list. That way, although the depth field is the basis for sorting, it carries with it other information for drawing, reducing the retrieval of additional data at a later stage to a minimum. Of course, to avoid slowing things down too much it's important to keep the record short. In the program a record is abstracted as a **RECORD** and is a new data type called a **structure,** which is a standard type in C but we will view it from our C++ perspective as having members which are all public by default, as compared to a class which has all members private by default. The concept of a class developed from the C structure. The structure data type is declared like a class except that the word **struct** replaces class in the declaration. In C++ programming it assumes a somewhat lesser importance, being a special case of a class. Here a structure is used to hold the information taken from the tiles on the map.

The new classes interfaces are shown in file DECL_06.H and implemented in file DEFN_06.CPP. We will examine them before moving on to other aspects of the graphics.

12.2.1 RECORD Structure

A structure in C++ is a class with members, which by default are public. We will hold the data associated with a visible tile in the form of a **struct** data type called RECORD. In this all the data types are **int** and so it could have been an array. However the elements of an array are only identifiable by their indices whereas a structure has data members with identifiers. Here are its data members.

int RECORD::type

The type of object on the tile. These are the primitives that populate the world. There are nine types currently but you can add as many as you wish. Their data is listed in the file CREATURE.H.

int RECORD::bck_col

The background colour of a tile. This serves to colour the landscape and show important urban features such as roads pavements and grassland. There are 16 possible colours for the background taken from the default palette

int RECORD::centrex

The x coordinates of the centre of a tile in World coordinates. Remember the World is where all things exist. The current view of the world is determined by the position and orientation of the viewframe. We will discuss how the orientation of the viewframe can be used as a transform to see the correct view of the World for projection onto the screen.

int RECORD::centrey

The y coordinates of the centre of a tile in World coordinates.

int RECORD::yV

The y coordinate of the centre of a tile in view frame coordinates. The view frame is the frame of reference from which we observe the world so it is important to know the y coordinate of a visible object. In particular we will wish to depth sort objects so that ones with the largest y values in the view frame will be drawn first. That way objects in the distance will be drawn before those in the foreground and be obscured, as they should.

This structure holds all the information we need to draw an object.

12.2.2 Class Node

A **RECORD** has the data but it does not contain sufficient data to constitute an element in a sorted list. Remember we need to draw distant graphics objects first and so the **RECORD**s must be put in a sorted list.

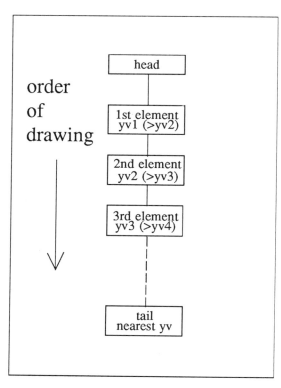

Figure 12.3: Schematic of sorted list.

A sorted list is a way of holding information in the order it is most useful. There are many occasions in life when a sorted list is essential: it would be impossible to find a telephone number if the directory were not sorted alphabetically in name order. Likewise it wouldn't be easy to find the spelling of a word if dictionaries were not similarly sorted. In our case we want the list of visible objects sorted in yv-order with the largest value of view frame y coordinate at the head.

Figure 12.3 shows schematically what we want from a sorted list. The sorted list we will in fact use is constructed from elements which are not just the yv numbers but instances of a class, **Node**, whose job it is to encapsulate the **RECORD**s and provide links between them. In addition the list is itself an abstraction, **Sorted_List**, which holds a pointer to the first,

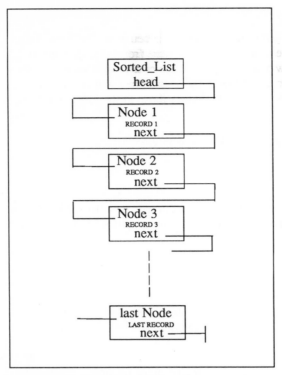

Figure 12.4: Implementation of a sorted list: a list of nodes.

or head, **Node** and has the task of dealing directly with other objects. Thus the **Sorted_list** controls the **Node**s, the **Node**s encapsulate the **RECORDS** and they encapsulate the data. Figure 12.4 shows the **Sorted_List** providing access to chain of **Nodes**. Notice in particular how each Node contains a **RECORD** together with a pointer, called *next*, to the next **Node** in the chain.

Using **Nodes** this way makes it possible to have a list where each member knows only the link to next element. There is a great advantage to making a list this way since if it is necessary to remove a **Node** or add a new one, only the link needs to be adjusted, as shown in Figure 12.5.

As you will see, in such a list it is not even necessary to carry a count of the total number of elements; the very existence of the pointer to the next node tells you whether the end of the chain has been reached. When the pointer to the next **Node** reads NULL, the end of the list has been reached. The class **Iterator**, the control abstraction, will walk along the list of **Nodes** gathering data. It goes without saying that memory for the **Nodes** will be allocated dynamically using **new** since the length of the list cannot be exactly known at compilation.

Here is a Node:

Node* Node::next

An important data member since it points to the next **Node** in the list. If this data member is NULL in an instance it means that it is the last **Node** and therefore the end of the list.

RECORD Node::record

Here's the data in the form of a **RECORD**.

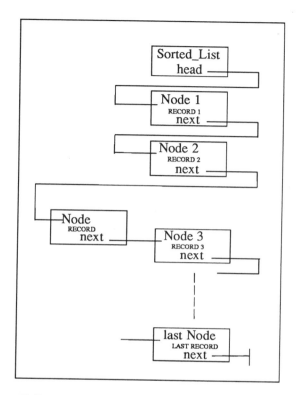

Figure 12.5: Inserting a new Node: only the links need be changed.

Node::Node(RECORD,Node*)

The constructor. This is a very odd-looking constructor but you will understand its form more fully when the **Sorted_List** is explained. It takes a **RECORD** as you would expect, and a pointer to a **Node**. The **RECORD** is the data for the **Node** and the pointer is to the next **Node** in the **Sorted_List** and will be assigned to *next*. More of this shortly.

Node::~Node()

The destructor which deletes the pointer, *next*, to the next **Node**.

void Node::insert(RECORD)

Be careful for there are two insert functions: one for the **Node** class and another for the **Sorted_List** class. This one inserts a **Node** after another **Node**. It doesn't know anything about **Sorted_List**s and doesn't care. First it checks if the pointer *next* is null. If so then this must be the last **Node** in the list so a new **Node** must be instantiated to hold the **RECORD**. The new **Node** is itself the end of the list.

If there is a next **Node** then it checks whether the viewframe y coordinate, yV, of the **RECORD**, *R*, under consideration is greater than that of the next **Node** (the one pointed to by *next*). The **RECORD** it is considering must have a viewframe y value smaller than its own or else it wouldn't have got this far. If the viewframe y value passed is greater than that of the next **Node**, then a new **Node** must be instantiated and inserted between this **Node** and the next. The new **Node** is passed the pointer to the next **Node** as its link and its pointer (to the memory allocated) is passed to this **Node**'s *next* data member. It does so with the instruction

```
next = new Node(R,next);
```

where *R* is the **RECORD** identifier. This means instantiate a new **Node** with the **RECORD** and the pointer, *next*, to the next **Node**. The pointer to the memory location of this new **Node** is then returned to *next*. So *next* appears twice in this statement but on the right hand side it means the old *next* and on the left hand side it means the new *next*. Confusing isn't it! All that has happened is that the link chain has been broken to insert the new **Node** as shown in Figure 12.5. If on the other hand the *yV* of the **RECORD** is less than that of the next **Node** it must be passed on down the list until it finds its rightful place with the statement

```
next->insert(R);
```

Observe what this means; *next->* means the **Node** that *next* points to, so the full statement says "next **Node** insert *R*". This means that the next **Node** **insert()** function is being called. Remember each Node is a different instance of the Node class and has its own perception of *next*. In this way the **RECORD** passes down the line.

The **Node** class thus possesses the ability to create new **Nodes** and make an ordered list. As we will see the other type **Sorted_List** controls the head of the list and so manages the whole list.

RECORD Node::get_record()

The access function to return the RECORD.

Node::friend Iterator

The Iterator class is a friend of the **Node** class. It needs to be, since it must walk the chain of **Nodes** in the linked list to return the **RECORD** data. This is how data is retrieved from the list.

12.2.3 Class Sorted_List

The **Sorted_List** holds a list of **Nodes** in order of decreasing *yv*, which is the depth into the viewframe. The list must be in this order so that the farthest graphics objects will be drawn first and not overwrite those in the foreground. It has an important data member, *head*, which is a pointer to the **Node** at the head of the list. Its function is to take **RECORD**s and put them in the list though the ordering is in fact done by the **Nodes** themselves as we have already seen. It has an important friend class, **Iterator**, which will walk along the list keeping a record of its position, and get data from the **RECORD**s.

Node* Sorted_List::head

The pointer to the **Node** at the head of the list.

Sorted_List::Sorted_List()

The constructor which doesn't do much. All of the work is done by the next function.

Sorted_List::insert(RECORD)

Add a new **RECORD**, *R*, to the list. It has several checks to do. First if *head* is NULL, this must be the first **RECORD** and a **Node** must be instantiated and put at the head of the list and a pointer to its memory location returned to *next*.

If there is already a *head* then it checks to see if the **RECORD** *yV* is greater than that of the head **Node**. If it is it must be inserted at the top of the list and become the new **head**. It does this with the instruction

```
head = new Node(R,head);
```

which means instantiate a new **Node** with *R* and the list *head*, and return a pointer to it to the list *head*. Similar to **Node::insert()**, it swaps the old *head* for the new *head* and passes the old *head* on to the new **Node**. What is confusing is that *head* appears twice in this statement but on the left hand side it means the old *head* whereas on the left hand side it means the new *head*.

If the **RECORD** *yV* is too small it is passed on down the line with

```
head->insert(R)
```

which invokes the insert function of the **Node** at the list head. The **Sorted_List** has lost control of the **RECORD** at this point and it is the responsibility of the list **Nodes** to insert it in order. In this way the list is truly a sorted-list since it inserts each new record in order as it arrives. It is an insertion sort.

12.2.4 Class Iterator

This is the control abstraction. It performs a service on another class. It's function is to traverse the **Sorted_list**, keeping a record of its position. **Sorted_List** is not otherwise disturbed by the **Iterator**. Because it keeps check of its progress through the list, it is very useful as a loop counter to traverse the list and can be used in a **while** loop. For this reason its stepping through the list is nicely described by an overloaded increment operator **++**.

Its constructor binds it to a particular **Sorted_List** object at instantiation. Here is the **Iterator** class.

Node* Iterator::pncurrent

The pointer to the current **Node**. This data member keeps count of where the **Iterator** is as it traverses a **Sorted_List**. By testing this data member the **Iterator** can be used to control a **while** loop and terminate when *pncurrent* becomes NULL.

Iterator::Iterator(Sorted_List&)

The constructor which binds it to an instance of **Sorted_List**, i.e. the list to traverse.

Node* Iterator::operator++()

The overloaded operator to increment along the list. It first checks to see if the pointer to the current **Node**, *pncurrent*, is NULL which means the end of the list has been reached. If it has, it returns zero which is NULL for the pointer. If it is not at the end of the list, it returns the pointer to the current **Node** and makes the pointer to the next **Node** the new current **Node** pointer. In this way it moves along the list and signals its arrival at the end with a returned NULL pointer which can be used in a loop condition.

Node* Iterator::getnode()

The access function to return the pointer to the current **Node**.

12.3 Bringing a World to Life

We wish to create an artificial World inside the computer, a Virtual Reality, and do it in the OOP paradigm. We want the objects in the program to look and feel like the entities in a real World, including ourselves in our own special relationship as the observer. What classes can we design to fulfil this requirement? Here is one possibility:

class World	– a class to hold the complete description of the World, including the layout of the terrain and the arrangement of buildings,
class Observer	– a class to hold the idea of observer awareness, giving the World I live in and a description of my immediate environment, the means to navigate around it and see it,
class Environment	– a class to describe what is immediately visible to me, i.e. my immediate environment,
class Navigator	– a class to control movement in the World, including input from the keyboard and subsequent adjustments to my location and speed as I move.

These are the classes on which the example program of this section, EXPLORE is based. They provide a meaningful basis on which to write EXPLORE which finally ends up looking very much like

```
let the world exist
I exist
forever
        I see
        I explore
```

This is not quite what the program looks like, but similar, as you can see from the file EXPLORE.CPP.

Before we move on to the implementation of these classes let us look at some final pieces of machinery needed to complete the picture. In particular we want to know how the landscape we visualise inhabited by the different graphics objects can be "seen" in a coherent way by the observer looking at the screen of the monitor. Of course, we already have the coordinate transforms in place to do this, but there is a conceptual leap from the bare mathematics of rotation matrices to an algorithm for handling a complete scene. In addition, to complete the realism we want there to be a horizon and a sky, not just a bitmapped backdrop, but something which responds dynamically in the correct way to the manoeuvres controlled from the keyboard.

12.4 The World-to-View Transform

We examine here how it is possible to transform graphics objects from the world frame to the view frame so the perspective transform can be done and an image produced on the screen. In many aspects this is a rerun of the earlier discussions of the coordinate and geometric transforms of earlier chapters, but here it is specifically aimed at constructing the complete view of the World seen by the observer.

What we know before this view transform is made are the coordinates of vertices in the world frame. The viewing transform will enable us to find out what they are in the viewframe. This is a coordinate transform. Fortunately we need nothing new here; the groundwork has already been prepared in Chapter 9 when the composite rotation was developed. That transform consisted of the following single rotations in order:

1. A rotation of angle γ about the z axis,

2. A rotation of angle θ about the x axis and

3. A rotation of angle ϕ about the y axis.

It is no accident that the rotations were done in this order, it is precisely the order required for this viewing transform except that here there is no rotation about the y axis. Remember that the order of the rotations matters. It turn out that this sequence gives a simple simulation of free movement. Here's the way it works:

The keys used from the keyboard have the following functions:

s	speed up forwards
a	turn to the left (yaw left)
x	turn to the right (yaw right)
k	speed up in reverse (equivalent to slow down if already moving forwards)
m	nose down (pitch up)
l	nose up (pitch down)

The controls therefore give variable speed either forward or reverse, left or right turns and flying up or flying down. Figure 12.6 illustrates the aeronautical terms for rotations in flight.

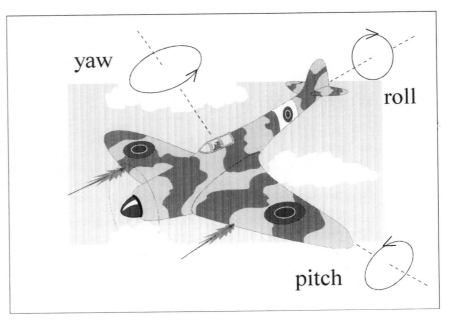

Figure 12.6 Aeronautical terms for rotations

Let us now see how the sequence of rotations gamma followed by theta can produce the observer's view of the World. Figure 12.7 shows an example scene of what an observer might see looking at three lap-top PCs. To start with there is no rotation of any kind and so the PCs appear horizontal and in the centre of the field of view.

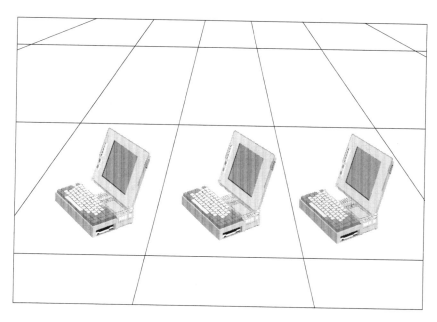

Figure 12.7: Initial view before rotation.

Figure 12.8 now shows the observer's view after he has rotated about his z axis by an angle γ, which to start with is also the world frame z axis. As a result of his rotation to the left, the PCs have appeared to rotate to the right and the rightmost PC has gone off the screen.

Figure 12.9 shows the observer's view after a successive rotation about his x axis by a negative angle –θ. This simulates the observer looking downwards and makes the two remaining PCs appear to rotate upwards..

At the end of these two rotations in order, a coordinate rotation about the z axis by γ, followed by a negative rotation about the x axis by –θ, the horizon is still horizontal but the observer has turned to the left and is looking down. There is no further rotation about the y axis, but if there were it would make the horizon tilt. We have no use for this additional rotation and it has been left out. You can put it in if you like simply by adding additional keys to the **switch** statement in the function **Navigator::keyboard()** which we will discuss shortly.

What happens in the program is that an instance of a **Navigator** class keeps a record of the angles γ and θ and uses them to construct a **Rotator called** *view* which is a compound rotational transform of the type just described. *view* is a compound rotation of the coordinate kind and so represents rotations of the observer. To see graphics objects from the observer's view, the transform *view* is applied to each in turn.

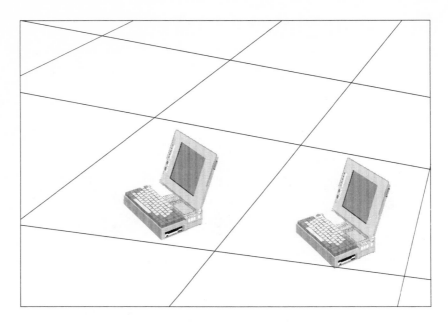

Figure 12.8: View after a rotation about the Z axis.

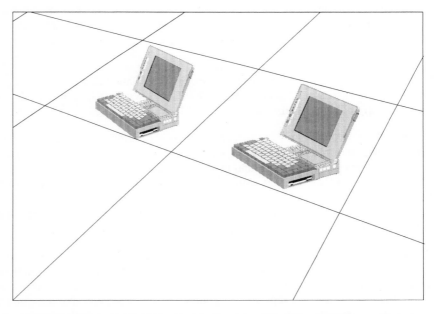

Figure 12.9: View after rotation about Z axis followed by rotation about x axis

12.5 Where's the Horizon?

The title is phrased this way because a horizon is a strange thing to think about. After all it doesn't really exist. You can always see the horizon but as you walk towards it, it moves into the distance. How do we get a horizon on the screen? It isn't sufficient to draw a fixed line somewhere on the screen because we want the horizon to move up and down as the view frame is tilted down or up respectively. Here's how it can be done.

Look at Figure 12.10. There you can see the view frame looking at the world frame.

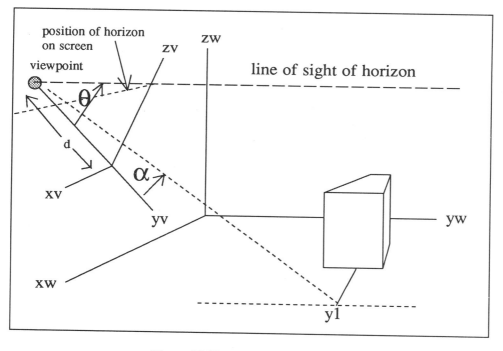

Figure 12.10: Drawing the horizon.

Consider an object at point y1 in the world frame. Now draw a line from the viewpoint of the view frame to y1. This line makes an angle α with the y axis of the view frame. Now the horizon occurs as we let y1 move off into the distance and the angle α grows until the line from y1 (now out of sight) to the viewpoint is horizontal. The angle becomes angle θ at this point which is the rotation of θ of the view frame about the x axis (which we can get from **Navigator::view**) and where the line cuts the screen is the horizon. The position of the horizon in the viewframe zvh is therefore given by

$$zvh = d*tan(\theta)$$

Its actual position on the screen depends on how viewframe coordinates have been converted to screen coordinates. In the example program we use

$$\text{horizon screen } y = 250 - d*tan(\theta)$$

which looks OK

The horizon is always horizontal since there is no rotation about the y axis.

Let us describe these classes in detail to see how they work.

12.6 Classes for the Virtual Reality

Now, all is in place for a description of the World inside the computer; a Virtual Reality. Armed with the methodology of OOP, it is possible to distil abstract data types from our perception of the problem so that instead of disintegrating into a mass of public data arrays serviced by a myriad of functions, we can describe the World almost in plain English. The classes we will invent will have an obvious and intuitive meaning in the World model. What classes come to mind immediately? For a start there could be a **World** class to contain the whole World and everything in it, with the exception of the observer. The observer is seen as in Classical Physics, as a disconnected and separate entity. The existence of the World doesn't in any way depend on the existence of the observer (this is not true in Quantum Mechanics). We will exemplify this abstraction in the **Observer** class.

The **Observer** has a particular view of the **World** which is restricted to what is nearby and of that only what is visible, in front; the Observer has an **Environment**. To move through the **World** as a free agent the **Observer** needs a **Navigator**.

These are the new classes which are now described in detail. The class interfaces are given in DECL_06.H and the their implementations in DEFN_06.CPP.

12.6.1 The World class

This class knows all about the World. It has a pointer to the map of the world giving the locations of all the graphics objects in it (in MAP.H), a pointer to the list of descriptions of each of the graphics objects (in CREATURE.H) and a pointer to a description of the unit of ground that each object sits on (also in CREATURE.H). It is global knowledge without being specific to any particular view. It contains all the information an observer needs to construct his scene. Since the data is accessed from files it can be changed without affecting the source code. Here are the class members.

int* World::tiles

A pointer to the map of the World showing where everything is placed. The *map* in MAP.H is assigned to this at instantiation.

DefPrim* World::primitives

An array of **DefPrims** containing the descriptions of the graphics objects. *zoo* from CREATURE.H is assigned to this at instantiation.

DefPrim* World::floor

A pointer to the **DefPrim** description of the way a unit of ground is designed, in this case a coloured square, and at instantiation is assigned the address of *ground* also in CREATURE.H.

World::World(int*,DefPrim*,DefPrim*)

The constructor which copies pointers into the data members.

int* World::get_tiles()

The inline access function to return *tiles*.

DefPrim* World::get_floor()

An access function to return *floor*.

Defprim* World::get_prim()

An inline access function to return *primitives*.

That's all there is to **World**. It is encapsulates World data.

12.6.2 Class Observer

The observer is you. You need to be able to move around the World under keyboard control and see things. The **Observer** class allows you to do that. Here is its interface. First the data members.

World* Observer::world

The World in which I exist.

Environment Observer::surroundings

My immediate surroundings as an instance of the **Environment** class. An environment holds a **Sorted_List** the objects I can see around me.

Navigator Observer::navigate

An instance of the **Navigator** class to keep count of my position in the World and provide motion through keyboard input.

Illuminator Observer::flashlight

A light to see my way. This also does hidden surface removal and shading on the visible objects and prepares them for display.

Observer::Observer()

The constructor which needs a **World** to bring the observer to life. It also sets up the flashlight direction to default fixed values.

void Observer::observe(Screen&)

This is a massive function which does most of the work. It constructs the environment and produces the image on the screen. It is so big it has a section to itself. It is necessary to describe the other classes before explaining how this function works.

Navigator Observer::Navigate()

The access function to get the data member *navigate*.

12.6.3 Class Navigator

This class provides the means of navigating round the world under keyboard control. You can move forwards and backwards with increasing speed, turn to the left or right and fly up or down, to a degree. Here are the members.

int Navigator::x

My x position in the World frame.

int Navigator::y

My y position in the World frame.

int Navigator::z

My z position in the World frame.

int Navigator::theta_inc

The angular amount by which I look up or down each key press.

int Navigator::phi_inc

The angular amount by which I look left or right each key press.

int Navigator::speed

My speed.

Rotator Navigator::view

A very important **Rotator** which you will remember is a rotational transform. This transform converts the coordinates in the world frame to coordinates seen from where I am, i.e. into viewframe coordinates. It represents my view. It is a very important transform, as described above, and is also discussed again in its own section later.

Navigator::Navigator

The constructor. Notice how it also calls the constructor for view with all angles set to zero to set off looking horizontal and straight ahead.

void Navigator::keyboard()

The member function that reads the keyboard and makes adjustments to position and speed. It checks to see if a key has been pressed since the last cycle and uses the switch-case statement to see which one. The keys 'a' and 'x' give rotation of the view frame to the left and right respectively and effect yaw and the 'l' and 'm' give rotation up and down and effect pitch, as shown in Figure 12.7. Both use the **angl_inc**() function of *view*. Key 's' gives speed increase up to a maximum of 50 and 'k' gives a reverse speed to the same limit, so pressing 'k' from rest produces reverse motion. 'q' causes the program to terminate in an orderly fashion and return to the caller which is either DOS or the IDE.

12.6.4 Class Environment

The **Environment** class is really just a holder for a **Sorted_List** which contains the information of the local surroundings. Here are the class members.

Sorted_List* Environment::patch_list

A pointer to the **Sorted_List** with the information of the immediate visible surroundings in the form of a linked list of **Nodes**. The list is sorted so that graphics objects which are farthest away in the view frame are at the top and are drawn first. That way near objects overwrite far objects, which is correct.

Environment::Environment()

The constructor which creates a new **Sorted_List** instance in free memory and returns the pointer to *patch_list*.

Environment::~Environment()

The destructor which releases the memory taken by the **Sorted_List**.

12.7 Observer::observe()

This is the function which does most of the work in producing an image of the World on the screen and it has a section all to itself. It is long and incorporates all of the other classes. Here's how it works. Notice at the start how a **Sorted_List** *patch_list* is instantiated ready for the list of visible objects, later.

1. Update Speed and Position

First, it identifies the tile in the map that the observer is located on and examines which of the surrounding 16 tiles are visible in front of the observer. There are several subsections to this first part. At the beginning the speed is used to update the position in the World. Remember that motion is not confined to the horizontal and the direction of motion is whatever direction is being looked in currently which is a vector. Now it turns out, very conveniently, that this vector is nothing more that the second row of the *view* transform matrix of *navigate*. This rather useful result comes about because of how that transform is made. Remember that it is the compound rotation of the view frame resulting from keyboard input. As such each row of the matrix is one of the unit vectors (base vectors) of the view frame x axis expressed in world frame coordinates. The first row is the base vector of the view frame expressed in terms of the world frame base vectors, and so on. Being able to just take the second row of that matrix as the direction that the view frame y axis is pointing in the World is very convenient. Its components are used to update the observer's position in the World. Notice how this information is assigned to a **Vector** *ky* and then overloaded subscripting is used to get the elements. At the end the position coordinates are bitwise **AND**ed with 4096, written in hexadecimal, to stay on the 4096 x 4096 size World and ensure "wrap". The z coordinate (height) is constrained to lie within the range 0 to 200.

2. Which Tile am I on?

The next task is to find out which tile in the 16x16 array from which the World is made I am on. This is done quickly with a bitwise right shift 8 times. Since 2^8 is 256, this is a fast way of dividing 4096 by 256 and getting the result mod 16. This result is the coordinates of the corner of a tile in the reduced 16x16 world and is the local world origin. I must now find my (the observer's) coordinates in this frame. To do so I have to scale up the tile origin to world coordinates again and subtract the result from my world coordinates. Now I have a working set of coordinates with which to do geometry.

3. What can I see?

Here's a large block of code to do a lot of things. It must examine to locality for what objects are visible and insert them in the **Sorted_List**. They are placed in order of displaying during the insertion.

There are three loops here, two **for**s and an **if**. The **for**s set the range of how many rows and columns of tiles around the observer will be examined. If these ranges are too large, the final picture will have many objects but be very slow to display. The ranges shown work OK on a 486 at 33 MHz. For each tile in the list, its centre coordinates relative to the observer are determined to see if it is in front and therefore visible. If it is visible several data are collected. The type of the graphic object is and its background colour are indexed from the map and then together with the coordinates used to instantiate a **RECORD** which is inserted into the **Sorted_List** *patch_list*. There's a great deal going on here but the code is not excessively long largely as a result of the OOP paradigm which hides the complexity in the abstract data types.

4. Start Drawing

Now the display begins. First the horizon is drawn. The section above the horizon is drawn as blue sky and the section below is drawn as grey background.

Then an instance of the Iterator class called *nextf* is bound to *patch_list*. This will enable us to walk along the sorted list to the end drawing each object in turn, starting with those farthest away. Because the increment operator ++ has been overloaded for the **Iterator** class, it is possible to write

```
Node* npf
while(npf=nextf++){
```

to enclose all of the subsequent code, which draws everything in sight. The **Iterator** gets the next **Node** pointer from the list and assigns it to *npf* ready for use in the drawing, but if it reaches the end of the list the assignment will be null and the **while** will fail, bringing the drawing to a close. This is how the main drawing loop is controlled. Here's the Iterator doing its job.

Inside the loop first a **Translator** named *world_displace* is instantiated to place each graphics object and the floor it sits on in the correct place in the world, and another **Translator** named *view_displace* instantiated to place it in the correct place in the view frame. Each record is examined to find the background colour for the tile and the floor data structure is fetched and used to instantiate a **DefPrim** called *floor*. *floor* is positioned in the correct place in the view frame, rotated into view, illuminated, projected and finally shown. These steps happen in single statements as a consequence of the effort we have already put in the development of the classes.

With the floor finished for a given tile it is now possible to go on and draw the object sitting on it. Once again an **Iterator** called *nextp* is bound to *patch_list* and through the list we go again. The type of the object on each tile is fetched, first translated into the World and then the view frame, rotated into view, illuminated, projected and shown on the screen. That's it! The whole job done, finished!

The last 30 lines of **observe**() don't seem very long but they are only so because of the great efforts we have made to generate meaningful classes that do what's required. That's the glory of OOP, the effort invested in producing useful classes is never wasted. Each class is a data type which can be used over and over again. The increasing complexity of the program does not result in increasing confusion; each new data type is a building block for higher building blocks. There is no limit. Just as language in general encapsulates concepts within concepts, so OOP encapsulates classes within classes. Using OOP is just like using a spoken language.

12.8 Example Program EXPLORE.CPP

The final example program is called EXPLORE. It is shown in the file EXPLORE.CPP. It is so simple that it is repeated here.

```
Screen screen(shadings);
World exist(map,zoo,&ground);    // Big Bang!
Observer I(&exist);              // I exist therefore I am
for(;;){                         // Evolve
     screen.swap screen();
     I.observe(screen);          // I see
     I.navigate.keyboard();      // I explore

}
```

By using instances and functions with meaningful identifiers it has been possible to make the program look like a short piece of English prose.

What EXPLORE does is allow you to move around a Virtual Reality city populated with objects listed in the file CREATURE.H in an arrangement given by the map in MAP.H. The city is called, unsurprisingly, PC-CITY and you will find its name over the entrance to the city. Moving through the city you will pass the various objects in a completely arbitrary arrangement. At the moment it has two major roads crossing at a main junction. No great effort has been made to make an architectural masterpiece; that is left to you.

Unfortunately the policy of sticking rigidly to standard Borland functions has left this large and complex program rather slow on anything less than 486 running at 33 MHz. That is partly the consequence, stated at the outset, of staying within the environment of a commercial library where everything is well documented and robust. It is also a consequence of making the code as easy to follow as possible, whilst utilising OOP techniques, for a learner. Now that you have reached the end of the book, regard it as a graduating exercise to re-examine the classes and programs and rewrite them so they run faster.

The project you need to create, EXPLORE.PRJ, must contain the following files

```
EXPLORE.CPP
DEFN_00.CPP
DEFN_01.CPP
DEFN_02.CPP
DEFN_03.CPP
DEFN_04.CPP
DEFN_05.CPP
DEFN_06.CPP
```

Here is a discussion of the various objects in the World and the World layout.

12.9 The Zoo

zoo is the identifier of the array of **DefPrim**s that make up the existing graphics objects in the World. They are listed in the file CREATURE.H. Here they are in the order of the index in the array zoo. For example, the first entry in *zoo* is *tree* which is *zoo*[0]. This is how the types are recognised by the program and how they are entered on the map.

tree is a tree. Not a very pretty tree, but recognisable. It has a trunk made from three sides and a foliage similarly constructed. Thus there are 6 polygons altogether in *tree*:

column is a column. It has 6 sides and a top. It's quite tall.

pc-city is the sign PC-CITY. It appears at only one place in the World, over the columns at the point of entry. As you pass through the columns it passes overhead.

stripef (stripe forward) is a road marking for showing the direction of the road in the y direction.

stripes (stripe sideways) is another stripe to mark roads going in the x direction.

house is a house with four walls and a roof.

block is a large high-rise building which could be an office block or an apartment building.

Look at how these buildings are constructed and design your own.

12.10 The Map

map, as shown in MAP.H is the layout of the World. It gives the background colour of each 256x256 tile and the type of object on it in the form of two nybbles of information. Since the map is an array of integers, this leaves additional unused space to enter more information if required. The information is in the order: primitive type = nibble 1, background colour = nibble 2.

Looking at *map* you will notice that the primitive type on the first tile is PC-CITY. To convert this array into what you see on the screen note that the primitive types going down the first column are *zoo*[3] which is *stripef*, or forward stripe. So moving forward takes you down the first column. Because "wrap" occurs, when you get to the bottom you come back in at the top. Of course, using the keyboard controls you can always turn around and head in the opposite direction.

```
//EXPLORE.CPP
// Exploring a Virtual Reality

#include "C:\TC\3D\DECL_00.h"
#include "C:\TC\3D\DECL_01.h"
#include "C:\TC\3D\DECL_02.h"
#include "C:\TC\3D\DECL_03.h"
#include "C:\TC\3D\DECL_04.h"
#include "C:\TC\3D\DECL_05.h"
#include "C:\TC\3D\DECL_06.h"
#include "C:\TC\3D\MAP.H"
#include "C:\TC\3D\SHADES.H"
#include "C:\TC\3D\CREATURE.H"
#include <graphics.h>
#include <stdlib.h>
#include <stdio.h>
#include <conio.h>


void main(void){

    Screen screen(shadings);

    World exist(map,zoo,&ground);        // Big Bang!

        Observer I(&exist);              // I exist therefore I am

    for(;;){                             // Evolve

        screen.swap_screen();

        I.observe(screen);               // I see

        I.navigate.keyboard();           // I explore

    }

}
```

```
// DECL_06.H
// Declarations of classes for a Virtual Reality


// A data record for a visible primitive

struct RECORD{
    int type;                   //what it is
    int bck_col;                //background colour
    int centrex;                //tile centre in World coords
    int centrey;                //
    int yV;                     //tile depth in Viewframe coords
    int angle;                  //angle of rotation to world
};


// Holder of the RECORD in a Sorted_List

class Node{
public:
    Node* next;                 // the one before
    RECORD record;              // this Node's RECORD
    Node(RECORD R,Node* Next=0){record=R;next=Next;}// make one
    ~Node(){delete next;}       // kill one
    void insert(RECORD);        // add a new Node
    RECORD get_record(){return record;}// public access
    friend Iterator;            // can get a Node
};


// A Sorted_List to hold the RECORDS in depth-sorted order

class Sorted_List{
    Node* head;                         // top of the list
public:
    Sorted_List(Node* pn=0){head=pn;}// start a new list
    ~Sorted_List(){delete head;}        // kill one
    void insert(RECORD);                // add a new Node
        friend Iterator;                // can walk the list
};


// Tools to navigate through the World

class Navigator{
public:
    int x,y,z;                      // where I am
    int theta_inc,gamma_inc;        // reorientation increments
    int speed;                      // my speed
    Rotator view;                   // my view reference frame
    Navigator():view(0,0,0)
                    {theta_inc=gamma_inc=5;speed=3;x=128;y=0;z=20;}
    void keyboard();                //read the keyboard-update vars

};
```

```
// The World in which I live

class World{
    int* tiles;                      // list of World inhabitants
    DefPrim* primitives;             // how they are assembled
    DefPrim* floor;                  // the ground beneath us
public:
    World(int* ,DefPrim* ,DefPrim* );     // make it
    int* get_tiles(){return tiles;}       // public access
    DefPrim* get_floor(){return floor;}
    DefPrim* get_prim(){return primitives;}
};


// My immediate environment - what can be seen

class Environment{
public:
    Sorted_List* patch_list;         // what I can see, depth-sorted
    Environment(){patch_list=new Sorted_List;}
    ~Environment(){delete patch_list;}
};


// The abstraction of myself

class Observer{                              // me
public:
    World* world;                            // where I exist
    Environment surroundings;                // what is there
    Navigator navigate;                      // whereabouts I am
    Illuminator flashlight;                  // let there be light
    Observer(World*);                        // I am born
    void observe(Screen&);                   // look at that
    Navigator Navigate(){return navigate;}   // public access
};


// A Sorted_List iterator

class Iterator{                              // walk the sorted list
    Node* pncurrent;                         // the current Node
public:
    Iterator(Sorted_List& L){pncurrent=L.head;}  //bind to a list
    Node* operator++();                      // get the next one
    Node* get_Node(){return pncurrent;}
};


//nonmember functions

void color(DefPrim&,int);                    // set the color
```

```cpp
// DEFN_06.CPP
// Implementation of classes for a Virtual Reality

#include "C:\TC\3D\DECL_00.H"
#include "C:\TC\3D\DECL_01.H"
#include "C:\TC\3D\DECL_02.H"
#include "C:\TC\3D\DECL_03.H"
#include "C:\TC\3D\DECL_04.H"
#include "C:\TC\3D\DECL_05.H"
#include "C:\TC\3D\DECL_06.H"
#include <conio.h>
#include <stdlib.h>
#include <math.h>
#include <graphics.h>


// Instantiate a World ...........................................
World::World(int* tp,DefPrim* p,DefPrim* f){
    tiles=tp;primitives=p;floor=f;
}


// Instantiate an Observer .......................................
Observer::Observer(World* reality):flashlight(.392,-.94,0){
    world=reality;
}


// The big function. Draw everything I can see ...................
void Observer::observe(Screen& S){
    Sorted_List patch_list;         // instantiate the Sorted_List

    Vector ky=navigate.view[1];     //the direction I'm going
    navigate.x+=(ky[0]*(navigate.speed))/30;// update my x position
    navigate.y+=(ky[1]*(navigate.speed))/30;//             y


// update my height but keep it below 200
    if((navigate.z+=(ky[2]*(navigate.speed)/30))>200)navigate.z=200;
// and above the ground
    if(((navigate.z)<0))navigate.z=0;

// stay on the map
    navigate.x=(navigate.x)&0xfff;  // keep in range 4096
    navigate.y=(navigate.y)&0xfff;  // keep in range 4096

// Find coords of patch centre = local world coords Tx,Ty,Tz
    // in a world 16x16 tiles.
    // A bitwise right shift gives a fast divide by 256
    // to locate me on the 16 x 16 tile array.
    int Tx=(navigate.x)>>8;         // x/256
    int Ty=(navigate.y)>>8;         // y/256
    int Tz=navigate.z;              // the height
// Coords of view frame referenced from this origin
    // I see the World from where I'm standing on a tile
    int Ovx=navigate.x-(Tx<<8);//observer coords in frame:x-256*Tx
    int Ovy=navigate.y-(Ty<<8);     // etc
    int Ovz=navigate.z;             // just the height
```

```
// Make a List of the tiles around me which are centred at Tx,Ty
    for(int row=-2;row<=2;row++){    //   rows - in front and behind
        for(int col=-2;col<=2;col++){//   columns - to the sides

// Get the actual tile centre coords in the World frame
// = 256*col+128 etc.   needed to position things for display
            int tileWx=(row<<8)+128,tileWy=(col<<8)+128;

// get tile coords from the viewframe origin i.e. me
            int tileVx=tileWx-Ovx,tileVy=tileWy-Ovy,tileVz=0-Ovz;
// make a Vector from these = current tile centre in world
            Vector tileWc(tileVx,tileVy,tileVz);
// transform (rotate) the tile centre to my view ie can I see it?
            Vector tileVc=(navigate.view)*tileWc;//rotated to my view
            tileVc[0]/=30;tileVc[1]/=30;tileVc[2]/=30;//cut to size


// Elementary clipping in 3D so objects too far away are ignored
// and if I can see it, then add it to the Sorted_List
            if(tileVc[1]>60&&tileVc[1]<1000&&tileVc[0]>-1000
            &&tileVc[0]<1000&&tileVc[2]<500&&tileVc[2]>-100){
            // So add it to the list
            // get what's on the tile, look in the map.
            // Offset is the index into the map array
            int map_offset=(((Ty+col)&0xf)*16)+((Tx+row)&0xf);
            // here's what,s on this tile
            int bkgcol_type=(world->get_tiles())[map_offset];
            int temp=bkgcol_type;            // save it
            int Bck_col=(bkgcol_type>>4)&0xf; // shift out the type
            int Type=temp&0xf;              //mask off background colour

            // make a new RECORD entry in the list
            RECORD next={Type,Bck_col,tileWx,tileWy,tileVc[1],0};
// The Sorted_List places RECORDS in depth sorted order as it goes
            patch_list.insert(next);            // add new entry
            }
        }
    }

// Start drawing the visible World
// Draw the sky and ground
    int vpoint=200,theta=-navigate.view.get_theta();
    int yh=vpoint*tan(theta*2*3.142/360);//in radians
    int ys=250-yh;

    // Sky
    int polys[]={0,0,640,0,640,ys,0,ys};//vertices
    setfillstyle(1,9); // solid line and color
    fillpoly(4,polys);// go to it

    // Ground
    int polyg[]={0,ys,640,ys,640,350,0,350};
    setfillstyle(1,8);
    fillpoly(4,polyg);

// Draw all the primitives in order of the list: farthest first
// Ground first - objects can't be drawn 'til this is down
    Iterator nextf(patch_list); // bind Iterator to list
    Node* npf;                      // moving node pointer
```

```
    // For all the Nodes in the list
    while(npf=nextf++){
        RECORD Rcurrent=npf->get_record();   // current RECORD
        int bck_col=Rcurrent.bck_col;        // background colour
        int x=Rcurrent.centrex,y=Rcurrent.centrey;// coords
        Translator world_displace(x,y,0);// to position in world
        Translator view_displace(-Ovx,-Ovy,-Ovz);// ditto my view
        DefPrim floor=*(world->get_floor());// design for a floor
        *(floor.colors)=bck_col;             //set floor the colour
        world_displace>>floor;               //locate in the world
        view_displace>>floor;                //locate in my frame
        DefPrim VW_Floor=(navigate.view)*floor;//rotated to view
        ViewPrim shining_floor=flashlight<VW_Floor;// illuminate it
        shining_floor.project();             // project
        shining_floor.show(S);               // display
    }                                        // for all visible tiles


// Second the Visible objects
    Iterator nextp(patch_list); // bind iterator to list
    Node* npp;                  // moving Node
    // For all the Nodes in the list
    while(npp=nextp++){
        RECORD Rcurrent=npp->get_record();   // current RECORD
        int type=Rcurrent.type;              // current primitive
        int x=Rcurrent.centrex,y=Rcurrent.centrey;// position
        Translator world_displace(x,y,0);    // to position in world
        Translator view_displace(-Ovx,-Ovy,-Ovz);// ditto my view
        DefPrim object((world->get_prim())[type]);// type's design
        world_displace>>object;              // locate in World
        view_displace>>object;               // locate in my frame
        DefPrim Object=(navigate.view)*object; // rotated to view
        ViewPrim shining_object=flashlight<Object;// illuminate it
        shining_object.project();            // project it
        shining_object.show(S);              // display it
    }
// done the lot!
}

// Walk the Sorted_List ........................................
Node* Iterator::operator++(){   //get the next node and move on
    if(pncurrent){                           // if any left
        Node* pnthis_one=pncurrent;          // present one
        pncurrent=pncurrent->next;           // move to next one
        return pnthis_one;                   // return present
    }
    return 0;                                // end of list
}

// Add a RECORD to the Sorted_List ............................
void Sorted_List::insert(RECORD R){  //High z at the top
    if(head){                            // If there's at least one link
        if(R.yV>=(head->record.yV)){ //this is farther away than head
            head=new Node(R,head);   // so make it the new head.
        }                            // It's closer than the head so
        else head->insert(R);        //  compare the next node.
    }                                //there's not even a head so
    else head=new Node(R);           // it must be the first node
}
```

```cpp
// Insert a Node in the list ......................................
void Node::insert(RECORD R){     //if farther than next it becomes next
    if(next){                               //if there is one
        if(R.yV>=(next->record.yV)){//and if this is farther
            next=new Node(R,next);  // insert it before next
        }                           // otherwise
        else next->insert(R);       // go on to next node
    }                               // There is no next Node so
    else next=new Node(R);          // this must be last Node
}


// Read the keyboard and update location and orientation ...........
void Navigator::keyboard(){
    if(kbhit()){
        char c=getch();                 // check for a key hit
        switch(c){                      // if so, get it
            case 'a':                   // find which key
                    view.angl_inc(0,0,gamma_inc);
                    break;  // left
            case 'x':
                    view.angl_inc(0,0,-gamma_inc);
                    break;  // right
            case 'l':
                    view.angl_inc(theta_inc,0,0);
                    break;  // up
            case 'm':
                    view.angl_inc(-theta_inc,0,0);
                    break;  // down
            case 's':
                    if((speed+=2)>50)speed=50;
                    break;  // speed up
            case 'k':
                    if((speed-=2)<-50)speed=-50;
                    break;  // slow down
            case 'q':
                    exit(EXIT_SUCCESS);                 // quit program
        }
    }
}
```

```
// CREATURE.H
// All the creatures in the World



// The ground - a square

int xg[]={-128,128,128,-128};                   // x values
int yg[]={128,128,-128,-128};                   // y
int zg[]={0,0,0,0};                             // z
int edglstg[]={0,1,2,3};                        // edge connections
int nedgesg[]={4};                              // edge number
int colorsg[]={3};                              // temporary colour
int nvtxg=4;                                    // 4 vertices
int nedgcg=4;                                   // 4 edges
int npolyg=1;                                   // 1 polygon
int *rg[]={xg,yg,zg};                           // pointer array


//a simple block

int x0[]={-70,70,70,-70,-70,70,70,-70};         // x values
int y0[]={50,50,-50,-50,50,50,-50,-50,};        // y
int z0[]={300,300,300,300,0,0,0,0};             // z
int edglst0[]={0,4,5,1,1,5,6,2,3,2,6,7,0,3,7,4,7,6,5,4,0,1,2,3};
int nedges0[]={4,4,4,4,4,4};
int colors0[]={15,15,15,15,15,15};
int nvtx0=8;
int nedgc0=24;
int npoly0=6;
int *r0[]={x0,y0,z0};


// thing1 an inverted pyramid

int x1[]={0,-20,-20,20,20};                     // x values
int y1[]={0,-20,20,20,-20};                     // y
int z1[]={0,100,100,100,100};                   // z
int edglst1[]={1,4,0,2,1,0,3,2,0,4,3,0,1,2,3,4};
int nedges1[]={3,3,3,3,4};
int colors1[]={2,3,4,5,6};
int nvtx1=5;
int nedgc1=16;
int npoly1=5;
int *r1[]={x1,y1,z1};


// tree - a conifer

int xt[]={0,-5,0,5,0,50,-10,50,-50,10,-50}; // x values
int yt[]={0,-5,7,-5,0,30,-40,15,10,-60,20}; // y
int zt[]={100,0,0,0,200,40,35,25,30,30,35}; // z
int edglstt[]={0,1,2,0,2,3,0,3,1,4,5,6,4,9,10,4,8,7};
int nedgest[]={3,3,3,3,3,3};
int colorst[]={4,4,4,10,2,1};
int nvtxt=11;
int nedgct=18;
int npolyt=6;
int *rt[]={xt,yt,zt};
```

```
// a column

int xc[]={-20,-20,0,20,20,0,-20,0,20,20,0,-20};        // x values
int yc[]={-20,20,35,20,-20,-35,20,35,20,-20,-35,-20};   // y
int zc[]={240,240,240,240,240,240,0,0,0,0,0,0};         // z
int edglstc[]={0,5,10,11,1,0,11,6,2,1,6,7,3,2
              ,7,8,4,3,8,9,5,4,9,10,0,1,2,3,4,5};
int nedgesc[]={4,4,4,4,4,4,6};
int colorsc[]={14,14,14,14,14,14,14};
int nvtxc=12;
int nedgcc=30;
int npolyc=7;
int *rc[]={xc,yc,zc};



// pc_city - the sign over the gate

int x_c[]={-255,-195,-195,-240,-240,-255,-240,-210,-210,-240,-165
          ,-135,-120,-120,-135,-135,-165,-165,-135,-135,-120,-120
          ,-135,-165,-180,-180,-105,-75,-75,-105,-60,-45,-15,0,0
          ,-15,-15,-45,-45,-15,-15,0,0,-15,-45,-60,30,45,45,30,75
          ,150,150,120,120,105,105,75,180,195,218,240,255,225,225
          ,210,210};
int y_c[]={0,0,0,0,0,0,0,0,0,0,0,0,0,0,0,0,0,0,0,0,0,0,0,0,0,0,0,0,0,0
          ,0,0,0,0,0,0,0,0,0,0,0,0,0,0,0,0,0,0,0,0,0,0,0,0,0,0,0,0,0,0
          ,0,0,0,0,0,0,0,0,0,0,0,0,0};
int z_c[]={360,360,300,300,240,240,345,345,315,315,360,360,345,315
          ,315,330,330,270,270,285,285,255,240,240,255,345,315,315
          ,285,285,345,360,360,345,315,315,330,330,270,270,285,285
          ,255,240,240,255,360,360,240,240,360,360,345,345,240,240
          ,345,345,360,360,315,360,360,300,240,240,300};
int edglst_c[]={0,1,2,3,4,5,6,7,8,9,10,11,12,13,14,15,16,17,18,19,20
               ,21,22,23,24,25,26,27,28,29,30,31,32,33,34,35,36,37,38,39
               ,40,41,42,43,44,45,46,47,48,49,50,51,52,53,54,55,56,57,58
               ,59,60,61,62,63,64,65,66};
int nedges_c[]={6,4,16,4,16,4,8,9};
int colors_c[]={15,9,15,15,15,15,15,15};
int nvtx_c=67;
int nedgc_c=67;
int npoly_c=8;
int *r_c[]={x_c,y_c,z_c};



// stripe forwards

int xsf[]={-16,16,16,-16};      // x values
int ysf[]={64,64,-64,-64};      // y
int zsf[]={0,0,0,0};            // z
int edglstsf[]={0,1,2,3};
int nedgessf[]={4};
int colorssf[]={15};
int nvtxsf=4;
int nedgcsf=4;
int npolysf=1;
int *rsf[]={xsf,ysf,zsf};
```

```
// stripe sideways

int xss[]={-64,64,64,-64};          // x values
int yss[]={16,16,-16,-16};          // y
int zss[]={0,0,0,0};                // z
int edglstss[]={0,1,2,3};
int nedgesss[]={4};
int colorsss[]={15};
int nvtxss=4;
int nedgcss=4;
int npolyss=1;
int *rss[]={xss,yss,zss};


// house

int xh[]={-64,-64,64,64,-64,-64,64,64,0,0};        // x values
int yh[]={-64,64,64,-64,-64,64,64,-64,-64,64};     // y
int zh[]={0,0,0,0,200,200,200,200,250,250};        // z
int edglsth[]={0,4,8,7,3,1,5,4,0,2,6,9,5,1,3,7,6,2,5,9,8,4,8,9,6,7};
int nedgesh[]={5,4,5,4,4,4};
int colorsh[]={12,12,12,12,1,1};
int nvtxh=10;
int nedgch=26;
int npolyh=6;
int *rh[]={xh,yh,zh};



// All the creatures

    DefPrim ground(rg,edglstg,nedgesg,colorsg,nvtxg,nedgcg,npolyg);
    DefPrim block(r0,edglst0,nedges0,colors0,nvtx0,nedgc0,npoly0);
    DefPrim thing1(r1,edglst1,nedges1,colors1,nvtx1,nedgc1,npoly1);
    DefPrim tree(rt,edglstt,nedgest,colorst,nvtxt,nedgct,npolyt);
    DefPrim column(rc,edglstc,nedgesc,colorsc,nvtxc,nedgcc,npolyc);
    DefPrim pc_city(r_c,edglst_c,nedges_c,colors_c,nvtx_c,nedgc_c,npoly_c);
    DefPrim stripef(rsf,edglstsf,nedgessf,colorssf,nvtxsf,nedgcsf,npolysf);
    DefPrim stripes(rss,edglstss,nedgesss,colorsss,nvtxss,nedgcss,npolyss);
    DefPrim house(rh,edglsth,nedgesh,colorsh,nvtxh,nedgch,npolyh);

// The array of them

    DefPrim zoo[]={tree,column,pc_city,stripef,stripes,house,block};
```

```
// MAP.H
// The World layout


int map[256]=
 {0x82,0xc1,0xa5,0x20,0x31,0x40,0xc1,0x11,0xc1,0x83,0xc1,0x90,0xa1,0xb1,0xa5,0xc1,
  0x83,0xc0,0x25,0x41,0x51,0x61,0xc1,0x81,0xc1,0x83,0xc1,0xc1,0xd0,0xe0,0x26,0xc0,
  0x83,0xc0,0xa5,0x50,0x61,0x70,0xc1,0x90,0xc1,0x83,0xc1,0xe0,0xf1,0x20,0xa5,0xc0,
  0x83,0xc0,0xa6,0x11,0x11,0x11,0xc1,0x11,0xc1,0x83,0xc1,0x11,0x11,0x11,0xa5,0xc0,
  0x83,0xc0,0x11,0x11,0x11,0x11,0xc1,0x11,0xc1,0x83,0xc1,0x11,0x11,0x11,0x11,0xc0,
  0x83,0xc0,0x11,0x11,0x11,0x11,0xc1,0x11,0xc1,0x83,0xc1,0x11,0x11,0x11,0x11,0xc0,
  0x83,0xc0,0xc0,0xc0,0xc0,0xc0,0xc1,0xc0,0xc1,0x83,0xc1,0xc0,0xc0,0xc0,0xc0,0xc0,
  0x83,0x84,0x84,0x84,0x84,0x84,0x84,0x84,0x84,0x84,0x84,0x84,0x84,0x84,0x84,0x84,
  0x83,0xc0,0xc0,0xc0,0xc0,0x80,0xc0,0xc1,0x83,0xc1,0xc0,0xc0,0xc0,0xc0,0xc0,
  0x83,0xc0,0x11,0x11,0x11,0x11,0x81,0x11,0xc1,0x83,0xc1,0x11,0x11,0x11,0x11,0xc0,
  0x83,0xc0,0x11,0x11,0x11,0x11,0x81,0x11,0xc1,0x83,0xc1,0x11,0x11,0x11,0x11,0xc0,
  0x83,0xc0,0x11,0x11,0x11,0x11,0x81,0x11,0xc1,0x83,0xc1,0x11,0x11,0x11,0x11,0xc0,
  0x83,0xc0,0x11,0x11,0x11,0x11,0x81,0x11,0xc1,0x83,0xc1,0x11,0x11,0x11,0x11,0xc0,
  0x83,0xc0,0x11,0x11,0x11,0x11,0x81,0x11,0xc1,0x83,0xc1,0xf1,0x11,0x11,0x11,0xc0,
  0x83,0xc0,0xd1,0xe1,0x51,0x81,0x81,0xe1,0xc1,0x83,0xc1,0xd1,0x41,0x71,0xa1,0xc0,
  0x83,0xc0,0xb1,0xc1,0x31,0x61,0x80,0xc1,0xc1,0x83,0xc1,0x50,0x61,0x70,0x80,0xc0};
```

Appendix 1

Turbo C++

The Integrated Development Environment is the platform which Turbo C++ provides to write, debug and run programs. This appendix describes some basic operations of the IDE together with tips that will help you overcome common problems. For a full description consult the Turbo C++ User's Guide supplied with the software.

Turbo C++ is a very powerful C++ compiler that gives you both the full features of ANSI C and AT&T v.2.1 C++ so you can program in C or move into full Object-Oriented Programming (OOP) in C++. This book is written to launch you speedily into OOP with all its advantages of abstract data types, inheritance and the many other features which just make it a "better C"

1.Installing Turbo C++

The installation program is on DISK 1. Insert it in drive A: (or B:) and enter

```
A:
INSTALL
```

This will change the drive to A: and start the installation. You will be guided through the installation and prompted for the remaining disks as they are required.

2. Running Turbo C++

When you have finished the installation make sure you include the path to the Turbo C++ program in your PATH in the DOS AUTOEXEC.BAT file. Your PATH should include

```
C:\TC\BIN
```

so that you can just type tc from any directory and run the program. If you do that you will have the directory you started from as the default directory that Turbo C++ will look in for source code files. To change the directory you will need to select **File|Change dir...** (**File** means the menu command and **Change dir..** means the menu option from that menu) from the IDE menu bar and then enter the new directory. Normally you will wish to have as the working directory the one containing the files you are writing so that they can be quickly loaded into the Editor.

3. The IDE

When Turbo C++ starts up you are in the IDE. Although much effort has gone into making the IDE as simple as possible, for the beginner it is still at times confusing. What we will do here is briefly discuss the overall picture before going on to a more detailed study.

To start a new program simply click on **File|new** and a window will open ready to receive the source code. When you are ready to save the source code **File|save as...** will offer the current directory listing and have the cursor set to type in the name of the new file.

There can be many windows open simultaneously (as many as there are FILES in your DOS CONFIG.SYS). As is usual with a graphical user interface, many open windows can result in a cluttered mess with the one you're interested in buried at the bottom. There is a cure for this in the **Window** menu where the **tile** option will make them all visible side by side. Each window has a zoom box which is a vertical arrow which can be toggled to either enlarge or reduce the window. It is always necessary to retile at regular intervals to bring all windows back into view. At the top of the screen is the menu bar where each of the main menus is listed. Some menus selections open smaller menus and some dialog boxes where you are asked for input. At the bottom of the screen is the status line which gives information regarding the current menu selection. It is possible to navigate all menus in the IDE from the keyboard but we will assume a mouse is being used.

Whilst the IDE has been made very user-friendly, it is still confusing for the beginner. In this section we'll look each of the many menus, and the submenus that appear in several of them. Much of the information contained in these menus is meaningless and not really very important to the beginner but to the experienced programmer allows the system to be fine tuned . For the programs in this book actually very little needs to be changed from the default values found when the IDE is first entered. There are however a few important settings which are not there by default and without the programs will not compile. This is not a guide for the experienced user but, rather, an introductory guide.

4.Windows

The IDE is a GUI (graphical user interface) though it is not Windows. It has many of the features that Windows uses but is really a graphical DOS – close to Turbo Vision. That doesn't mean you can't run it under Windows, you can, but in a DOS box with a PIF file. That's actually quite useful if you want to capture screen shots and touch them up in a paint program like Paintbrush.

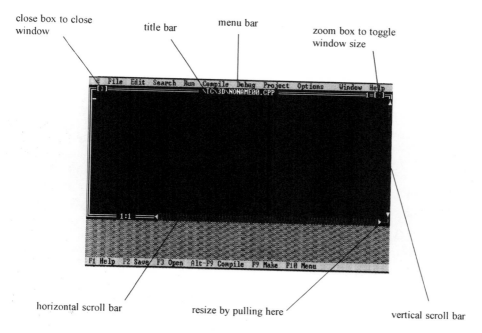

Figure A1.1 A Windows in the IDE

Figure A1.1 shows a screen shot of the IDE with an empty window ready to write a program. Notice there is a close box to quickly close the window and a zoom box to toggle the size of the window. Many of the actions you will want to do with windows are given in the Window menu which is discussed fully later. If you have several windows open you will probably want to tile them from this menu so they fit side by side and are all visible. The text is not constrained to lie in the immediately visible window and by clicking on the scroll bars, vertical and horizontal, with the mouse you can scroll through a long and wide file. The line the top is the menu bar and below that the title bar to show what file window is active. With several windows, the one you have most recently clicked on is the active one and is highlighted. The bar at the bottom is the status bar which gives additional information to supplement the active menu.

5.Menus

The menus give you choices to choose from so as to relieve you of having to remember obscure instructions. To operate a menu all you have to do is click on it and the menu will drop down revealing the choices, some of which may lead to further menus. Then click on your choice. Many times a dialogue box will appear asking for input.

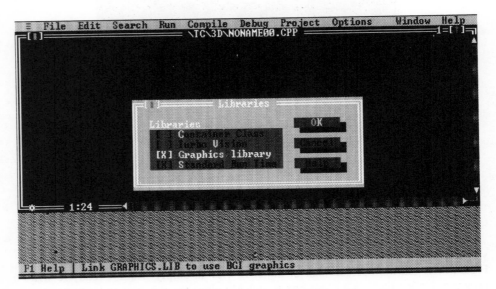

Figure A1.2 A dialogue box

Figure A1.2 shows just such a box which came from the Options menu and then from the Linker option in it and then for the Libraries option in that; three layers deep. For convenience I have written this path as Options|Linker|Libraries. This is a useful illustration since by default the Graphics Library is not selected but without it you can't use the graphics functions which are essential to our programs. This is one important option you must set. We'll now look at the menus one by one though not exactly in the order they appear on the menu bar since that is not the order they are usually used in.

5.1 Help Menu

When you don't understand something, here's where you can go for help. It's at the end of the menu bar but offers a guide to everything about the system. In fact you don't need the Help menu since Help is context sensitive which means you can place the cursor on the word you don't understand in the text of a file, click with the right mouse button and Help will try to open on the explanation, i.e. Help is intelligent. It will either take you right to the relevant section or open the Help index. The expanded menu is shown in Figure A1.3.

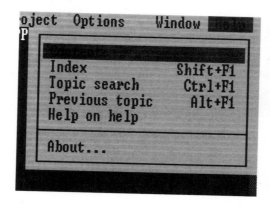

Figure A1.3 The Help menu

In **Contents** you are presented with four menus, three of which deal with the IDE and one which deals with handles general topics including aspects of the C++ language. The remaining headings take you straight to the index and handle queries.

5.2 File Menu

This menu is the first and handles the opening and saving of program files. It is used a lot; Figure A1.4 shows it expanded. The first option, **New** will open a new window. If you keep opening, but never closing windows the IDE will get very cluttered (you can tidy up with **Tile** from the Windows menu). The second, **Open**, will open an already existing file for further work and will give you a selection from the current directory (selected from the **Change dir...** option). The current directory for the graphics programs will be C:\TC\3D to use the full path. Unless you have changed to this directory before entering Turbo C++, you won't be in it and will have to change to it. Frequently you will work on an existing file and want to save it under a different name; **Save as...** will do this. **Save all** will save all the opened windows. **Print** will give a listing on your printer, though you may wish to import it into your word processor for better formatting. **DOS shell** gets you into DOS to do such things as making new directories or deleting unwanted files with a quick return to the IDE on typing EXIT without disturbing your current work. **Quit** terminates you session in Turbo C++.

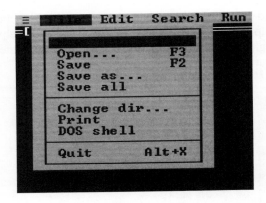

Figure A1.4 The File menu

5.3 Edit Menu

This menu has several very useful basic word processing commands to help in writing programs. Figure A1.5 shows it expanded. The most useful of these are **Cut**, **Copy** and **Paste**. Very frequently you will wish to cut out a block of code and paste it in somewhere else. **Cut** and **Paste** will do this. First you highlight the text by clicking with the mouse at the start of the text and dragging to the end. The selecting **Cut** from the menu will remove the text to the clipboard, which is a text buffer. The text can be retrieved from the buffer by moving the cursor to the new location and selecting **Paste** form the menu. The code will reappear at the new location, pushing the existing code down to make room. Sometimes you may wish to duplicate a block of code whilst leaving the original in tact. For this use **Copy** and **Paste**; the clipboard will still be used to hold the copy.

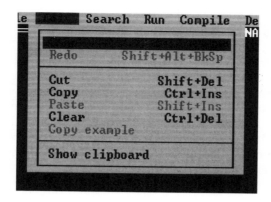

Figure A1.5 The Edit menu

5.4 Run Menu

Having written a program you will be anxious to see if it will run. If it is a short program that does not require a Project, it can be run immediately from this menu shown expanded in Figure A1.6. Run will run the program immediately, producing at the same time an .EXE file which you could run directly from DOS. Run is the short cut to running a program and most of the time you will wish to use it. The other options are very useful in debugging which we will discuss in the Debug menu.

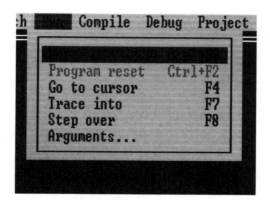

Figure A1.6 The Run menu

5.5 Options Menu

Having looked at the easy start the IDE provides to run a program, it's time to take a closer look at the many details which can be adjusted to fine-tune the system for specific applications. The default setting are of course what you find when you first enter the IDE but some of these at least must be changed to run even the elementary graphics programs in this book. The options menu and its several submenus are shown in Figures 7, 8, 9, 10 and 11. We'll discuss these in turn paying attention to only those aspects which are of importance to the book. The more advanced programmer will find much scope here for his creative talents.

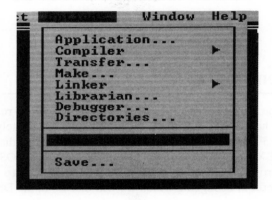

Figure A1.7 Options menu

In the first expanded menu in Figure A1.7 you'll note that three of the headings have small arrows at the side; these are the ones that expand to menus at the lower levels. The first option is **Application** which specifies what kind of program it is We want **Standard** which means a plain .EXE file.

The next option **Compiler** expands to a list of further options. The first of these, **Code Generation**, asks principally what kind of memory model which is small in our case, with near pointers. Also enums should be integers. Then in **Advanced Code Generation** you should set for floating point emulation if you don't have a maths coprocessor and probably choose the 80286 instruction set. Other setting take as default. **Entry/Exit Code** take as default. In **C++ Options** choose C++ always, smart virtual tables and out-of-line inline functions. In **Optimizations** choose automatic register variables and optimize for speed. In **Source** check Turbo C++. Messages expands to another menu as in Figure A1.9. These are settings for messages which will be displayed to alert you to possible problems and errors. There are many of these and are covered by the default values. It is useful to read them to understand what they mean. When it comes to debugging programs these messages and the help that comes with them are very important. How well you can understand what the messages are talking about is also a useful guide to your understanding of the C++ language.

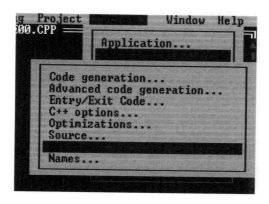

Figure A1.8 Options/Compiler menu

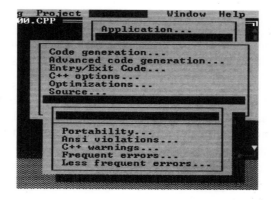

Figure A1.9 Options/Compiler/Messages menu

Back in the main **Options** menu the next entry is **Transfer**. This allows you to temporarily transfer control to any program listed under the triple horizontal bar at the top left of the screen without leaving the IDE. You can add new transfer programs to the list, providing of course they are loaded.

Make, Librarian and **Debugger** can be left as default. **Linker** expands into a menu with two choices as shown in Figure A1.10 and the one to look out for here is **Libraries** which is shown in Figure A1.2 and must include the graphics library. In **Directories** you are given the paths where **include** and **library** files will be sought. If your own include files are placed elsewhere you can add additional paths separated by a semicolon. In the programs in this book the paths have been written in explicitly in the source code. Also note the output and source directories which if you make no entry will be placed in the current directory set in **File|Change dir..**

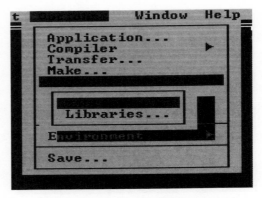

Figure A1.10 Options/Linker menu

Environment expands to give several choices as shown in Figure A1.11. In preferences you can usefully increase the number of code line visible in the editor by changing from 25 to 43/50. You also want to autosave everything. The default values in **Editor** are OK but you may wish to reduce the tab size so that code is not pushed off the right hand side of the screen in nested loops. I use a setting of 4.

In **Mouse Options** you can change what the right button does. The default topic search is very useful but in debugging Inspect is very handy. Also if your "clicking" speed is slow you can set it here. **Desktop** and **Startup** may need attention depending on your computer model and **Colors** will enable you to have an IDE different from anyone else's

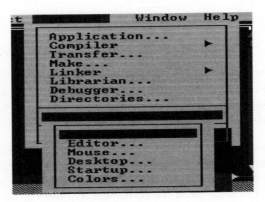

Figure A1.11 Options/Environment menu

At the bottom of the main **Options** menu is the **Save** choice in which you should check everything and where you should explicitly click OK at any point where a particular configuration is to be saved.

5.6 Project Menu

Running a single file program is easy. When your program has several source files, as do those in this book, you need to link them together in a Project file. The menu is shown in Figure A1.12. All you have to do is click on **Open Project..** and then use **Add item..** to add in the .CPP source files one by one until you are finished. The project is then run from the **Run** menu and the separate source files will be compiled and linked to produce the combined .exe file.

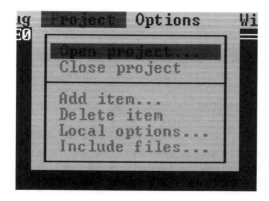

Figure A1.12 Project menu

5.7 Compile Menu

This will allow you to do in stages what is done all in one go in **Run**. It is shown in Figure A1.13. **Compile** will compile the file in the active window and **Build all** will go through all the files in a project as if it were the first time, but run it.

Figure A1.13 Compile menu

5.8 Debug Menu

The options here are invaluable for finding why your program won't run. Figure A1.14 shows this.

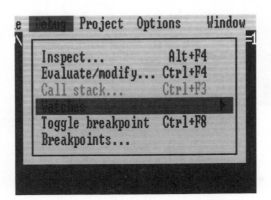

Figure A1.14 Debug menu

The error messages provide the explanations for why your program won't compile and link, but when it does all that but behaves in an unexpected way or, worse, crashes, the debugger is all you have left. Programmers spend many hours debugging. Generally novice programmers shy away from the debugger and prefer to stare at the source code praying for inspiration. It is a sign of increasing programming skill when this approach is abandoned and instead the debugger is used for a careful step-by-step examination of the faulty program. The most useful things you can do are **Inspect** variables as you **Trace into** the program as one of the options in the **Run** menu. Here these two menus are used together. Run allows you to step line by line (F7) whilst F8 does the same thing most of the time but will step over large enclosed blocks of code such as functions. You can get to the part of the program you want to inspect by setting a breakpoint (where the program halts) using **Toggle breakpoint** and once there use inspect, with the name of the variable, to see how the data is changing. You can also keep a continual **Watch** on particular variables to see how they change, particularly in a loop, with the **Watch** submenu in Figure A1.14.

Figure A1.15 Debug/Watches menu

5.9 Search Menu

This, shown in Figure A1.16, works in conjunction with **Edit** allows you to find and alter lines of code globally throughout a file, without having to remember where each one is. The searching is done automatically.

5.10 Window Menu

Finally the **Window** menu in Figure A1.17 helps you to control how and what is visible in the IDE. **User screen** will display the otherwise hidden screen where your graphics output is displayed in brief programs. If you can't find it, **Project** will reveal the window that contains the list of files in your project. When many files have disintegrated into a chaotic mess, you can clean up with **Tile** to lay them side-by-side, or **Cascade** to lay them in a pile. Zoom (or clicking on the zoom box) will blow up the active window to fill the screen. You can restore it with the zoom box or retiling.

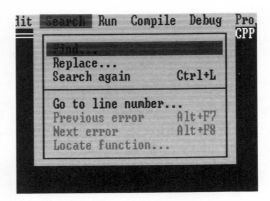

Figure A1.16 Search menu

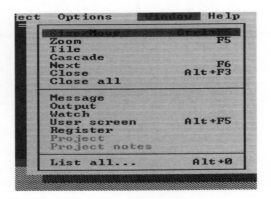

Figure A1.17 Windows menu

That is a very brief summary, touching only superficially on the many aspects of writing and running a program. Consult the *User's Guide* for the full story.

Appendix 2

ASCII Codes

On the next page are ASCII (American Standard Code for Information Interchange) codes. The control (ctrl) character is shown as ^. In this way the backspace character is ctrl-H or ^H. The table shows only the original 128 characters of the 7-bit code and does not include the IBM extended (128 - 255) characters.

0	null	32	space	64	@	96	`
1	^A	33	!	65	A	97	a
2	^B	34	''	66	B	98	b
3	^C	35	#	67	C	99	c
4	^D	36	$	68	D	100	d
5	^E	37	%	69	E	101	e
6	^F	38	&	70	F	102	f
7	^G	39	'	71	G	103	g
8	^H	40	(	72	H	104	h
9	^I	41	)	73	I	105	i
10	^J	42	*	74	J	106	j
11	^K	43	+	75	K	107	k
12	^L	44	,	76	L	108	l
13	^M	45	-	77	M	109	m
14	^N	46	.	78	N	110	n
15	^O	47	/	79	O	111	o
16	^P	48	0	80	P	112	p
17	^Q	49	1	81	Q	113	q
18	^R	50	2	82	R	114	r
19	^S	51	3	83	S	115	s
20	^T	52	4	84	T	116	t
21	^U	53	5	85	U	117	u
22	^V	54	6	86	V	118	v
23	^W	55	7	87	W	119	w
24	^X	56	8	88	X	120	x
25	^Y	57	9	89	Y	121	y
26	^Z	58	:	90	Z	122	z
27	escape	59	;	91	[	123	{
28		60	<	92	\	124	|
29		61	=	93	]	125	}
30		62	>	94	^	126	~
31		63	?	95	_	127	del

Appendix 3

C++ Operator Precedence

In writing C++ code you will often find find adjacent operators in an expression. What exactly the expression means will depend on which operator acts first, i.e. which has precedence. The following table gives the order of precedence of operators as specified by Borland. This table does not exactly agree with that specified by Stroustrup (*The C Programming Language* – see Appendix 4) – which might be taken as the final word.

If you are in doubt in an expression, then it is best to use parenthesis () to enclose an operator and its operand and to force precedence. This will also make the code easier to follow, although it will be longer.

There are 16 categories starting with the highest. In a category the operators have equal precedence.

1. Highest

()	function call
[]	subscripting
–>	select a member from a pointer indirectly
::	scope resolution
.	select a member directly

2. Unary

!	NOT
~	bitwise 1's complement
+	unary plus
−	unary minus
++	pre- or post-increment
--	pre- or post-decrement
&	address of
*	indirection of pointer
sizeof	size of operand (bytes)
new	dynamic allocation
delete	dynamic deallocation

3. Multiplicative

*	multiply
/	divide
%	modulo (remainder)

4. Member access

.*	dereference
−>	dereference

5. Additive

+	binary plus
−	binary minus

6. Shift

<	bitwise shift left
>	bitwise shift right

7. Relational

<	less than
<=	less or equal
>	greater than
>=	greater or equal

8. Equality

==	equal to ?
!=	not equal to ?

9.

&	bitwise AND

10.

^	bitwise XOR

11.

|	bitwise OR

12.

&&	logical AND

13.

||	logical OR

14. Conditional

?:	1st if TRUE, 2nd if FALSE

15. Assignment

=	simple assignment
*=	assign product
/=	assign quotient
%=	assign remainder
+=	assign sum
−=	assign difference
&=	assign bitwise AND
^=	assign bitwise XOR
|=	assign bitwise XOR
<=	assign bitwise left shift
>=	assign bitwise right shift

16.

,   comma, evaluate

Note that all the operators in this table can be overloaded except
.   member selection direct
.*   member dereference
::   scope resolution
?:   conditional

Appendix 4

Bibliography

The object of this book has been to provide a practical experience of the language whilst exploring graphics in (real) time. Whilst many books describe OOP through classes, they do not provide a practical demonstration of the style of the language in a real context. I hope this book has done that.

There is an explosion of books on C++ at the present time, many of which simply recycle the collective wisdom. The shelves of bookstores are packed with such books which, though initially valuable, rapidly become too trivial. Here are a few references which I have found valuable. None of them is really suitable for the novice, but they fill the space beyond which real programming has to be done. For the most part it is not possible to work in sequence, following first one book then another. Progress is usually made by moving backwards and forwards across the bibliography, seeing how different authors have perceived the same issue.

The C++ Programming Language. Bjarne Stroustrup. Addison-Wesley.
ISBN 0-201-53992-6

Surely this must be on the bookshelf of every C++ programmer. Words from the Master himself, the inventor of C++. A densely-packed tome, almost impenetrable to the novice, but a source of wisdom and reference.

Turbo C++ User's Guide V 3.0. Borland.

The manual with Turbo C++. At 772 pages it's more than a book and very readable. It contains much practical information about the implementation of C++.

Programming in C++. Stephen C. Dewhurst and Kathy T. Stark. Prentice-Hall. ISBN 0-13-723156-3

A delightful book. It explains how to program in C++ as opposed to simply chanting the syntax of the language. It concentrates on the implementation of the language and emphasises the C++ style, rising above the minutia of the language and taking a broad view whilst including plenty of practical examples.

C++ for Scientists and Engineers. James T. Smith. Intertext/McGraw-Hill 1991

Perhaps outdated by his more recent *C++ Aplications Guide*, this book shows how to program mathematical data types in C++ down to the last detail.

Journals: Look at the *Journal of Object Oriented Programming* and *Byte* and *Dr Dobbs' Journal* over the past three years. There you will find a rich source of introductory, general and specialised articles on the subject of OOP, far more informative than any one book.

Index

Words for the wise - from
Sigma Press

Sigma publish what is probably the widest range of computer books from any independent UK publisher. And that's not just for the PC, but for many other popular micros – Atari, Amiga and Archimedes – and for software packages that are widely-used in the UK and Europe, including Timeworks, Deskpress, Sage, Money Manager and many more. We also publish a whole range of professional-level books for topics as far apart as IBM mainframes, UNIX, computer translation, manufacturing technology and networking.

A complete catalogue is available, but here are some of the highlights:

Amstrad PCW
The Complete Guide to LocoScript and Amstrad PCW Computers – Hughes – £12.95
LocoScripting People – Clayton and Clayton – £12.95
The PCW LOGO Manual – Robert Grant – £12.95
Picture Processing on the Amstrad PCW – Gilmore – £12.95
See also Programming section for *Mini Office*

Archimedes
A Beginner's Guide to WIMP Programming – Fox – £12.95
See also: *Desktop Publishing on the Archimedes* and *Archimedes Game Maker's Manual*

Artificial Intelligence
Build Your Own Expert System – Naylor – £11.95
Computational Linguistics – McEnery – £14.95
Introducing Neural Networks – Carling – £14.95

Beginners' Guides
Computing under Protest! – Croucher – £12.95
Alone with a PC – Bradley – £12.95
The New User's Mac Book – Wilson – £12.95
PC Computing for Absolute Beginners – Edwards – £12.95

DTP and Graphics
Designworks Companion – Whale – £14.95
Ventura to Quark XPress for the PC – Wilmore – £19.95
Timeworks Publisher Companion – Morrissey – £12.95
Timeworks for Windows Companion – Sinclair – £14.95
PagePlus Publisher Companion – Sinclair – £12.95
Express Publisher DTP Companion – Sinclair – £14.95
Amiga Real-Time 3D Graphics – Tyler – £14.95
Atari Real-Time 3D Graphics – Tyler – £12.95

European and US Software Packages
Mastering Money Manager PC – Sinclair – £12.95
Using Sage Sterling in Business – Woodford – £12.95
Mastering Masterfile PC – Sinclair – £12.95
All-in-One Business Computing (Mini Office Professional) – Hughes – £12.95

Game Making and Playing
PC Games Bible – Matthews and Rigby – £12.95
Archimedes Game Maker's Manual – Blunt – £14.95
Atari Game Maker's Manual – Hill – £14.95
Amiga Game Maker's Manual – Hill – £16.95
Adventure Gamer's Manual – Redrup – £12.95

General

Music and New Technology – Georghiades and Jacobs – £12.95
Getting the Best from your Amstrad Notepad – Wilson – £12.95
Computers and Chaos (Atari and Amiga editions) – Bessant – £12.95
Computers in Genealogy – Isaac – £12.95
Multimedia, CD-ROM and Compact Disc – Botto – £14.95
Advanced Manufacturing Technology – Zairi – £14.95

Networks

$25 Network User Guide – Sinclair – £12.95
Integrated Digital Networks – Lawton – £24.95
Novell Netware Companion – Croucher – £16.95

PC Operating Systems and Architecture

Working with Windows 3.1 – Sinclair – £16.95
Servicing and Supporting IBM PCs and Compatibles – Moss – £16.95
The DR DOS Book – Croucher – £16.95
MS-DOS Revealed – Last – £12.95
PC Architecture and Assembly Language – Kauler – £16.95
Programmer's Technical Reference – Williams – £19.95
MS-DOS File and Program Control – Sinclair – £12.95
Mastering DesqView – Sinclair – £12.95

Programming

C Applications Library – Pugh – £16.95
Starting MS-DOS Assembler – Sinclair – £12.95
Understanding Occam and the transputer – Ellison – £12.95
Programming in ANSI Standard C – Horsington – £14.95
Programming in Microsoft Visual Basic – Penfold – £16.95
For **LOGO**, *see Amstrad PCW*

UNIX and mainframes

UNIX – The Book – Banahan and Rutter – £11.95
UNIX – The Complete Guide – Manger – £19.95
RPG on the IBM AS/400 – Tomlinson – £24.95

HOW TO ORDER

Prices correct for 1993.
Order these books from your usual bookshop, or direct from:

SIGMA PRESS,
1 SOUTH OAK LANE,
WILMSLOW, CHESHIRE, SK9 6AR

PHONE: 0625 – 531035; FAX: 0625 – 536800

PLEASE ADD £1 TOWARDS POST AND PACKING FOR ONE BOOK.
POSTAGE IS FREE FOR TWO OR MORE BOOKS.
OVERSEAS ORDERS: please pay by credit card; we will add airmail postage at actual cost

CHEQUES SHOULD BE MADE PAYABLE TO **SIGMA PRESS.**

ACCESS AND VISA WELCOME – 24 HOUR ANSWERPHONE SERVICE.

√

3-5-96

A000024971201